The Measurement of Efficiency of Production

Studies in Productivity Analysis

Ali Dogramaci, Editor
Cornell University

Titles in the Series:

Adam, Dogramaci; Productivity Analysis at the Organizational Level

Dogramaci, Adam; Aggregate and Industry-Level Productivity Analysis

Dogramaci; Productivity Analysis: A Range of Perspectives

Dogramaci; Developments in Econometric Analyses of Productivity: Measurement and Modelling Issues

Sudit; Productivity Based Management

The Measurement of Efficiency of Production

by
Rolf Färe,
Shawna Grosskopf,
and C. A. Knox Lovell

Springer Science+Business Media, LLC

Library of Congress Cataloging in Publication Data

Färe, Rolf, 1942-
The measurement of efficiency of production.

(Studies in productivity analysis)
Bibliography: p.
Includes index.
1. Production (Economic theory) 2. Efficiency, Industrial. I. Grosskopf, Shawna. II. Lovell, C.A. Knox. III. Title. IV. Series.
HB241.F335 1984 338'.06'072 84-872
ISBN 978-90-481-5813-3 ISBN 978-94-015-7721-2 (eBook)
DOI 10.1007/978-94-015-7721-2

Originally published by Kluwer-Nijhoff Publishers in 1985
Softcover reprint of the hardcover 1st edition 1985

To

Carolina, Claire, and Ian

TABLE OF CONTENTS

1 INTRODUCTION

1.0 Introduction

The subject matter of this inquiry is efficiency in production. We hold the view that efficiency is an important characteristic of producer performance, one that has suffered considerable and unfortunate neglect in the economic literature. The purpose of this inquiry, then, is to redress that neglect by constructing a model of the producer in which inefficiency is allowed to play a meaningful role. This construction enables us to systematically explore the various ways in which a producer might depart from overall efficiency, and to explore the structural relationships among the component types of inefficiency. It also enables us to derive indexes, or measures, of the degree of producer efficiency, both overall and by component, and to examine the properties each of these efficiency indexes satisfies. Finally, this approach suggests ways in which the incorporation of inefficiency into a model of the producer enriches the set of testable hypotheses concerning producer behavior.

It seems desirable at the outset to explain what we mean by efficiency. Formal definitions will appear in due course, but for now an informal definition is that efficiency is the quality or degree of producing a set of desired effects.[1] Thus a producer is efficient if the producer's behavioral objectives are achieved, and inefficient if they are not. The efficiency of a producer is measured by some index of observed and desired performance. Since we decompose a producer's performance into a number of components, these notions apply with equal force to each component of overall performance.

Most modern writing on producer theory assumes, often explicitly, that producers are efficient. From this and other assumptions on the structure of production technology and the structure of commodity markets are derived testable hypotheses on producer behavior. The treatment of efficiency in this literature is briefly reviewed in section 1.1. In recent years, however, a small but growing number of writers have begun to turn their attention to the possibility of inefficiency in production, with emphasis typically placed on measurement of the degree of inefficiency. Some have even gone so far as to suggest that the notion of efficient production employed by most writers is not always the relevant economic concept.[2] It is unfortunate but hardly surprising that this relatively young body of literature is best characterized by its eclectic nature, and by its development without coherent and comprehensive theoretical underpinnings. This development is briefly surveyed in section 1.2.

Even prior to the development of much theoretical literature on efficiency in production, the idea that variation in efficiency might exist in some systematic fashion and might therefore be a phenomenon of some consequence, appeared in a wide range of applied literature. Indeed it might be argued that these ideas encouraged the development of the theoretical foundations that do exist. The role of producer efficiency in a selected number of applied areas is surveyed in section 1.3.

It is our view that the neglect of inefficiency in the modern mainstream literature, the rather disparate development of a heterogeneous fringe literature on efficiency measurement, and the role played by efficiency considerations in a wide range of applied fields, all point to the need for the development of a coherent theory of the producer in the presence of inefficiency. This is our goal. However, aside from the simple desire to fill a large gap in the literature, we are guided by another more empirically relevant motivation. That productive inefficiency exists cannot be denied. To ignore it in constructing theories of producer behavior is to put the predictive content of such theories at considerable risk. Moreover, inefficiency is costly, both to the producer under investigation and to society at large. The cost of inefficiency is ultimately an empirical question, a question well worth asking. But reliable answers to the question require econometric investigation, and sound econometric investigation cannot proceed in advance of the development of a coherent and adaptable theory. It is hoped that the theory developed in this book will provide the requisite foundation for useful applied work.

The core of our investigation, contained in chapters 3–8, is concerned with the identification of various ways in which a producer might depart from efficiency, the specification of an appropriate method of measuring each type of inefficiency, and an exploration of the implications for producer behavior of each type of inefficiency. To maintain consistency with much of the extant literature, the producer we study is fairly conventional. The producer uses many inputs to produce many outputs. Inputs are purchased and outputs sold in competitive markets at strictly positive unit prices over which the producer has no control. Inputs are transformed into outputs by means of a well-behaved production technology, the structure of which is developed in chapter 2. Finally, the producer has a well-defined behavioral goal that is pursued, but of course not always attained. Depending on what variables (in addition to prices) are assumed to be exogenous, a number of goals can be specified, but we focus primarily on the three conventional goals of cost minimization, revenue maximization, and profit maximization. Our techniques are much more widely applicable, however, and can be employed in the investigation of efficiency in a broad range of economic environments. As we shall frequently demonstrate, our techniques are readily adaptable to noncompetitive situations and to alternative behavioral goals.

We measure the efficiency of a producer by comparing any given situation with a (or the) situation that satisfies the producer's behavioral goal. The comparison may be conducted in terms of quantities (inputs and outputs) or values (cost, revenue, and profit). We also decompose the overall efficiency measure in the most suggestive way possible, a way designed to point to an informative set of sources of any measured inefficiency. Relative to any behavioral goal, we identify three basic sources of private inefficiency. Beginning with chapter 3 we will provide precise definitions (and somewhat different terminology), but for now we call them technical inefficiency, structural inefficiency, and allocative inefficiency. A producer is said to be technically efficient if production occurs on the boundary of the producer's production possibilities set, and technically inefficient if production occurs on the interior of the production possibilities set.[3] A technically efficient producer is said to be structurally efficient if production occurs in the uncongested or "economic" region of the boundary of the production possibilities set, and structurally inefficient if production occurs in a congested or "uneconomic" region of the boundary of the production possibilities set. Structural inefficiency can occur only if some nonzero subvector of inputs and outputs is not freely disposable. If all inputs and outputs are freely disposable, as is often assumed in production theory, structural inefficiency cannot occur. Finally, a technically and structurally efficient producer is said to be allocatively efficient if production occurs in a subset of the uncongested boundary of the production possibilities set that satisfies the producer's behavioral objective. The location of this subset is determined by the prices faced by the producer and by the producer's behavioral goal. Thus a technically and structurally efficient producer is said to be allocatively inefficient if production occurs at the wrong point on the uncongested boundary of the production possibilities set, wrong in relation to the prices faced by the producer and the behavioral goal pursued by the producer. These three types of private inefficiency are mutually exclusive and exhaustive, so that a producer can be privately inefficient in any one way, in any two ways, or in all three ways, but in no other way. Thus a producer is completely efficient in a private sense if, and only if, the producer is technically, structurally, and allocatively efficient. The presence of each type of inefficiency, independently and adversely, affects the producer's ability to solve the postulated behavioral optimization problem.

The notions of technical and structural efficiency are independent of the behavioral goal postulated for the producer. That is, a producer is either technically and structurally efficient or inefficient, regardless of the producer's behavioral goal. However, the notion of allocative efficiency is clearly goal-related, in the sense that different goals generate different allocative efficiency requirements. One example occurs when goals are related in a hierarchical fashion. In that event, allocative efficiency relative to the lower-level goal (e.g., cost minimization) is necessary but not sufficient for allocative efficiency relative to the higher-level goal (e.g., profit maximization). Another example occurs when alternative behavioral goals are not nested. In that event allocative efficiency relative to one goal (e.g., profit maximization) is neither necessary nor sufficient for allocative efficiency relative to the other goal (e.g., revenue maximization subject to a minimum profit constraint). Thus allocative, and hence overall, private efficiency can be defined and measured only with respect to a particular behavioral objective of the producer.

Even if a producer is completely efficient in a private sense, and so succeeds in solving the postulated optimization problem, the resulting configuration of input usage and output supply may be suboptimal in a social sense. That is, there may exist a divergence between the actual size, somehow measured, of a privately efficient producer and the ideal size, similarly measured, of that producer. The notion of ideal size is slippery at best, leaving much room for choice. However, we choose to call a producer's input-output decision scale efficient if it corresponds to the inputs and outputs that would arise from a zero profit long run competitive equilibrium situation, and scale-inefficient if it diverges from such a situation. Scale inefficiency is not necessarily the result of private error on the part of the producer, and it may be unfair to refer to such a phenomenon as inefficiency. Nonetheless, privately efficient production that leads to something other than the long-run competitive equilibrium outcome is socially inefficient, and it is worthwhile to define and measure this type of inefficiency. We shall constantly stress the fact that this inefficiency is social, and not necessarily private.[4]

1.1 The Treatment of Efficiency in Modern Production Theory

The possibility that producers might operate inefficiently is typically ignored, and occasionally acknowledged and dismissed, in modern neoclassical production theory. In this literature, as exemplified by the works of Carlson (1939), Hicks (1946), Samuelson (1947), Frisch (1965) and Danø (1966), it is assumed that the producer successfully allocates all resources in a privately efficient manner, efficient relative to the constraints imposed by the structure of production technology and by the structure of input and output markets, and relative to whatever behavioral goals are attributed to the producer. The technology constraint in the producer's behavioral optimization problem is binding, eliminating technical inefficiency.[5] Satisfaction of the first-order conditions necessary for optimization eliminates behavioral inefficiency. Monotonicity and curvature assumptions on production technology sufficient to guarantee satisfaction of the second-order optimization conditions eliminate structural inefficiency.[6] Testable hypotheses about producer behavior then refer to the behavior of efficient producers only, and derive from assumptions on the structure of technology and of markets, on behavioral motivation, and on full efficiency. Since modifying assumptions on the structure of technology, as well as of markets, and on behavioral motivation, influences the richness of the resulting testable hypotheses, it is to be expected that relaxing the full efficiency assumption will do likewise. This expectation has not, however, been explored by any of these writers.

The proponents of the more recent duality approach to producer theory that originated with Shephard (1953, 1970) have not shown much more interest in the efficiency issue. This is because duality theory is concerned with the establishment of conditions under which the production possibilities set and certain value functions (such as the cost, revenue, and profit functions) provide equivalent characterizations of the structure of production technology. Duality theory is also concerned with the uses to which this equivalence might be put, such as the derivation of testable hypotheses concerning producer behavior. However, the conditions required for the establishment of a duality relationship–optimizing behavior in competitive markets with a well-behaved production technology–effectively preclude all three types of inefficiency.[7] However, a partial or restricted duality relationship can be derived if some of the more restrictive regularity conditions on the technology (such as global monotonicity and curvature) are relaxed, since the value duals remain well-behaved despite these relaxations. This is because efficient production with strictly positive input and output prices eliminates the possibility of operation in regions of the technology that fail to satisfy the monotonocity or curvature conditions. What results is a restricted duality between the value function and a well-behaved envelope of the true production possibilities set. So, the very characteristics of technology that generate structural inefficiency are discarded on efficiency grounds! Consequently, testable hypotheses about producer behavior based on duality theory also ignore the potentially fruitful role of inefficiency. However, as we shall demonstrate in subsequent chapters, duality theory remains a powerful under-exploited tool for the analysis of inefficiency, precisely because inefficiency is costly. Since it is costly, we can examine it by looking to the value duals for evidence of extra cost, foregone revenue, or foregone profit.

1.2 The Recognition of Inefficiency in Modern Production Theory

Somewhat outside the mainstream of modern neoclassical production theory, the study of efficiency and its measurement has been undertaken by a number of writers, so we are not exactly starting from scratch. We are, however, confronted by a wide variety of models set up to investigate a wide range of efficiency-related topics in a wide range of environments. The literature, thin as it is, is by no means homogeneous.

Early efforts in the investigation of efficiency and its measurement were made by Koopmans (1951, 1957) and Debreu (1951). Both only studied what we have called technical inefficiency. Koopmans (1951, p. 60) defined a feasible input-output vector to be technically efficient if it is technologically impossible to increase any output and/or to reduce any input without simultaneously reducing at least one other output and/or increasing at least one other input. Using this definition, he was able to prove that an input-output vector is efficient if, and only if, it possesses a positive normal to the production possibilities set, and he provided an economic interpretation to this normal as a set of shadow prices. (This interpretation is valid for the tightly structured technology Koopmans uses, but it does not survive the generalization to less restrictive technologies.) While Koopmans offered a definition and characterization of technical efficiency, it was Debreu who first provided a measure or an index of the degree of technical efficiency with his "coefficient of resource utilization." This coefficient is computed as one minus the maximum equiproportionate reduction in all inputs consistent with continued production of existing outputs, and from it Debreu obtained measures of the magnitude and the cost of technical inefficiency. It is a simple matter to modify Debreu's measure to obtain a measure of the technical efficiency of an output vector produced from any given input vector, or to obtain an overall measure of technical efficiency with both inputs and outputs variable, although these three measures of technical efficiency do not in general have the same value. This is important because all three variants of Debreu's coefficient are widely used, as can be seen in Chapter 6.

More recently Eichhorn (1972, 1978a, 1978b), following Vincze (1960), has modeled a production process involving many variable inputs, one fixed input, many variable outputs, and a time dimension. Within this framework he defined the price-dependent notions of technical and economic "effectiveness" of a production process in terms of systems of functional equations, and derived closed form parametric indexes of technical and economic effectiveness as solutions to the respective systems. His index of technical effectiveness compares processes on the basis of the time dimension, the output vector, and variable input cost, while his index of economic effectiveness compares processes on the basis of the time dimension, the fixed input, and two measures of profitability. Apart from the time dimension, each of the indexes measures what we have called overall private efficiency which is the sum of technical, structural, and behavioral efficiency. The only difference between them is the different behavioral motivations of variable cost minimization and profit maximization. Neither index provides for a decomposition of overall efficiency into its constituent parts.

By far the most influential writer on the subject has been Farrell (1957), who first obtained a partial decomposition of private efficiency into technical and allocative components. Farrell also proposed indexes of technical, allocative, and overall private efficiency, the first being a direct descendent of Debreu's coefficient of resource utilization. However, Farrell confined his attention to a single-output production technology having strong scale, monotonicity, and curvature properties, and these properties rule out the possibility of structural inefficiency. Although Farrell's decomposition of efficiency into technical and allocative components, and his indexes of each, are entirely appropriate for the restrictive technology he considers, they are not suitable for less restrictive technologies. This difficulty with the Farrell approach to efficiency measurement is analyzed in detail at various points in chapters 3–5.

The shortcomings of the Farrell approach to measuring efficiency in complex technologies have led to two separate developments. In the first, Farrell's two-way decomposition of efficiency into technical and allocative components is retained, and the measure of technical efficiency is generalized to allow for disproportionate input reductions and/or disproportionate output increases. This has the virtue of preserving the two-way decomposition, but it assigns different shares to the technical and allocative components of overall private efficiency than does the Farrell approach, unless technology satisfies Farrell's strong monotonicity conditions. This generalization was originally developed in a single-output context by Färe (1975), and was modified by Färe and Lovell (1978), and again by Zieschang (1984). It was later extended to multiple-output technologies by Färe, Lovell and Zieschang (1983), and is explored in some detail in Chapter 7.

In the second development, Farrell's measure of technical efficiency is augmented, rather than generalized, with the addition of a separate measure of structural efficiency. This leads to the decomposition of overall private efficiency into technical, structural, and allocative components discussed earlier. Although the nature of the generalization of Farrell's two-way decomposition differs from that mentioned above, it enjoys the same desirable property of collapsing to Farrell's approach when his strong monotonicity conditions hold. This three-way decomposition was first suggested by Färe and Grosskopf (1983a, b). In their 1983b article they consider a multiple-output producer with a behavioral goal of cost minimization, and they obtain a three-way decomposition. In their 1983a article they consider a multiple-output producer with an unspecified behavioral goal, and show how the presence of output congestion requires the inclusion of both technical and structural efficiency measures. This approach to efficiency measurement is discussed at length in chapters 3–5.

The idea of gauging the performance of a producer by comparing actual to optimal size, and the association of optimal size with input-output vectors satisfying constant returns to scale, is due to Frisch (1965). An index of scale efficiency based on this notion of technically optimal firm size was proposed by Førsund and Hjalmarsson (1974), and has been implemented by Førsund and Hjalmarsson (1979a), Banker (1984), and Banker, Charnes, and Cooper (1983). Färe, Grosskopf and Lovell (1983) showed how this measure relates to measures of private efficiency, and showed how to determine whether scale inefficiency is due to increasing or decreasing returns to scale. This technique has been applied to U.S. coal mining by Byrnes, Färe, and Grosskopf (1984) and by Byrnes, Färe, Grosskopf, and Lovell (1984), and to Philippine agriculture by Färe, Grabowski, and Grosskopf (1984). The measurement of scale efficiency is discussed in chapter 8.

Despite a common theme, the studies cited in this section have little else in common. They consider production technologies that satisfy different sets of regularity conditions: 1. some technologies produce a single output and others produce multiple outputs, 2. some have fixed inputs and a time dimension, 3. some producers seek maximum profit, while others have different behavioral objectives, 4. some writers focus on technical efficiency, others focus on overall private efficiency with or without a concern for its decomposition, and still others focus on scale efficiency with or without a concern for private efficiency, and 5. different writers propose different measures for each type of efficiency. What is clearly needed is a unified treatment of efficiency and its decomposition in a multiproduct setting with a fairly general technology. This is the purpose of this study.

1.3 The Introduction of Inefficiency in Applied Production Theory

The basic notions of technical and allocative efficiency of Koopmans, Debreu, Farrell and others have been used to shed light on a number of phenomena in applied production theory. Indeed it is remarkable that the full efficiency formulation of modern production theory has remained intact for so long, in light of this small but rapidly growing body of literature that both suggests hypotheses concerning inefficiency in production, and presents evidence in support of these hypotheses. In the following paragraphs a few of the many areas of research in which both hypotheses and evidence bearing on inefficiency are summarized. The fact that some of these topics are far removed from the traditional theory of the firm illustrates the widespread applicability of the ideas.

1.3.1 *Average and Best Practice Technologies*. In addition to introducing the notions of technical and allocative efficiency to reflect the performance of firms, Farrell also proposed the notion of the structural efficiency of an industry. Structural efficiency is essentially a reflection of the dispersion in overall private efficiency among the constituent firms in an industry. It measures the extent to which an industry keeps up with the performance of its own most efficient firms. Salter (1966) drew a remarkably similar distinction between average-practice and best-practice technologies. The latter are defined as "... the techniques at each date which employ the most recent technical advances, and are economically appropriate to current factor prices. They correspond to the idea of the most up-to-date techniques currently available" (1966, p. 26). Salter recognized the variation between input requirements in average-practice and best-practice firms as an important characteristic of industry performance, and offered hypotheses concerning the determinants of this variation and evidence on its magnitude. However it seems natural to replace Salter's input requirements with Farrell's technical or overall private efficiency measures, and to replace Salter's comparison between average-practice and best-practice firms with a more informative analysis of the entire distribution of firm efficiencies, in the measurement of the structural efficiency of an industry. This would provide better evidence on the ability of an industry to keep pace with its most efficient firms. Such an approach has been partially developed by Førsund and Hjalmarsson (1974) and successfully applied by Førsund and Jansen (1977) to the Norwegian pulp industry, by Førsund and Hjalmarsson (1979a, b) to Swedish dairy plants, by Albach (1980) to German industrial firms, and by many others.[8]

1.3.2 *Competitive Pressure*. Many years ago Hicks suggested that "... people in monopolistic positions ... are likely to exploit their advantage much more by not bothering to get very near the position of maximum profit, than by straining themselves to get very close to it. The best of all monopoly profits is a quiet life" (1935, p. 8). Ever since, the quiet life hypothesis has suggested that productive efficiency can be expected to vary inversely with market power. While strong competitive pressures impose productive efficiency on firms as a survival condition, under a monopoly sheltered from such pressures the pursuit of productive efficiency is an option rather than a necessity. The degree of competitive pressure is a crucial determinant of "X-efficiency" in Leibenstein's (1966, 1973, 1976, 1978b) micro-micro approach to the theory of the firm.[9] Empirical tests by Primeaux (1977) for U.S. electric utilities provide support for the hypothesized inverse relationship between efficiency (as measured by average cost) and market power.

Since the costs associated with inefficiency stemming from market power are really the costs of sheltering, or the costs of protection, it is not surprising that another area in which the efficiency-market power nexus has been repeatedly subjected to empirical test is that of the cost of protection in international trade. Protection affects relative prices, thereby generating inter-industry allocative inefficiencies by inducing a country to produce a different product mix than it would under free trade. But protection also leads to intra-industry "X-inefficiency" both by permitting domestic production that cannot compete with imports and by permitting domestic production that could compete with imports if such competition were present. Some recent studies that focus on the "X-inefficiency" costs of protection include Carlsson (1972) for Sweden, Bergsman (1974) for six Less Developed Countries (LDC), White (1976) for Pakistan, and Martin and Page (1983) for Ghana, among many others. A thorough analysis of the effect of trade liberalization on productive efficiency can be found in Pelkmans (1982).

1.3.3 *Type of Ownership*. A closely related hypothesis, arising from the property rights literature, asserts that public ownership is inherently less efficient than private ownership. The argument, due originally to Alchian (1965), holds that the broadly dispersed ownership of the public organization, combined with the inability of the public owners to transfer ownership shares, dampens the incentive of public owners to monitor the performance of management. The ownership of private firms is both more concentrated and transferable, and this generates an incentive for private owners to monitor managerial performance. Hence public firm management is hypothesized to be less efficient than private firm management. This hypothesis has been subjected to many empirical tests that have, on balance, provided only modest support for the hypothesis. Some recent examples include Davies (1971) for Australian airlines, Tyler (1979) for Brazilian plastics and steel producers, Crain and Zardkoohi (1980) for U.S. water utilities, Caves and Christensen (1980) for Canadian railroads, Levy (1981) for three Iraq industries, and Gillis (1982) for Bolivian and Indonesian mining. For a good survey, see Borcherding, Pommerehne, and Schneider (1982).

1.3.4. *Efficiency and Firm Size*. For a number of reasons unrelated to either type of ownership or market power, an association between firm size and some measure of efficiency is frequently postulated. Knight (1965) emphasized the importance of the relationship, noting that cost-increasing inefficiency of large firms might provide a useful deterrent to excessive growth in pursuit of monopoly profit. Robinson (1962) offered three reasons why efficiency might be expected to decline with increases in firm size, at least after some threshold size is reached. First the gradual replacement of gains to the division of labor with costs as routine causes boredom and stifles creativity, secondly a reduced speed and flexibility of decision-making, and thirdly an increased difficulty and cost of coordination. The role of coordination costs, particularly hierarchical control costs, is central to most current models that associate increases in firm size with altered efficiency.[10] The postulated association is important for both private and public policy reasons because, depending on its direction, cost-reducing efficiency gains could be realized through splintering of large firms or merger of small firms. Although the theoretical foundations of the association are a bit shaky, the hypothesis is sufficiently interesting to have generated a large and growing body of empirical literature, one that has not surprisingly reached conflicting conclusions. Among the more prominent recent works are those of Lau and Yotopoulos (1971), Yotopoulos and Lau (1973), Bharadwaj (1974), and Sidhu (1974) for Indian agriculture, Meller (1976) for Chilean manufacturing, Page (1979) for Indian soap manufacturing, Herdt and Mandac (1981) for Philippine rice farming, Tyler (1979) for the Brazilian plastics and steel industries, Pitt and Lee (1981) for Indonesian weaving firms, Trosper (1978) for American Indian ranching, Färe, Grosskopf, Logan, and Lovell (1984) for electric utilities in the U.S., and van den Broeck (1983) for Belgian manufacturing.

1.3.5. *Regulatory Effects*. Various types of government regulation, in addition to achieving their stated objectives, frequently have favorable or unfavorable secondary effects on the performance of regulated firms. For example, Averch and Johnson (1962) were able to show that effective rate of return regulation has the unfortunate side effect of inducing the regulated firm to become allocatively inefficient by selecting inefficiently large capital-labor and capital-fuel ratios for the rate of output it produces. The magnitude and cost of this "A-J bias" depend on the severity of the constraint, and on the extent to which capital is substitutable for other inputs. Gollop and Karlson (1978) later showed that a fuel adjustment clause, allowing the regulated firm to pass through fuel cost increases, has partially offsetting allocative effects in that it induces the regulated firm to adopt inefficiently large fuel-capital and fuel-labor ratios for the rate of output it produces, a result that has been verified by Cowing and Stevenson (1982) using simulation experiments. An empirical test of both types of regulation-induced allocative inefficiency has been conducted by Atkinson and Halvorsen (1980) for U.S. electricity generation.[11]

1.3.6. *The Economics of Discrimination*. A wide variety of models has been developed in an effort to explain various types of discrimination against minorities. Although the literature has a long history dating back at least to Edgeworth, its recent development was initiated by Becker (1957). According to Becker, if an individual has a "taste" for discrimination, then that individual must act as if he were willing to pay for the opportunity to avoid associating with those against whom he has a taste for discrimination. These subjective tastes are given quantitative representation through the use of "discrimination coefficients," which reflect the amount by which prices must be adjusted to induce a person to associate with those against whom he has a taste for discrimination. For example, an employer with a taste for discrimination against minority employees would act as if the minority wage exceeds the majority wage by an amount determined by the discrimination coefficient, and hire an inefficiently small percentage of minority labor. The result is what we have termed an allocatively inefficient input choice that raises cost; the magnitude of each depends on the size of the discrimination coefficient and the substitutability of minority labor for other inputs. The excess cost is a measure of what the employer is willing to pay to indulge his prejudice. Since non-discriminating firms are more profitable than discriminating firms, the former will tend to grow relative to the latter, and the ability of the latter to sustain their indulgence depends on the competitive pressures imposed by the marketplace.

1.3.7. *Land Tenure in Agriculture*. There exist a large number of contractual arrangements by which agricultural land is cultivated, with the most prominent types being cropsharing, fixed rental payments, wage contracts, and owner cultivation. The importance of agriculture in most developing economies, together with the pressures for land reform in these economies, makes the relative performance of these different contractual arrangements important to policy makers. An argument originally made by Adam Smith asserts that cropsharing is an allocatively inefficient form of tenure, since payment of a share of the crop to the owner reduces the tenant's incentive to work and invest in the land. Consequently, share tenancy involves an inefficiently small ratio of labor to land and other inputs, as well as lower output, relative to other forms of contractual arrangement. A good derivation and analysis of this popular result is provided by Bardhan and Srinivasan (1971). However this outcome is disputed by Cheung (1969), who asserts that "... different contractual arrangements do not imply different efficiencies of resource use as long as these arrangements are themselves aspects of private property rights.... The allocation of resources will differ, however, if property rights are attenuated or denied as private, or if the government overrides the market process of allocation" (1969, p. 4). Cheung relies on competition among land owners to induce efficient contracts, and on competition among tenants to assure the employment of the contracted amount of tenant inputs, in an environment of protected private property rights to generate efficient resource allocation in cropsharing. Empirical testing of the efficiency hypothesis has become increasingly popular, although the results have been largely inconclusive. Currie (1981) discusses the logic of various types of land tenure and examines the British experience, while Cheung (1969) uses data on Asian agriculture. The performance of alternative land tenurial arrangements in the post-bellum U.S. South is investigated by DeCanio (1974), Higgs (1977), and Ransom and Sutch (1977).

1.3.8 *Surplus Labor and Choice of Technology in Developing Countries*. The economies of developing countries are frequently characterized by the simultaneous occurrence of surplus labor and positive wage rates in the traditional agricultural sector, and of high capital costs and capital-intensive techniques in the modern industrial sector. The adoption of such seemingly inappropriate technologies in the industrial sector is widely attributed to the limited range of technologies actually available for adoption, to the selection of technologies on the basis of input prices that are distorted by government policies, or to the absence of competitive pressure that would force selection of an appropriate technology. Whatever the reasons, this scenario gives the appearance of allocative inefficiency, both within each sector and between the two sectors. Theoretical investigations of the surplus labor and choice of technique hypotheses appear in Sen (1966, 1975) and Leibenstein (1978a), and recent empirical investigations have been undertaken by Pack (1974) for a sample of individual firms in a number of countries, by Pack (1976) for Kenyan manufacturing firms, and by Lecraw (1979) for firms in Thailand, among many others.

1.3.9. *Uncertainty*. If management is uncertain about some of the input prices it faces, then even under risk-neutrality, management can be expected to use relatively more of the risk-free inputs, and relatively less of the risky inputs, as compared to the cost minimizing outcome under certainty (see Perrakis, 1980). Moreover, Stewart (1978) has shown that risk-aversion reinforces this effort. Each of these effects presumably carries over to output price uncertainty in the multiproduct firm, and similar effects can be shown to result from uncertainty about input supplies and about the outputs that can be produced from given inputs, the latter resulting from an erratic environment or technological uncertainty. Holtman (1983) has incorporated uncertainty into a model of the firm in an effort to shed light on the "X-inefficiency" issue, and risk plays an important role in the choice of land tenurial arrangements in Cheung (1969). The effects of uncertainty on the efficiency of resource allocation have been examined empirically by Cheung (1969) for Asian agriculture, by Roumasset (1976) for Philippine rice production, and by Wu (1979) for Taiwan family rice farms, among many others.

1.3.10. *Total Factor Productivity Growth*. The rate of total factor productivity growth is commonly calculated as the share-weighted sum of the rates of growth of outputs minus the share-weighted sum of the rates of growth of inputs. This corresponds roughly to the distinction Solow (1957) drew between output growth attributable to movements along a production surface (input growth) and output growth attributable to shifts in the production surface (technical change). Indeed, the concepts of total factor productivity change and technical change are frequently used synonomously. However, the correspondence assumes that production is continuously technically efficient. If the full efficiency assumption is relaxed, then the rate of total factor productivity growth can be decomposed into the rate of technical change and the rate of change of efficiency. If such a decomposition is possible, it enables one to enrich Solow's dichotomy by attributing observed output growth to movements along a path on or beneath the production surface (input growth), movement toward or away from the production surface (efficiency growth or retardation), and shifts in the production surface (technical change). The distinction between efficiency growth and technical change is important because they are fundamentally different phenomena with different sources, and so different policies may be required to address them. The decomposition of total factor productivity growth into technical change and efficiency growth has been modeled by Nishimizu and Page (1982), who apply their technique to the postwar Yugoslav economy.

1.4. The Plan of the Book

In chapter 2 we describe the structure of the production technology we shall be working with in the rest of the book. The technology by which inputs are transformed into outputs is modeled by an input correspondence specifying the subset of input vectors capable of producing a certain output vector or, inversely, by an output correspondence specifying the subset of output vectors obtainable from a certain input vector. We then state and interpret weak and strong axiom systems that the two correspondences must satisfy if they are to model a production technology. For future use in efficiency measurement, we identify various types of efficient subsets of these correspondences. We also introduce the graph of the production technology, defined in terms of the input and output correspondences. The graph of the production technology specifies the subset of all technologically feasible input and output vectors, and so for purposes of efficiency measurement we specify various efficient subsets of the graph as well.

In chapter 3 we introduce a family of radial input efficiency measures defined on the technology. These measures are termed "input" measures because they measure the efficiency of an input vector in the production of a given output vector, using the input correspondence to represent the technology. Since they hold the output vector fixed, these measures are appropriate to situations in which a firm takes its outputs as being exogenous, as in a cost minimization context. These measures are termed "radial" since the search for smaller feasible input vectors is constrained to proportionally smaller feasible input vectors relative to which the efficiency of an observed input vector can be calculated. The core of the chapter consists of a decomposition of a radial measure of overall input efficiency into technical, two types of structural and allocative components, and an investigation of the properties of the overall measure and each of its components.

In chapter 4 we introduce a family of radial output efficiency measures defined on the technology. These measures are called "output" measures because they measure the efficiency of an output vector produced by a given input vector, using the output correspondence to represent the technology. Since they hold the input vector fixed, these measures are appropriate to situations in which the firm takes inputs as exogenous, as in a revenue-maximizing context. The radial measure of overall output efficiency is decomposed, and its decomposition interpreted, in much the same manner that the radial measure of overall input efficiency is.

In chapter 5 we permit both inputs and outputs to be freely variable, and we introduce a family of hyperbolic graph efficiency measures. These measures are appropriate to situations in which neither inputs nor outputs are taken to be exogenous by the firm, as in the case of profit maximization. The measures are called "hyperbolic" because they seek the maximum proportionate change in all variables (decrease for inputs, increase for outputs) consistent with the technology as represented by its graph. Although these measures are natural extensions of the radial input and output efficiency measures introduced in chapters 3 and 4, they are not radial, or even linear, in input-output space. They are hyperbolic. As in the case of the radial input and output measures, however, the hyperbolic graph efficiency measure can be decomposed into technical, two types of structural and allocative components, and such a decomposition occupies much of the chapter.

In chapter 6 we establish some relationships among various input, output, and graph efficiency measures. We seek to establish conditions on the technology under which input, output, and graph measures of a certain type of efficiency attach the same efficiency value to a given input-output vector. We also seek conditions under which the three measures of a certain type of efficiency can be ordered, as well as conditions under which an input-output vector labeled efficient by one measure is also identified as being efficient by another measure.

The efficiency measures introduced in chapters 3–5 and compared in chapter 6 are all either radial or hyperbolic. That is, they impose proportional changes on all variables of interest, inputs or outputs, or both.

Such a restriction is convenient and in keeping with tradition, but it is not without its drawbacks. Unless the technology is extremely well-behaved, these measures can lead to an input-output vector being called efficient when it is not, as well as to the efficiency of an input-output vector being measured relative to an inefficient input-output vector. These drawbacks can be avoided by defining nonradial input and output efficiency measures, and non-hyperbolic graph efficiency measures. Indeed, in the absence of severe restrictions on the structure of technology, the only way to avoid these two drawbacks is to force reference vectors to belong to efficient subsets, and this in turn requires the use of nonradial or nonhyperbolic efficiency measures. Accordingly, in chapter 7 we introduce families of nonradial input and output efficiency measures and a family of nonhyperbolic graph efficiency measures. We also derive their decompositions, and compare their properties to those of the radial or hyperbolic measures introduced in chapters 3–5. Although these nonradial measures contain their radial counterparts as testable special cases, they are somewhat more difficult to calculate, and their decomposition is not so transparent.

In chapter 8 we introduce a measure of scale efficiency as an indicator of the firm's departure from what is often called technically optimal scale, that input-output vector that would be generated by long run competitive equilibrium. We also demonstrate how to tell whether a scale-inefficient firm is operating at too large or too small scale. A measure of scale efficiency is a logical complement to the previously obtained measures of technical, structural and allocative efficiency, although as we noted above, scale efficiency is more of a social or external notion than a private or internal notion of efficiency in production.

At the end of chapters 3, 4, 5, 7 and 8 we show how all of the efficiency measures we develop can be calculated. This is accomplished by specifying linear programming models (and a non-linear programming model in chapter 7) to capture the structure of efficient technology. These programming models also provide a means by which each measure of efficiency (e.g., input, output, graph, and scale), and the components of each measure, can be calculated. Small artificial data sets are employed to illustrate the ability of the programming models to construct an efficient technology and to measure various types of efficiency relative to that technology. The programming models themselves are extensions of models of Afriat (1972), Hanoch and Rothschild (1972), Shephard (1974b), Diewert and Parkan (1983), and Varian (1984) designed to serve somewhat different purposes. The numerical examples are intended to illustrate and facilitate the practical application of these efficiency measures, which is one of the basic motivations of this study.

In chapter 9 we accomplish three tasks. First, we summarize the results on efficiency measurement obtained in preceding chapters. Next, we discuss some unfinished business and suggest some potentially fruitful areas for further research. Finally, we provide a brief survey of the various approaches to the empirical estimation of efficiency that have been proposed during the past three decades. A somewhat arbitrary but useful allocation rule yields four approaches to estimation; two of them programming techniques and two of them statistical techniques. All four approaches have been employed, with varying degrees of success; their performance can be expected to improve as the techniques are refined. The survey is neither exhaustive nor detailed. It is intended as a brief reader's guide for those interested in empirical application of the measures developed in this book.

Notes

1. This definition is a blend of the definitions of "efficient" and "efficiency" found in *Webster's New Collegiate Dictionary*, which also contains the suggestive phrase "productive without waste." Some early ruminations on the meaning and measurement of efficiency appear in Hall and Winsten (1959).

2. See, for example, Hildenbrand (1981), who cites others as well.

3. Technical inefficiency corresponds to what some writers call waste. Stigler (1976) is arguably one such writer, and he suggests that waste is a useless economic concept that will remain so until we have a theory of error. Although we do not claim to be proposing a theory of error, we do offer a taxonomy, a measurement scheme, and a set of implications of error.

4. Our benchmark against which to measure scale efficiency corresponds to Chamberlin's (1933) "ideal output," to the notion of "technically optimal scale" advanced by Frisch (1965), to the "most productive scale size" of Banker (1984), and to the "M-locus" of Baumol, Panzar, and Willig (1982).

5. In this regard Danø (1966, pp. 14–15) invokes a division of labor between the technician and the economist; it being the job of the technician to provide the boundary of the production possibilities set to the economist responsible for selecting an optimal point on the boundary. Carlson (1939, pp. 14–15) states that "If we want the production function to give only one value for the output from a given service combination, the function must be so defined that it expresses the *maximum product* obtainable from the combination at the existing state of technical knowledge. Therefore, the purely *technical* maximization problem may be said to be solved by the very definition of our production function." However, neither argument denies the fruitfulness of associating a production function with the boundary of a production possibilities set while at the same time permitting production to occur on the interior of that set.

6. Indeed for Samuelson (1947, Chap. 1) the equivalence between equilibrium conditions (i.e., satisfaction of the first-order conditions) for the optimization of some magnitude, and the stability of that equilibrium (i.e., satisfaction of the second-order conditions) constitute the two sources of operationally meaningful theorems. However, this does not deny the possibility that these conditions might fail in a way that permits inefficiency, while at the same time allowing for the development of testable hypotheses.

7. The mathematical basis for the economic theory of duality is Minkowski's Theorem, which in this context states that under certain conditions a closed, convex production possibilities set can be represented as the intersection of the halfspaces generated by the iso-value surfaces tangent to the production possibilities set. The key words are "convex" and "tangent." Thorough explorations of the structure and implications of duality theory can be found in Diewert (1974, 1982), and in Fuss and McFadden (1978).

8. The recent monograph of Førsund and Hjalmarsson (1979c) contains a number of studies of average-practice vs. best-practice variation.

9. Although his main focus is on intra-firm pressures, in keeping with his micro-micro orientation, Leibenstein does not ignore the role of inter-firm pressures. "Considerable X-inefficiency may arise as a result of low pressure for performance from the environment. Monopoly is a case in point. There is no need for monopolists to minimize costs or transmit pressure through the organization to improve performance, since higher costs can be passed on to consumers." (Leibenstein 1975, p. 604). This line of reasoning has, however, come under attack; see, for example, Schwartzman (1973) and Stigler (1976).

10. A good example of a model of this sort is given in Williamson (1967), who also briefly traces the history of thought on the subject.

11. Two related claims are worthy of mention. One is that it is frequently claimed that rate of return regulation has a tertiary effect: by inducing the firm to expand its rate base, such regulation also induces the firm to expand output, a desirable offset to the undesirable A–J bias. The validity of this claim, however, rests on the satisfaction of severe restrictions on the structure of production technology. The second claim is that regulatory lag tends to dampen allocative inefficiencies. These and other aspects of rate of return regulation are discussed in Baumol and Klevorick (1970).

2 THE STRUCTURE OF PRODUCTION TECHNOLOGY

2.0 Introduction

Any investigation of efficiency in production must begin with a description of the structure of the technology that constrains production activities. The purpose of this chapter is to provide such a description.

Consider a production unit transforming a vector of nonnegative inputs into a vector of nonnegative outputs, subject to the constraint imposed by a known, fixed technology. This transformation process is modeled by an input correspondence specifying the subset of input vectors capable of producing a certain output vector or, inversely, by an output correspondence specifying the subset of output vectors obtainable from a certain input vector. An input correspondence provides the basis for various measures of input efficiency (the efficiency of an input vector in the production of a certain output vector), while an output correspondence provides the basis for various measures of output efficiency (the efficiency of an output vector produced by a certain input vector). In section 2.1 we introduce a dual pair of axiom sets that these two correspondences must satisfy if they are to model a production technology. These dual axiom sets are assumed to hold throughout the monograph. We also introduce three additional axiom pairs relating to disposability of inputs or outputs, quasiconcavity of the two correspondences, and attainability of outputs. One or more of these additional axiom pairs are occasionally used to strengthen the basic axiom sets.

Input and output correspondences specify subsets of technologically feasible input and output vectors, respectively. Efficiency measurement requires that we be able to identify subsets of efficient feasible input and output vectors, and to provide a basis against which to evaluate the efficiency of any observed feasible input-output vector. Accordingly, in section 2.2 we specify three different candidates for efficient feasible subsets of each correspondence. In order of increasing restrictiveness, they are isoquants, weak efficient subsets, and efficient subsets. We discuss the distinctions among the three candidates and state conditions under which they coincide. Each of these three subsets of the input and output correspondences is price-independent. However, since some efficiency measures are price-dependent, we also introduce two price-dependent subsets, namely the input cost minimizing subset of the input correspondence, and the output revenue maximizing subset of the output correspondence.

In section 2.3 we consider the possibility of representing production technology by means of a production function or a transformation function. For a production unit producing a single output we define a scalar valued production function in terms of the input and output correspondences. For a production unit producing a vector of outputs, many writers, beginning with Hicks (1946), have used a transformation function to provide a functional representation of production technology. We take a somewhat different approach, following Shephard (1970), by defining an Isoquant Joint Production Function (IJPF) in terms of the input and output correspondences, and we obtain necessary and sufficient conditions for the existence of an IJPF.

In section 2.4 we introduce a variety of special production structures that prove useful in illustrating various efficiency measures later on in the monograph. Four of these structures (ray-homotheticity, homotheticity, ray-homogeneity, and homogeneity, of either the input correspondence or the output correspondence or both) serve to simplify various efficiency measures. The fifth special structure is a piecewise linear input-output structure. This type of structure is of particular interest because it can be readily used in the numerical calculation of the efficiency measures discussed and developed in this study. This piecewise-linear technology is used in the numerical examples throughout the text.

In section 2.5 we introduce the graph of the production technology, defined in terms of the input and output correspondences. The graph of the technology provides the basis for various measures of input-output efficiency, or what is called graph efficiency. The axiom set satisfied by the graph is, of course, equivalent to the axiom sets satisfied by the input and output correspondences. The graph specifies the set of all technologically feasible input-output vectors, and for efficiency measurement it is necessary to identify subsets of efficient feasible input-output vectors. Accordingly, we introduce three price-independent efficient subsets of the graph (the isoquant, the weak efficient subset, and the efficient subset), and one price-dependent efficient subset of the graph (the profit maximizing subset).

2.1 The Input and Output Correspondences

A production technology transforming factors of production (inputs) $x = (x_1, x_2, \ldots, x_n) \in R^n_+$ into net outputs $u = (u_1, u_2, \ldots, u_m) \in R^m_+$ is modeled by an input correspondence $u \to L(u) \subseteqq R^n_+$ or inversely by an output correspondence $x \to P(x) \subseteqq R^m_+$. For any $u \in R^m_+$, $L(u)$ denotes the subset of all input vectors $x \in R^n_+$ which yield at least u. Inversely, for any $x \in R^n_+$, $P(x)$ denotes the subset of all (net) output vectors obtainable from x. The inverse relationship between L and P is given by

$$x \in L(u) \Longleftrightarrow u \in P(x), \tag{2.1.1}$$

and may be computed by

$$P(x) = \{u: x \in L(u)\} \text{ and } L(u) = \{x: u \in P(x)\}. \tag{2.1.2}$$

An input set $L(u)$ and an output set $P(x)$ are illustrated for the case $m = n = 2$ in Fig. 2–1. In panel (a) the subset of all input vectors $x \in R^2_+$ capable of producing at least output u is labeled $L(u)$, and consists of the subset of input vectors on or above the curve AB. In panel (b) the subset of all output vectors obtainable from input vector x is labeled $P(x)$, and consists of the subset of nonnegative output vectors on or below the curve AB.

If the correspondences L and P are to model a production technology, they must satisfy certain properties (axioms). It is assumed here that the input correspondence L satisfies the following subset of axioms suggested by Shephard (1974a)

L.1 $0 \notin L(u)$ for $u \geq 0$, and $L(0) = R^n_+$,

L.2 If $\| u^l \| \to +\infty$ as $l \to +\infty$, then $\bigcap_{l=1}^{+\infty} L(u^l)$ is empty,

L.3 If $x \in L(u)$, $\lambda x \in L(u)$ for $\lambda \geqq 1$,

L.4 L is a closed correspondence,

L.5 $L(\theta u) \subseteqq L(u)$ for $\theta \geqq 1$.

The axioms (L.1–L.5) are taken as valid for any production technology, and are assumed to hold throughout this monograph. L.1 states that semipositive output cannot be obtained from a null input vector (i.e., free production is excluded), and that any nonnegative input yields at least zero output. L.2 states that finite inputs cannot produce infinite outputs. L.3 states

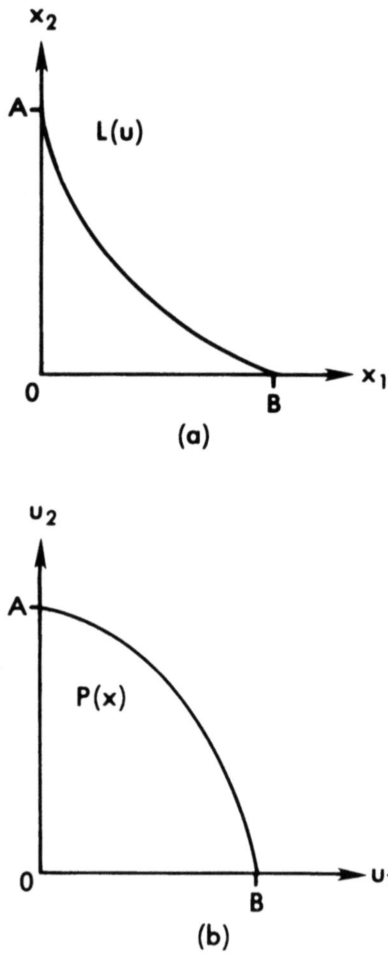

Figure 2-1

that proportional increases in inputs do not decrease outputs. This axiom is referred to as "weak disposability of inputs." L.4 is a mathematical requirement imposed to enable us to define input isoquants as subsets of the boundaries of the input sets L(u). It is equivalent to assuming that the graph of the input and output correspondences is closed (Shephard, 1970). The graph is defined as

$$\text{GR}: = \{(x, u): x \in \text{L}(u), u \in R_+^m\} = \{(x, u): u \in \text{P}(x), x \in R_+^n\} \tag{2.1.3}$$

and is examined further in section 2.5. The last property, L.5, states that a proportional increase in outputs cannot be obtained if inputs are reduced. This axiom is referred to as "weak disposability of outputs."

From the inverse relationship between the input and the output correspondences it follows that there exists a set of axioms on P that is equivalent to (L.1–L.5). This set is

P.1 $\text{P}(0) = \{0\}$,

P.2 $\text{P}(x)$ is bounded for $x \in R_+^n$,

P.3 $\text{P}(\lambda x) \supseteqq \text{P}(x)$ for $\lambda \geqq 1$,

P.4 P is a closed correspondence,

P.5 $u \in \text{P}(x) \Rightarrow \theta u \in \text{P}(x)$ for $\theta \in [0, 1]$.

Property P.1 states that the null input vector yields zero output. P.2 states that finite input cannot produce infinite output. P.3 states that a proportional increase in inputs does not reduce output (i.e., "weak disposability of inputs"). P.4 allows the definition of output isoquants as subsets of the boundaries of the output sets P(x), and is equivalent to closure of the graph. P.5 states that a proportional decrease in outputs remains producible with no change in inputs (i.e., "weak disposability of outputs").

In places in this monograph, stronger axioms than L.3 and L.5 are needed. These axioms are

L.3.S $y \geqq x \in \text{L}(u) \Rightarrow y \in \text{L}(u)$,
L.5.S $v \geqq u \Rightarrow \text{L}(v) \subseteqq \text{L}(u)$,

or equivalently

P.3.S $y \geqq x \Rightarrow \text{P}(y) \subseteqq \text{P}(x)$,
P.5.S $u \leqq v \in \text{P}(x) \Rightarrow u \in \text{P}(x)$.

Properties L.3.S and P.3.S strengthen L.3 and P.3 by imposing strong disposability of inputs, while properties L.5.S and P.5.S strengthen L.5 and P.5 by imposing strong disposability of outputs. Thus, by L.3.S and P.3.S, an increase in inputs, including but not limited to a proportional increase, cannot lead to a reduction in output. By L.5.S and P.5.S, any reduction in outputs, including but not limited to a proportional reduction, remains producible with no change in inputs. Clearly, if inputs or outputs are strongly disposable they are also weakly disposable. Of course, the converse is not true. Although the strong disposability axiom excludes congestion in the technology, such a property is often justified on socio-economic grounds, provided inputs and outputs can be fully adjusted. Thus, if the option is available, producers simply dispose of congesting inputs or outputs. In this case, instead of assuming that the technology only satisfies (L.1–L.5), an additional assumption is made, namely that if an input vector $x \in R^n_+$ is available, then each $y \in R^n_+$, $y \leqq x$ may also be used in production. The formal definition of this strongly disposable input correspondence is

$$L^{SI}(u) := \{x: u \in P(y),\ 0 \leqq y \leqq x\}. \tag{2.1.4}$$

To show that L^{SI} satisfies (L.1–L.5) and L.3.S, we note that $L^{SI}(u) = \{x: y \in L(u), 0 \leqq y \leqq x\}$. Next we show that $\{x: y \in L(u), 0 \leqq y \leqq x\} = L(u) + R^n_+$. Thus let $x \in L^{SI}(u) = \{x: y \in L(u), 0 \leqq y \leqq x\}$, then $x \geqq y$ for some $y \in L(u)$. Define $z: = x - y$, since $z \in R^n_+$ it follows that $x \in L(u) + R^n_+$. Conversely if $x = y + z$ where $y \in L(u)$ and $z \in R^n_+$, then $x \in L^{SI}(u)$. Thus (2.1.4) can be written as $L^{SI}(u) = L(u) + R^n_+$. Formally, from Färe (1975) and Teusch (1983) it is true that

Theorem: If L satisfies (L.1–L.5) then the input correspondence (2.1.4) satisfies (L.1–L.5 and L.3.S). (2.1.5)

Frequently, again on socio-economic grounds, it is assumed that outputs are freely (strongly) disposable. However, such an assumption is not always justified, since outputs may be "bads," such as toxic chemical wastes, as well as "goods." The formal definition of such a strongly disposable output correspondence is

$$P^{SO}(x) := \{u: x \in L(v),\ v \geqq u \geqq 0\}. \tag{2.1.6}$$

Regarding this output correspondence we have

Theorem: If P satisfies (P.1–P.5), and P(B) is bounded for each bounded set $B \subset R^n_+$, then the correspondence (2.1.6) satisfies (P.1–P.5 and P.5.S). (2.1.7)

Proof: It is straightforward to show that P.1–P.3 and P.5.S hold. To show that P is a closed correspondence, let $x^l \rightarrow x^0$, $u^l \rightarrow u^0$ with $u^l \in \mathrm{P}^{\mathrm{SI}}(x^l)$. Then there is a sequence v^l with $v^l \geqq u^l$ and $v^l \in \mathrm{P}(x^l)$ for all l. Since the set $\{x^0, x^1, x^2, \ldots\}$ is bounded, $\mathrm{P}(\{x^0, x^1, x^2, \ldots\})$ is bounded and thus its closure is compact. Therefore v^l has a convergent subsequence $v^{l_k} \rightarrow v^0$. Since P is a closed correspondence, $v^0 \in \mathrm{P}(x^0)$. $v^{l_k} \geqq u^{l_k}$ for all l_k, thus $v^0 \geqq u^0$. Therefore, $u^0 \in \mathrm{P}^{\mathrm{SI}}(x^0) = \{u{:}v \in \mathrm{P}(x^0),\ v \geqq u \geqq 0\} = \{u{:}x^0 \in \mathrm{L}(v),\ v \geqq u \geqq 0\}$. ■

In some sections of this monograph, two convexity assumptions will also be used. These are

L.6 $\mathrm{L}(u)$ is convex for all $u \in R^m_+$,

L.7 The input correspondence is quasi-concave on R^m_+,

or equivalently

P.6 The output correspondence is quasi-concave on R^n_+,

P.7 $\mathrm{P}(x)$ is convex for all $x \in R^n_+$.

By L.6 and P.6 if $x \in \mathrm{L}(u)$ and $y \in \mathrm{L}(u)$ then $(\lambda x + (1 - \lambda)y) \in \mathrm{L}(u)$ for $\lambda \in [0, 1]$, implying that u can also be produced with a convex combination of x and y. Similarly, by L.7 and P.7, if $u \in \mathrm{P}(x)$ and $v \in \mathrm{P}(x)$ then $(\lambda u + (1 - \lambda)v) \in \mathrm{P}(x)$ for $\lambda \in [0, 1]$, implying that x can also produce a convex combination of u and v.

Finally, an output attainability assumption will occasionally be used. This assumption is

L.8 If $x \in \mathrm{L}(u)$ for some $u \geq 0$, then the ray $\{\lambda x{:}\ \lambda \geqq 0\}$ intersects all $\mathrm{L}(\theta u)$ for $\theta \geqq 0$,

or equivalently

P.8 If $u \in \mathrm{P}(x)$, $u \geq 0$, then for each $\theta \geqq 0$ there is a $\lambda \geqq 0$ such that $\theta u \in \mathrm{P}(\lambda x)$.

By L.8 and P.8, if input vector x can produce output vector u, then all proportional scalings of u can be produced by some proportional scaling of x.

2.2 Subsets of the Input and Output Correspondences

To measure efficiency it is important to isolate certain subsets of $L(u)$ and $P(x)$, since different efficiency measures relate an observed feasible input-output vector to different subsets of $L(u)$ and $P(x)$.

Definition: The Input Isoquant of $L(u)$ is defined for $u \geq 0$, as Isoq $L(u)\!: = \{x\!: x \in L(u), \lambda x \notin L(u), \lambda \in [0, 1)\}$ and Isoq $L(0)\!: = \{0\}$. (2.2.1)

Definition: The Weak Efficient Subset of $L(u)$ is defined for $u \geq 0$, as WEff $L(u)\!: = \{x\!:\ x \in L(u),\ y \overset{*}{<} x \Rightarrow y \notin L(u)\}$ and WEff $L(0)\!: = \{0\}$. (2.2.2)

Definition: The Efficient Subset of $L(u)$ is defined for $u \geq 0$, as Eff $L(u)\!: = \{x\!:\ x \in L(u),\ y \leq x \Rightarrow y \notin L(u)\}$ and Eff $L(0)\!: = \{0\}$. (2.2.3)

Definition: The Output Isoquant is defined for $P(x) \neq \{0\}$ as Isoq $P(x)\!: = \{u\!:\ u \in P(x),\ \theta u \notin P(x),\ \theta > 1\}$ and for $P(x) = \{0\}$, Isoq $P(x)\!: = \{0]$. (2.2.4)

Definition: The Weak Efficient Subset of $P(x) \neq \{0\}$ is WEff $P(x)\!: = \{u\!:\ u \in P(x),\ v \overset{*}{>} u \Rightarrow v \notin P(x)\}$ and for $P(x) = \{0\}$, WEff $P(x)\!: = \{0\}$. (2.2.5)

Definition: The Efficient Subset of $P(x) \neq \{0\}$ is Eff $P(x)\!: = \{u\!:\!u \in P(x),\ \ v \geq u \Rightarrow v \notin P(x)\}$ and for $P(x) = \{0\}$, Eff $P(x)\!: = \{0\}$. (2.2.6)

Definitions (2.2.1)–(2.2.6) yield the following relations

$$\text{Isoq } L(u) \supseteqq \text{WEff } L(u) \supseteqq \text{Eff } L(u), \tag{2.2.7}$$

and

$$\text{Isoq } P(x) \supseteqq \text{WEff } P(x) \supseteqq \text{Eff } P(x). \tag{2.2.8}$$

To further clarify definitions (2.2.1)–(2.2.6) let us consider an input set L(u) and an output set P(x).

In Fig. 2–2 of an input set L(u), the Isoq L(u) is given by the connected line segments $\overline{ABCD}$, the WEff L(u) is given by the connected line segments $\overline{BCD}$, and the Eff L(u) is given by the line segment $\overline{CD}$.

An example of a technology for which Isoq L(u) = WEff L(u) = Eff L(u) is provided by the Cobb-Douglas form for which the input set can be written as $L(u) = \{x: \Pi_{i=1}^{n} x_i^{\alpha_i} \geqq u, \alpha_i > 0\}$.

In Fig. 2–3 of an output set P(x), the connected line segments $\overline{EFGH}$ form the Isoq P(x), the connected line segments $\overline{FGH}$ form the WEff P(x), and the line segment $\overline{GH}$ forms the Eff P(x).

An example of a technology for which Isoq P(x) = WEff P(x) = Eff P(x) is provided by the constant elasticity of transformation (CET) form for which the output set can be written as $P(x) = \{u: (\Sigma_{i=1}^{m} \delta_i u_i^{-\rho})^{-1/\rho} \leqq x, \delta_i > 0, \rho < -1\}$.

It is of interest to know the most general conditions under which the different subsets of L(u) or P(x) coincide, respectively. To prove conditions

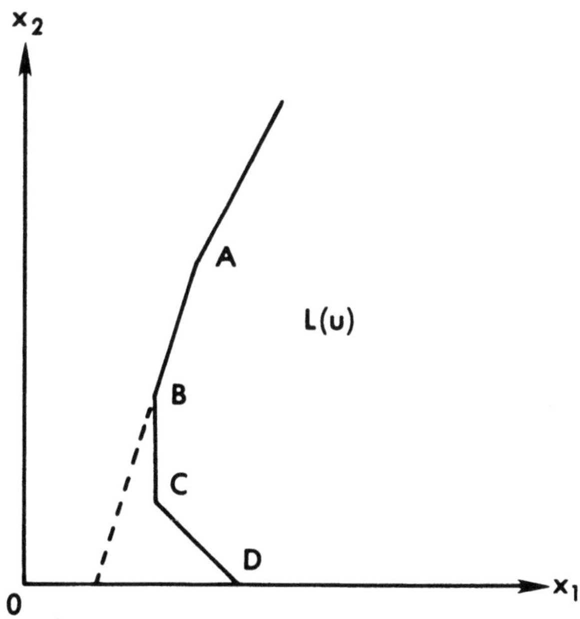

Figure 2-2

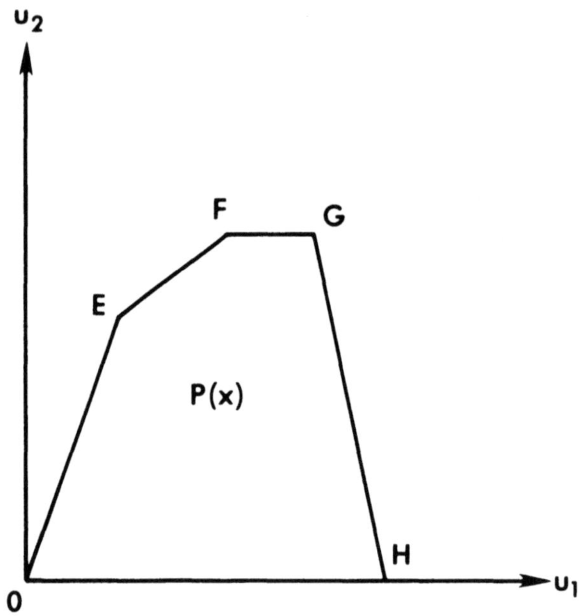

Figure 2-3

under which isoquants and weak efficient subsets coincide, consider the following properties of the input and output correspondences.

Definition: For all $x \geq 0$, $u \geq 0$ such that $\mathrm{P}(x) \neq \{0\}$, $\mathrm{L}(u) \neq \emptyset$, define (2.2.9)

I:1 $\text{Isoq L}(\theta u) \cap \text{Isoq L}(u) = \emptyset, \theta \neq 1,$

I:2 $\text{Isoq P}(\lambda x) \cap \text{Isoq P}(x) = \emptyset, \lambda \neq 1,$

I:3 $x \in \text{Isoq L}(u) \Rightarrow u \in \text{Isoq P}(x),$

I:4 $u \in \text{Isoq P}(x) \Rightarrow x \in \text{Isoq L}(u).$

The following relationship holds among these properties of the input and output correspondences:

Lemma: I:1 $\Leftrightarrow$ I:3 and I:2 $\Leftrightarrow$ I:4. (2.2.10)

Proof: Assume that I:3 holds and that $x \in (\text{Isoq L}(\theta u) \cap \text{Isoq L}(u))$, $\theta \neq 1$, then u and θu belong to Isoq $\mathrm{P}(x)$, which is a contradiction, showing that I:3

implies I:1. Conversely, assume that I:1 holds and that $x \in$ Isoq L(u) but $u \notin$ Isoq P(x). Clearly, $u \in$ P(x). Thus there exists a $\theta > 1$ such that $\theta u \in$ Isoq P(x). Thus $x \in$ L(θu). Since $\theta > 1$, L(θu) $\subseteqq$ L(u) by L.5, and hence $x \in$ Isoq L(θu) since $x \in$ Isoq L(u). However this contradicts I:1, thus I:1 implies I:3. Similar arguments apply to show that I:2 is equivalent to I:4. ■

We also need the following properties of the input and output correspondences

Definition: For all $x \geq 0, u \geq 0$, with P(x) $\neq \{0\}$, L(u) $\neq \emptyset$ define (2.2.11)

IW:1 $u \overset{*}{>} v \Rightarrow$ Isoq L(u) $\cap$ Isoq L(v) $= \emptyset$,

IW:2 $x \overset{*}{>} y \Rightarrow$ Isoq P(x) $\cap$ Isoq P(y) $= \emptyset$,

IW:3 Isoq L(u) = WEff L(u),

IW:4 Isoq P(x) = WEff P(x),

from which it can be proven that

Theorem: IW:1 and IW:2 imply IW:3 and IW:4. (2.2.12)

Proof: It is first shown that IW:1 and IW:2 imply IW:3. Since in general, WEff L(u) $\subseteqq$ Isoq L(u), it is sufficient to prove that Isoq L(u) $\subseteqq$ WEff L(u). Therefore, assume that $x \notin$ WEff L(u). If $x \notin$ L(u) then we are done, thus let $x \in$ L(u). Then there is a $y \overset{*}{<} x$, $y \in$ WEff L(u), (otherwise, $x \in$ WEff L(u)). Since WEff L(u) $\subseteqq$ Isoq L(u), $y \in$ Isoq L(u). Now, IW:1 implies I:1 of (2.2.9) and I:1 $\Leftrightarrow$ I:3, by lemma (2.2.10). Thus, $u \in$ Isoq P(y), then by IW:2, $u \notin$ Isoq P(x) implying that $x \in$ Isoq L(u), see I:3. Thus, $x \notin$ WEff L(u) $\Rightarrow x \notin$ Isoq L(u), showing that Isoq L(u) $\subseteqq$ WEff L(u). Similar arguments can be used to show that IW:1 and IW:2 also imply IW:4. ■

It is next shown that IW:3 and IW:4 do not imply IW:1 or IW:2. Let P(x): $= \{u \in R_+ : u \leqq \phi(x)\}$ and L(u): $= \{x \in R^n_+ : \phi(x) \geqq u\}$, where ϕ is given by example (2.2.13), and P(x) satisfies P.1, P.2, P.3.S, P.4, and P.5.S

$$\mathrm{P}(x) = [0, \phi(x)], \text{ where } \phi(x) := \begin{cases} x \text{ for } x \in [0, 1) \\ \text{and} \\ x + 1 \text{ for } x \in [1, +\infty). \end{cases} \qquad (2.2.13)$$

Clearly, Isoq $L(u)$ = WEff $L(u)$ and Isoq $P(x)$ = WEff $P(x)$, i.e., IW:3 and IW:4 hold. However, Isoq $L(1½)$ = Isoq $L(2)$, i.e., IW:1 does not hold.

To see that IW:3 and IW:4 do not imply IW:2, let $P(x)$ and $L(u)$ be defined as above but let ϕ be given by example (2.2.14)

$$P(x) = [0, \phi(x)], \text{ where } \phi(x) := \begin{cases} x \text{ for } x \in [0, 1) \\ 1 \text{ for } x \in [1, 2) \\ x - 1 \text{ for } x \in [2, +\infty). \end{cases} \tag{2.2.14}$$

Again, P has the required properties and IW:3 and IW:4 hold. However, Isoq $P(1½)$ = Isoq $P(2)$, i.e., IW:2 does not hold.

Recall that we are attempting to determine conditions under which the different subsets of $L(u)$ or $P(x)$ coincide. Theorem (2.2.12) is concerned with isoquants and weak efficient subsets, and states that the conjunction of IW:1 and IW:2 implies IW:3 and IW:4. That is, if output vector u is larger than output vector v in its positive components, it implies that Isoq $L(u)$ and Isoq $L(v)$ are disjoint, and if input vector x is larger than input vector y in its positive components, it implies that Isoq $P(x)$ and Isoq $P(y)$ are disjoint, then the isoquant of $L(u)$ coincides with the weak efficient subset of $L(u)$, and the isoquant of $P(x)$ coincides with the weak efficient subset of $P(x)$. But these conditions are only sufficient; they are not necessary, as examples (2.2.13) and (2.2.14) show.

Although the converse of theorem (2.2.12) is not true, we can prove

Theorem: I:4 and IW:3 imply IW:2. I:3 and IW:4 imply IW:1. (2.2.15)

Proof: Let $x \overset{*}{>} y \geq 0$ and $u \in$ Isoq $P(x)$. It must be shown that $u \notin$ Isoq $P(y)$. Since $u \in$ Isoq $P(x)$ it follows from I:4 that $x \in$ Isoq $L(u)$. Now, $y \overset{*}{<} x$, thus by IW:3, $y \notin L(u)$. Since $y \in L(u)$ if, and only if, $u \in P(y)$, $u \notin$ Isoq $P(y)$, proving the first part. A similar argument can be used to prove the second part. ■

Attention is next focused on the relationship between the weak efficient subsets and the efficient subsets. To prove conditions such that WEff $L(u)$ = Eff $L(u)$ and that WEff $P(x)$ = Eff $P(x)$, we first introduce

Definition: For $x \geq 0$, $v \geq 0$ with $P(x) \neq \{0\}$, $L(u) \neq \emptyset$, define (2.2.16)

W:1 $u \overset{*}{>} v \Rightarrow$ WEff $L(u) \cap$ WEff $L(v) = \emptyset$,

$$W:2 \;\; x \overset{*}{>} y \Rightarrow \text{WEff } P(x) \cap \text{WEff } P(y) = \emptyset,$$

$$W:3 \;\; x \in \text{WEff } L(u) \Rightarrow u \in \text{WEff } P(x),$$

$$W:4 \;\; u \in \text{WEff } P(x) \Rightarrow x \in \text{WEff } L(u).$$

Lemma: Let inputs and outputs be strongly disposable, then W : 1 $\Leftrightarrow$ W : 3 and W : 2 $\Leftrightarrow$ W : 4. (2.2.17)

Proof: Assume W : 1 holds and there exists an $x \in \text{WEff } L(u)$, $u \geq 0$, such that $u \notin \text{WEff } P(x)$. Clearly, $u \in P(x)$ and there exists a $v \overset{*}{>} u$, $v \in P(x)$, (otherwise, $u \in \text{WEff } P(x)$), implying that $x \in L(v)$. By strong disposability of outputs, $v \overset{*}{\geq} u \Rightarrow L(v) \subseteqq L(u)$. Thus, $x \in \text{WEff } L(v)$, contradicting W : 1. Conversely, assume W : 3 holds but there is an $x \in (\text{WEff } L(u) \cap \text{WEff } L(v))$, $u \overset{*}{>} v \geq 0$. Then, $u \in \text{WEff } P(x)$ and $v \in \text{WEff } P(x)$, contradicting the definition of WEff $P(x)$. Similar arguments apply to show that W : 2 $\Leftrightarrow$ W : 4. ■

Next, introduce

Definition: For all $x \geq 0, u \geq 0$ with $P(x) \neq \{0\}$, $L(u) \neq \emptyset$, define (2.2.18)

$$WE:1 \;\; u \geq v \Rightarrow \text{WEff } L(u) \cap \text{WEff } L(v) = \emptyset,$$

$$WE:2 \;\; x \geq y \Rightarrow \text{WEff } P(x) \cap \text{WEff } P(y) = \emptyset,$$

$$WE:3 \;\; \text{WEff } L(u) = \text{Eff } L(u),$$

$$WE:4 \;\; \text{WEff } P(x) = \text{Eff } P(x).$$

Note that if WE : 1 holds, so does W : 1, and if WE : 2 holds, so does W : 2. We can now prove a theorem showing sufficient conditions for the weak efficient subset to equal the efficient subset.

Theorem: Let inputs and outputs be strongly disposable. Then WE : 1 and WE : 2 imply WE : 3 and WE : 4. (2.2.19)

Proof: It is first shown that WE : 1 and WE : 2 imply WE : 3. Since in general, $\text{Eff } L(u) \subseteqq \text{WEff } L(u)$ it is sufficient to show that if $x \notin \text{Eff } L(u)$, then $x \notin \text{WEff } L(u)$. Thus, let $x \notin \text{Eff } L(u)$. If $x \notin L(u)$ we are done, therefore, let $x \in L(u)$. Then there is a $y \leq x$ such that $y \in \text{Eff } L(u)$, implying that $y \in \text{WEff } L(u)$. From WE:1 $\Rightarrow$ W:3 it follows that $u \in \text{WEff } P(y)$.

Then from WE : 2 we have that $u \notin$ WEff P(y), since $y \leq x$. Therefore, by W : 3, $y \notin$ WEff L(u). A similar argument can be used to show that WE : 1 and WE : 2 imply WE : 4. ■

Theorem (2.2.19) provides conditions under which weak efficient subsets and efficient subsets coincide for both L(u) and P(x). If both inputs and outputs are strongly disposable (i.e., L.3.S and P.5.S hold), and if output vector u is semi-larger than output vector v implies that WEff L(u) and WEff L(v) are disjoint, and if input vector x is semi-larger than input vector y implies that WEff P(x) and WEff P(y) are disjoint, then the weak efficient subset of L(u) coincides with the efficient subset of L(u), and the weak efficient subset of P(x) coincides with the efficient subset of P(x). However, examples (2.2.13) and (2.2.14) again serve to show that these conditions, although sufficient, are not necessary. However, concerning the converse of theorem (2.2.19), we can state

Theorem: W : 4 and WE : 3 imply WE : 2. W : 3 and WE : 4 imply WE : 1. (2.2.20)

Proof: Let $x \geq y \geq 0$ and $u \in$ WEff P(x). It has to be shown that $u \notin$ WEff P(y). Since $u \in$ WEff P(x) it follows by W : 4 that $x \in$ WEff L(u). Thus, since $y \leq x$ it follows from WE : 3 that $y \notin$ L(u). Hence, $u \notin$ P(y) $\supseteqq$ WEff P(y). A similar argument can be used to show that W : 3 and WE : 4 imply WE : 1. ■

Finally, the relationships between isoquants and efficient subsets are analyzed. Therefore, introduce

Definition: For all $x \geq 0, u \geq 0$ with P(x) $\neq \{0\}$, L(u) $\neq \emptyset$, define (2.2.21)

E : 1 $u \geq v \Rightarrow$ Eff L(u) $\cap$ Eff L(v) $= \emptyset$,

E : 2 $x \geq y \Rightarrow$ Eff P(x) $\cap$ Eff P(y) $= \emptyset$,

E : 3 $x \in$ Eff L(u) $\Rightarrow u \in$ Eff P(x),

E : 4 $u \in$ Eff P(x) $\Rightarrow x \in$ Eff L(u).

The following relationships are valid for a technology with inputs and outputs which are strongly disposable

Lemma: Let inputs and outputs be strongly disposable. Then E : 1 $\Longleftrightarrow$ E : 3 and E : 2 $\Longleftrightarrow$ E : 4. (2.2.22)

Proof: Assume E : 1 holds, but there is an $x \in \text{Eff L}(u)$, $u \geq 0$, such that $u \notin \text{Eff P}(x)$. Then there is a $v \geq u$ with $v \in \text{Eff P}(x)$, implying that $x \in \text{L}(v)$. Since $v \geq u$, $\text{L}(v) \subseteqq \text{L}(u)$ by strong disposability of outputs. Thus, $x \in \text{Eff L}(v)$, which contradicts E : 1. Conversely, assume E : 3 holds but $x \in (\text{Eff L}(u) \cap \text{Eff L}(v))$, $u \geq v \geq 0$. Then by E : 3, $u \in \text{Eff P}(x)$, $v \in \text{Eff P}(x)$. This contradicts the definition of Eff P(x). Similar arguments apply to show that E : 2 $\Longleftrightarrow$ E : 4. ■

To show sufficient conditions for isoquants to equal efficient subsets introduce

Definition: For all $x \geq 0$, $u \geq 0$, with $\text{P}(x) \neq \{0\}$, $\text{L}(u) \neq \emptyset$, define (2.2.23)

IE : 1 $u \geq v \Rightarrow \text{Isoq L}(u) \cap \text{Isoq L}(v) = \emptyset$,

IE : 2 $x \geq y \Rightarrow \text{Isoq P}(x) \cap \text{Isoq P}(y) = \emptyset$,

IE : 3 $\text{Eff L}(u) = \text{Isoq L}(u)$,

IE : 4 $\text{Eff P}(x) = \text{Isoq P}(x)$.

Based on these definitions, we can state the following

Theorem: IE : 1 and IE : 2 imply IE : 3 and IE : 4. (2.2.24)

Proof: It is first shown that IE : 1 and IE : 2 imply IE : 3. Since in general, $\text{Eff L}(u) \subseteqq \text{Isoq L}(u)$, it is sufficient to show that $\text{Isoq L}(u) \subseteqq \text{Eff L}(u)$. Assume $x \notin \text{Eff L}(u)$ but $x \in \text{L}(u)$. Then there is a $y \leq x$, $y \in \text{Eff L}(u)$. Since $\text{Eff L}(u) \subseteqq \text{Isoq L}(u)$, $y \in \text{Isoq L}(u)$. It now follows from IE : 1 $\Rightarrow$ I : 1 $\Longleftrightarrow$ I : 3 that $u \in \text{Isoq P}(y)$. Hence by IE : 2, $u \notin \text{Isoq P}(x)$. Thus by I : 3, $x \notin \text{Isoq L}(u)$. A similar argument can be used to show that IE : 1 and IE : 2 imply IE : 4. ■

Theorem (2.2.24) provides conditions under which isoquants and efficient subsets coincide, for L(u) and P(x). However, these conditions are only sufficient, and once again examples (2.2.13) and (2.2.14) show that they are not necessary. However, one has

Theorem: I : 4 and IE : 3 imply IE : 2. I : 3 and IE : 4 imply IE : 2. (2.2.25)

Proof: Let $x \geq y \geq 0$ and $u \in$ Isoq P(x). It must be shown that $u \notin$ Isoq P(y). Since $u \in$ Isoq P(x) it follows from I : 4 that $x \in$ Isoq L(u). Now, $y \leq x$ and thus by IE : 3, $y \notin$ L(u). Hence, $u \notin$ P(y) $\supseteqq$ Isoq P(y). A similar argument can be used to show that I : 3 and IE : 4 imply IE : 2. ■

The above subsets of L(u) and P(x) are all price independent. However, some efficiency measures are price dependent, hence their reference sets must also be price dependent. Therefore, we need to introduce the set of cost minimizing input vectors and the set of revenue maximizing output vectors. For this purpose let $p \in R^n_+$ denote a vector of input prices and $r \in R^m_+$ denote a vector of output prices. The cost minimizing set of input vectors at prices p and outputs u is then defined as

$$\mathrm{CM}(u,p) := \{x \in \mathrm{L}(u) : px = \mathrm{Q}(u,p)\}, \qquad (2.2.26)$$

where the cost function Q(u, p) is defined as

$$\mathrm{Q}(u,p) := \inf\{px : x \in \mathrm{L}(u)\}. \qquad (2.2.27)$$

Infimum is used in (2.2.27) since we do not insist on strictly positive prices.

The set of revenue maximizing output vectors at prices r and inputs x is given by

$$\mathrm{RM}(x,r) := \{u \in \mathrm{P}(x) : ru = \mathrm{R}(x,r)\}, \qquad (2.2.28)$$

where the total revenue function is defined as

$$\mathrm{R}(x,r) := \max\{ru : u \in \mathrm{P}(x)\}. \qquad (2.2.29)$$

Since P(x) is a compact set, see properties P.2 and P.4, R(x, r) is well-defined. CM(u, p) and RM(x, r) are illustrated in Fig. 2-4.

It is clear that the use of non-negative input and output prices $p \in R^n_+$ and $r \in R^m_+$, implies that

$$\mathrm{CM}(u,p) \subsetneqq \mathrm{WEff\ L}(u) \text{ and } \mathrm{RM}\,(x,r) \subsetneqq \mathrm{WEff\ P}(x), \qquad (2.2.30)$$

respectively.

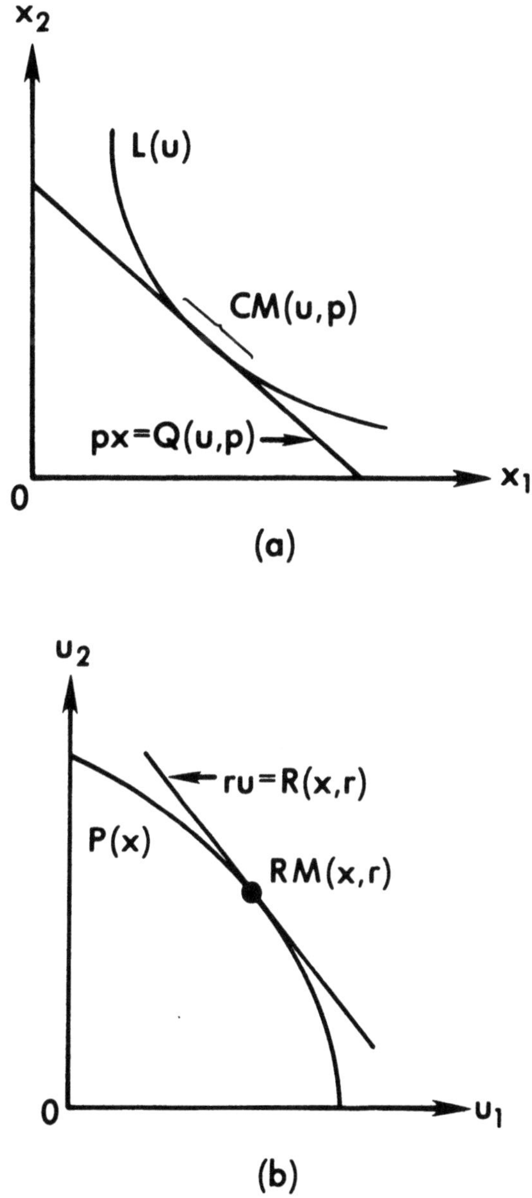

Figure 2-4

2.3 Production Functions

Suppose the production unit produces only a single output $u \in R_+$. In this case the structure of production technology is frequently represented by a scalar-valued production function. It is therefore of interest to establish the relationship of a scalar-valued production function to the input and output correspondences. Following Shephard (1970), we define a scalar-valued production function as

$$\phi(x) = \max\{u : x \in \mathrm{L}(u)\} = \max\{u : u \in \mathrm{P}(x)\}. \qquad (2.3.1)$$

Shephard (1970) has shown that if the production technology satisfies (L.1–L.5) or equivalently (P.1–P.5), then the production function (2.3.1) exists and has the following properties

ϕ.1 ϕ: $R^n_+ \to R_+$, $\phi(0) = 0$,

ϕ.2 ϕ is upper semi-continuous,

ϕ.3 $\phi(\lambda x) \geqq \phi(x)$ for $\lambda \geqq 1$.

In addition, given (ϕ.1–ϕ.3), the input correspondence

$$\mathrm{L}(u) := \{x: \phi(x) \geqq u\} \qquad (2.3.2)$$

satifies (L.1–L.5) and the output correspondence

$$\mathrm{P}(x) := [0, \phi(x)] \qquad (2.3.3)$$

satisfies (P.1–P.5).

Suppose now that the production unit produces a vector of outputs $u \in R^m_+$. It remains useful to have a functional representation of the structure of production technology in the multiple output case, and for this purpose several writers have introduced the notion of a transformation function, or a joint production function. Hicks (1946) proposed to write the transformation function in symmetric fashion as $T(u, x) = 0$. Samuelson (1966), Diewert (1973), Jorgenson and Lau (1974a, b) and others write the transformation functions asymmetrically as $Z_i = t(\hat{Z})$, where Z_i is the i-th component of $Z = (u, x)$ and $\hat{Z} = Z$ with the i–th component set to zero. However as Shephard (1970, p. 213) notes, "the existence of a joint production function has not been demonstrated, i.e., derived from the properties of the input and output sets of the production correspondence to which it refers." It turns out that some fairly strong monotonicity conditions are required in order to prove existence. We begin by defining a joint production function in definition (2.3.4); other definitions are available in Färe (1980).

Definition: (Shephard, 1970; Färe, 1980) The function I: $R_+^m \times R_+^n \to R_+$ such that (1) for $u^0 \geq 0$, $L(u^0) \neq \emptyset$, Isoq $L(u^0) = \{x \in R_+^n : I(u^0, x) = 0\}$, (2) for $x^0 \geq 0$, $P(x^0) \neq \{0\}$, Isoq $P(x^0) = \{u \in R_+^m : I(u, x^0) = 0\}$ is called an Isoquant Joint Production Function (IJPF). (2.3.4)

Bol and Moeschlin (1975) give the following characterization of the IJPF.

Lemma: An IJPF $I(u, x)$ exists, if and only if, for all $x \geq 0$, $u \geq 0$, $P(x) \neq \{0\}$, $L(u) \neq \emptyset$, $u \in$ Isoq $P(x) \Longleftrightarrow x \in$ Isoq $L(u)$. (2.3.5)

Proof: If an IJPF exists, then the following holds: $x \in$ Isoq $L(u) \Longleftrightarrow I(u, x) = 0 \Longleftrightarrow u \in$ Isoq $P(x)$. Conversely, assume that $u \in$ Isoq $P(x) \Longleftrightarrow x \in$ Isoq $L(u)$ and consider the sets

$$\{(u, x): x \geq 0, u \geq 0, P(x) \neq \{0\}, L(u) \neq \emptyset, u \in \text{Isoq } P(x)\} \tag{2.3.6}$$

and

$$\{(u, x): x \geq 0, u \geq 0, P(x) \neq \{0\}, L(u) \neq \emptyset, x \in \text{Isoq } L(u)\}. \tag{2.3.7}$$

Clearly these sets are equal. Denote them by A and define

$$I(u, x) := \begin{cases} 0 \text{ if } (u, x) \in A, \\ 0 \text{ if } u = 0, P(x) = \{0\}, \\ 1 \text{ otherwise.} \end{cases} \tag{2.3.8}$$

Then clearly, $I(u, x)$ is an IJPF. ■

It is not in general true, however, that for a production technology satisfying (L.1–L.5), an IJPF exists. To illustrate, recall examples (2.2.13) and (2.2.14) of the previous section

$$P(x) = [0, \phi(x)], \text{ where } \phi(x) := \begin{cases} x \text{ for } x \in [0, 1) \\ \text{and} \\ x + 1 \text{ for } x \in [1, +\infty) \end{cases} \quad (2.3.9)$$

and

$$P(x) = [0, \phi(x)], \text{ where } \phi(x) := \begin{cases} x \text{ for } x \in [0, 1) \\ 1 \text{ for } x \in [1, 2) \\ x - 1 \text{ for } x \in [2, +\infty). \end{cases} \quad (2.3.10)$$

Both (2.3.9) and (2.3.10) satisfy the axioms (L.1–L.5), and from (2.3.9) it is clear that $1\frac{1}{2} \notin$ Isoq P(1) but $1 \in$ Isoq L($1\frac{1}{2}$). From (2.3.10) it is clear that $1 \in$ Isoq P($1\frac{1}{2}$) but $1\frac{1}{2} \notin$ Isoq L(1). Thus we have two examples showing that, in general, an IJPF does not exist.

From these two examples it is clear that necessary and sufficient conditions for the existence of an IJPF follow from lemmata (2.3.5) and (2.2.10).

Theorem: (Al-Ayat and Färe, 1979) An IJPF exists if and only if I:1 and I:2 hold. (2.3.11)

Thus a necessary and sufficient condition for the existence of an IJPF is that the input and output correspondences from which it is obtained both have disjoint isoquants for proportional changes in inputs and outputs. This is the monotonicity condition mentioned above.

So far we have shown that given input and output correspondences we may derive an IJPF, and conversely, given an IJPF, we can obtain Isoq L(u) and Isoq P(x). The final step to recover L(u) and P(x) from the IJPF is given in the following proposition.

Proposition: $L(u) = \{x: x = \lambda y, y \in \text{Isoq } L(u), \lambda \geqq 1\}$, $u \geq 0$, $L(u) \neq \emptyset$ and $P(x) = \{u: u = \theta v, v \in \text{Isoq } P(x), 1 \geqq \theta \geqq 0\}$, $x \geq 0$, $P(x) \neq \{0\}$. (2.3.12)

Proof: Since inputs are weakly disposable (L.3), clearly $\{x: x = \lambda y, y \in \text{Isoq } L(u), \lambda \geqq 1\} \subseteq L(u)$. Conversely, let $x \in L(u)$. Then, since L(u) is closed (L.5), and $u \geq 0$ implying that $x \neq 0$, there exists a $\bar{\lambda}$, $0 < \bar{\lambda} \leqq 1$, such that $\bar{\lambda}x \in$ Isoq L(u). Thus $\lambda(\bar{\lambda}x) \in \{x: x = \lambda y, y \in \text{Isoq } L(u), \lambda \geqq 1\}$. Similar arguments can be used to show the second part of the proposition. ■

2.4 Special Production Structures

In this section some special production structures, useful for this monograph, are introduced. This section is not intended to be a complete catalog of special structures, but a sample of some important ones.

Definition: (Färe and Shephard, 1977) The input correspondence L is Ray-Homothetic if

$$L(u) := \frac{F(u)}{F(u/\|u\|)} \cdot L(u/\|u\|),$$

where $F\colon R_+^m \to R_+$ satisfies (1) $F(0) = 0$, (2) $F(\theta u) \geqq F(u)$ for $\theta \geqq 1$, (3) F is lower semi-continuous. (2.4.1)

Definition: (Shephard, 1970) The input correspondence L is Homothetic if $L(u) := F(u) \cdot L(1)$. (2.4.2)

Definition: (Shephard, 1974a) The input correspondence L is Ray-Homogeneous if $L(\theta u) := \theta^{A(u/\|u\|)} \cdot L(u)$, where $A(u/\|u\|)$ is positive and bounded, $\theta > 0$. (2.4.3)

Definition: The input correspondence L is Homogeneous of degree $+\alpha$ if $L(\theta u) := \theta^{\alpha} \cdot L(u)$, $\theta > 0$. (2.4.4)

In the definition of ray-homotheticity, let $L(u/\|u\|)$ take the special form of

$$L(u/\|u\|) = F(u/\|u\|) \cdot L(1),$$

then we find that (2.4.1) degenerates into $L(u) = F(u) \cdot L(1)$, i.e., into a homothetic input structure. Next, let $F(\theta u) = \theta^{A(u/\|u\|)} \cdot F(u)$ in the definition of ray-homotheticity, then it follows that the input structure is ray-homogeneous. Finally, if $A(u/\|u\|)$ equals a positive constant, α, then the homogeneous input structure is obtained.

As on the input structure, we can also define special structures for the output structure, P. Thus, introduce

Definition: (Färe and Shephard, 1977) The output correspondence P is Ray-Homothetic if

$$P(x) := \frac{G(x)}{G(x/\|x\|)} \cdot P(x/\|x\|),$$

where $G: R^n_+ \to R_+$ satisfies (1) $G(0) = 0$,
(2) $G(\lambda x) \geqq G(x)$ for $\lambda \geqq 1$,
and (3) G is upper semi-continuous. (2.4.5)

Definition: (Shephard, 1970) The output correspondence P is Homothetic if $P(x) = G(x) \cdot P(1)$. (2.4.6)

Definition: (Shephard, 1974a) The output correspondence P is Ray-Homogeneous if $P(\lambda x) := \lambda^{B(x/\|x\|)} \cdot P(x)$, where B is positive and bounded, $\lambda > 0$. (2.4.7)

Definition: The output correspondence P is Homogeneous of degree $+\beta$ if $P(\lambda x) := \lambda^{\beta} \cdot P(x)$, $\lambda > 0$. (2.4.8)

As for the input correspondence, it is easy to show that the homothetic, ray-homogeneous, and homogeneous output structures are special cases of the ray-homothetic output structure.

It has been shown elsewhere (Färe and Shephard, 1977; Eichhorn, 1978b) what assuming any of (2.4.1)–(2.4.4) on the input structure implies for the output structure, and what assuming any of (2.4.5)–(2.4.8) on the output structure implies for the input structure. One of these inversely related structures is of interest for this monograph, namely

Theorem: $L(\theta u) = \theta^{\alpha} \cdot L(u) \Leftrightarrow P(\lambda x) = \lambda^{1/\alpha} \cdot P(x)$, $\alpha > 0$. (2.4.9)

Proof: $x \in L(\theta u) = \theta^{\alpha} \cdot L(u) \Leftrightarrow x/\theta^{\alpha} \in L(u) \Leftrightarrow u \in P(x/\theta^{\alpha})$. Also, $u \in 1/\theta \cdot P(x)$. Thus, $1/\theta \cdot P(x) = P(x/\theta^{\alpha})$. Now take $\lambda^{1/\alpha} := 1/\theta$, then $P(\lambda x) = \lambda^{1/\alpha} \cdot P(x)$. Similar arguments can be used to show the converse. ■

This theorem states that if the input or output correspondence is homogeneous of a positive degree, then its inverse correspondence is homogeneous of the reciprocal degree. For example, if $\alpha = 1$, i.e., if either of the correspondences is homogeneous of degree one, then and only then, is the other correspondence homogeneous of the same degree, i.e., of degree one.

The linear technology introduced next will play an important role in this monograph. It is an example of a production technology that can be used to calculate the various efficiency measures using simple linear programming techniques. Throughout this monograph, we will include simple programming examples of the efficiency measures developed here using this piecewise linear technology.

We use M to denote a (k, m) matrix of (observed) outputs and N to denote a (k, n) matrix of (observed) inputs. There are k observations or activities and m different types of outputs and n different types of inputs.

As an illustration, consider the hypothetical example summarized in Table 2–1. There are four firms (or observations or activities) which produce two outputs (u_1 and u_2) with two inputs (x_1 and x_2). The corresponding output and input matrices would be

$$M = \begin{bmatrix} 1 & 2 \\ 2 & 1 \\ 1 & 1 \\ 2 & 2 \end{bmatrix}$$

and

$$N = \begin{bmatrix} 2 & 2 \\ 2 & 3 \\ 1 & 2 \\ 3 & 3 \end{bmatrix}$$

respectively.

Individual elements in the M matrix are denoted as m_{ij} which denotes the jth output of the ith firm or activity. In our example, m_{11} would be equal to one unit of the first output produced by firm 1. Individual elements of the N (or input) matrix are denoted as n_{ij} which denotes the quantity of the jth input

Table 2-1

Firm	*Output 1* (u_1)	*Output 2* (u_2)	*Input 1* (x_1)	*Input 2* (x_2)
1	1	2	2	2
2	2	1	2	3
3	1	1	1	2
4	2	2	3	3

used by the ith firm or activity. In our example, n_{11} would be equal to two, which is the amount of the first input (x_1) used by the first firm. We require that

$$m_{ij} \geqq 0 \text{ and } n_{ij} \geqq 0, \text{ and that}$$

$$\text{(i)} \sum_{i=1}^{k} m_{ij} > 0,\ j = 1, \ldots, m,$$

$$\text{(ii)} \sum_{j=1}^{m} m_{ij} > 0,\ i = 1, \ldots, k,$$

$$\text{(iii)} \sum_{i=1}^{k} n_{ij} > 0,\ j = 1, \ldots, n,$$

$$\text{(iv)} \sum_{j=1}^{n} n_{ij} > 0,\ i = 1, \ldots, k. \tag{2.4.10}$$

Thus assumption (i) means that each output is producible, (ii) means that each activity produces at least one output, (iii) means that each input is required by at least one activity and (iv) means that each activity uses at least one input.

Finally, let $z = (z_1, z_2, \ldots, z_k)$ denote the activity (intensity) level of each of the k activities. These k activities which use n inputs to produce m outputs are useful in modeling the reference technologies relative to which efficiency is measured.

There are several different piecewise linear reference technologies used in this monograph. These vary in the restrictions placed on the technology with respect to the disposability of inputs and outputs (weak or strong) and the scale properties of the technology (constant returns to scale, increasing returns to scale, and decreasing returns to scale). The most restrictive linear reference technology used here satisfies strong disposability of inputs and outputs, and constant returns to scale. This can be written as

$$\mathrm{L}^{\mathrm{S}}(u) := \{x : z \cdot \mathrm{M} \geqq u,\ x \geqq z \cdot \mathrm{N},\ z \in R_{+}^{k}\} \tag{2.4.11}$$

or inversely,

$$\mathrm{P}^{\mathrm{S}}(x) := \{u : z \cdot \mathrm{M} \geqq u,\ x \geqq z \cdot \mathrm{N},\ z \in R_{+}^{k}\}. \tag{2.4.12}$$

Shephard (1974b) has shown that the input correspondence (2.4.11) satisfies properties (L.1–L.5, L.3.S, L.5.S and L.6–L.8). In addition, L is homogeneous of degree +1. Thus, the output correspondence is also homogeneous of degree +1 (theorem 2.4.9) and satisfies (P.1–P.5, P.3.S, P.5.S and P.6–P.8).

If we replace the assumption of strong disposability of inputs and outputs with weak disposability, the linear reference technology becomes

$$\mathrm{L^W}(u) := \{x: \theta \cdot z \cdot \mathrm{M} = u, z \cdot \mathrm{N} = \lambda \cdot x, \theta, \lambda \in (0, 1], z \in R^k_+\} \tag{2.4.13}$$

or inversely,

$$\mathrm{P^W}(x) := \{u: \theta \cdot z \cdot \mathrm{M} = u, z \cdot \mathrm{N} = \lambda \cdot x, \theta, \lambda \in (0, 1], z \in R^k_+\}. \tag{2.4.14}$$

These correspondences satisfy all the above properties except L.3.S, L.5.S and P.3.S, P.5.S, respectively.

Technologies (2.4.13) and (2.4.14) allow for weak disposability through the θ and λ parameters and the strict equalities which replace the inequalities in (2.4.11) and (2.4.12). The θ and λ parameters allow for radial scaling of the original observations and their convex combinations.

To illustrate the distinction, consider Fig. 2-2. If A,B,C and D represented our observed points, then the technology in (2.4.11) would construct the boundary of L(u) as the segment DC and a vertical extension from point C, i.e., the backward-bending segments would be in the interior of L(u). On the other hand the technology in (2.4.13) would construct the boundary of L(u) as drawn in Fig. 2-2, i.e., it allows for backward-bending isoquants.

All of the technologies (2.4.11)–(2.4.14) satisfy constant returns to scale (or linear homogeneity). This assumption can be relaxed by changing the restriction of the z (intensity) vector. To allow for decreasing returns to scale (as well as constant returns to scale), the appropriate restriction is

$$\sum_{i=1}^{k} z_i \leqq 1, z \in R^k_+. \tag{2.4.15}$$

To allow for increasing, decreasing, or constant returns to scale, the appropriate restriction is

$$\sum_{i=1}^{k} z_i = 1, z \in R^k_+. \tag{2.4.16}$$

2.5 The Graph and Its Subsets

In section 2.1, the graph was defined in terms of either the input or equivalently in terms of the output correspondence. Recall that

$$\text{GR}:=\{(x,u): x\in \text{L}(u), u\in R_+^m\}=\{(x,u): u\in \text{P}(x), x\in R_+^n\}. \tag{2.5.1}$$

Conversely, if $(x, u) \in$ GR, then $x \in$ L(u) and $u \in$ P(x). From the properties assumed on L and P, the graph must satisfy

GR.1 $0 \in$ GR, $(0, u) \in \text{GR} \Rightarrow u = 0$,

GR.2 $(\text{GR} \cap \{(x, u): x \leqq \bar{x}\})$ is bounded for each $\bar{x} \in R_+^n$,

GR.3 If $(x, u) \in$ GR then $(\lambda x, u) \in$ GR for $\lambda \geqq 1$,

GR.4 GR is a closed set,

GR.5 If $(x, u) \in$ GR then $(x, \theta u) \in$ GR for $1 \geqq \theta \geqq 0$.

These properties are, of course, equivalent to (L.1–L.5). If, in addition, inputs and outputs are strongly disposable, then (and only then) we have

GR.6 $(x, u) \in \text{GR} \Rightarrow (y, v) \in$ GR for $(y, -v) \geqq (x, -u)$.

Three price-independent subsets of the graph are introduced next, namely

Definition: The Graph Isoquant is defined by Isoq GR: =
$\{(x, u): (x, u) \in \text{GR}, (\lambda x, \lambda^{-1}u) \notin \text{GR for } 0 < \lambda < 1\}$. (2.5.2)

Definition: The Weak Efficient Subset of GR is WEffGR: =
$\{(x, u): (x, u) \in \text{GR}, (y, -v) \overset{*}{<} (x, -u) \Rightarrow (y, -v) \notin \text{GR}\}$. (2.5.3)

Definition: The Efficient Subset of GR is EffGR: $= \{(x, u)$:
$(x, u) \in \text{GR}, (y, -v) \leq (x, -u) \Rightarrow (y, -v) \notin \text{GR}\}$. (2.5.4)

From these definitions it is clear that

$$\text{EffGR} \subseteqq \text{WEffGR} \subseteqq \text{IsoqGR}. \tag{2.5.5}$$

It is of interest to note that if $(x, u) \in$ IsoqGR, then $x \in$ Isoq L(u) or $u \in$ Isoq P(x) or both. In example (2.2.14), consider $x = 1½, u = 1$. Then (x, u) $\in$ IsoqGR and $u \in$ Isoq P(x), but $x \notin$ Isoq L(u). Therefore, we have that

$$\{(x, u): x \in \text{Isoq L}(u) \text{ and } u \in \text{Isoq P}(x)\} \subseteqq \text{IsoqGR},$$

but equality need not hold. The next theorem shows when equality holds.

Theorem: For all $x \geq 0, u \geq 0$ with $P(x) \neq \{0\}$, $L(u) \neq \emptyset$, let Isoq $L(\theta u) \cap$ Isoq $L(u) = \emptyset$ for $\theta \neq 1$ and Isoq $P(\lambda x) \cap$ Isoq $P(x) = \emptyset$ for $\lambda \neq 1$. $(x, u) \in$ IsoqGR if and only if $x \in$ Isoq $L(u)$ and $u \in$ Isoq $P(x)$. (2.5.6)

The proof of this theorem follows from lemma (2.2.10). In addition, the following theorems hold

Theorem: Let inputs and outputs be strongly disposable, and assume that W : 1 and W : 2 of definition (2.2.16) hold. $(x, u) \in$ WEffGR if and only if $x \in$ WEff $L(u)$ and $u \in$ WEff $P(x)$. (2.5.7)

Theorem: Let inputs and outputs be strongly disposable, and assume that E : 1 and E : 2 of definition (2.2.21) hold. $(x, u) \in$ EffGR if and only if $x \in$ Eff $L(u)$ and $u \in$ Eff $P(x)$. (2.5.8)

These theorems follow from lemmata (2.2.17) and (2.2.22) respectively.

Regarding the conditions under which the subsets of (2.5.5) are equal we have

Theorem: Let properties IW : 1 and IW : 2 of definition (2.2.11) hold, then IsoqGR = WEffGR. (2.5.9)

Theorem: Let properties WE : 1 and WE : 2 of definition (2.2.18) hold, then WEffGR = EffGR. (2.5.10)

Theorem: Let properties IE : 1 and IE : 2 of definition (2.2.23) hold, then IsoqGR = EffGR. (2.5.11)

Theorems (2.5.9)–(2.5.11) follow from theorems (2.2.12), (2.2.19) and (2.2.25) respectively.

The above subsets of GR are all price-independent. However, some efficiency measures are price-dependent, and so their reference sets must also be price-dependent. Therefore, we need to introduce the set of profit maximizing input-output vectors. The profit function is defined as

$$\pi(r, p) = \sup\{ru - px\colon (x, u) \in \text{GR}\}. \tag{2.5.12}$$

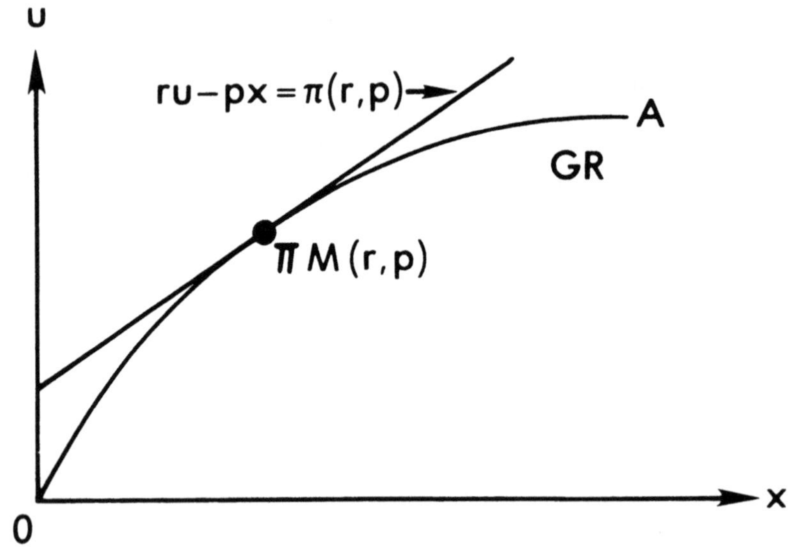

Figure 2-5

The set of profit maximizing input and output vectors is given by

$$\Pi M(r,p) = \{(x,u) \in GR\colon ru - px = \pi(r,p)\}. \quad (2.5.13)$$

$\Pi M(r,p)$ is illustrated for the case $m = n = 1$ in Fig. 2–5. The graph of the technology is the region bounded by the curve OA and the x-axis, the profit function is the supporting hyperplane, and the profit-maximizing input-output vector is located at their intersection.

3 RADIAL INPUT EFFICIENCY MEASURES

3.0 Introduction

Consider some feasible production plan $\{(u,x):x \in L(u)\}$. It is natural to inquire as to whether there exists some smaller input vector $0 \leq y \leq x$ that remains feasible for output vector u, i.e., $y \in L(u)$. A different, but related, question involves the existence of a less expensive, though not necessarily smaller, input vector $z:pz < px$, given input prices $p \in R^n_{++}$, that remains feasible for output vector u, i.e., $z \in L(u)$. If either y or z exists, then x is clearly inefficient for u, and the efficiency of x can be calculated relative to y or z respectively.

In this chapter we introduce and examine the properties of several radial input efficiency measures. The measures are dubbed "input" efficiency measures because they measure the efficiency of an input vector in the production of a certain output vector, using the input correspondence to represent the production technology. Hence they compare observed to smaller feasible input vectors in the production of a certain output vector. All measures considered in this chapter are "radial" measures in the sense that the search for smaller feasible input vectors is constrained to proportionally smaller, or radially smaller, feasible input vectors relative to which the efficiency of an observed input vector can be computed. The restriction to radial input efficiency measurement has the advantage of being consistent with the original formulation of Farrell (1957). It has the further advantage that all radial efficiency measures have a straightforward cost interpretation, since proportional input reductions translate directly into corresponding cost reductions at fixed input prices. The disadvantages of radial efficiency measurement, and the consequent interest in nonradial efficiency measurement, are deferred to chapter 7.

In section 3.1 we provide an intuitive geometric portrayal of each of the five radial input efficiency measures. This geometric portrayal is a straightforward generalization of the ideas originally introduced by Farrell. The generalization involves extending his radial measurement of three types of input efficiency to a radial measurement of five types of input efficiency.

The intuitive notions of section 3.1 are given a more rigorous treatment in sections 3.2–3.6. Farrell's input measure of technical efficiency is examined in section 3.2, and a weak input measure of technical efficiency is examined in section 3.3. These two measures differ because they measure the technical efficiency of $x \in L(u)$ relative to different subsets of $L(u)$. The overall input efficiency measure is examined in section 3.4. In contrast to the Farrell and the weak input measures of technical efficiency, the overall measure of input efficiency is input price-dependent. The overall measure was introduced by Farrell (1957), and corresponds to Eichhorn's (1978a, b) notion of the "technical effectiveness" of a production process, absent a time dimension.

From these three primary measures of input efficiency, two additional measures can be derived. The input congestion measure is examined in section 3.5, and the allocative input efficiency measure is examined in section 3.6. The former measure extends the analysis of Färe and Svensson (1980) and Färe and Grosskopf (1983b), while the latter is a generalization of Farrell's (1957) notion of input price efficiency. Like the overall measure of input efficiency, the allocative measure is input price-dependent.

Section 3.7 concludes the chapter with a linear programming example designed to illustrate the calculation of each of the five measures of input efficiency.

3.1 Radial Input Efficiency Measures

The five radial input efficiency measures discussed in this chapter can be divided into two groups. The first group consists of Farrell's input efficiency measure, the weak input efficiency measure, and the overall input efficiency measure. The second group consists of the congestion measure and the allocative measure. The measures in the first group are "primary," and the measures in the second group are "derived" from those of the first group. The measures in the first group measure the efficiency of an observed (u, x) relative to three different subsets of the input set $L(u)$; the Farrell input measure relates the efficiency of (u, x) to the Isoq $L(u)$, the weak input efficiency measure relates the efficiency of (u, x) to the WEff $L(u)$, and the overall input measure relates the efficiency of (u, x) to the set of cost minimizing input vectors $CM(u, p)$.

To illustrate these measures, consider Fig. 3–1.

In Fig. 3–1 point P denotes an input vector x used to produce output vector u. Note that x belongs to the interior of $L(u)$. Now imagine a nonpositive orthant R^2_- with origin at point P, and translate this nonpositive orthant R^2_- down as far as possible along the ray OP corresponding to the observed input mix, maintaining a nonempty intersection with $L(u)$. The translated nonpositive orthant is labeled R′ − R − R″, and the intersection with $L(u)$ occurs at point T. Finally, the input prices $p \in R^2_{++}$ faced by the production

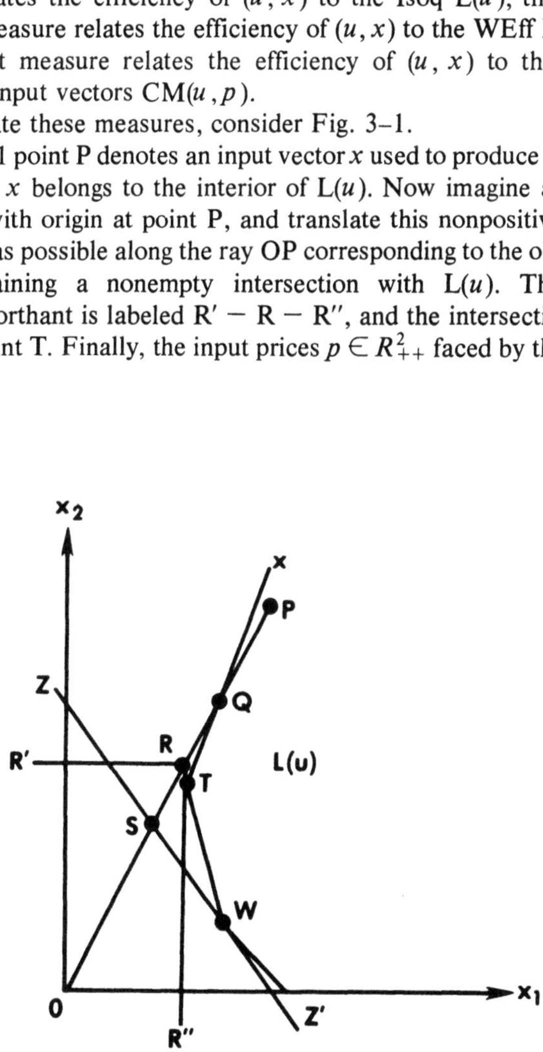

Figure 3-1

unit are portrayed by the line Z − Z′. Input cost is minimized when Z − Z′ intersects L(u) at point W. The first group of radial input efficiency measures can now be identified.

First, input technical efficiency (ITE), in the sense of Farrell, is represented by ITE = OQ/OP. If both elements of the observed input vector x are scaled down proportionally by the scalar OQ/OP, the resulting input vector located at point Q $\in$ Isoq L(u) is technically efficient in Farrell's sense. Moreover, ITE = OQ/OP also measures the cost saving that results from moving from point P to point Q: input cost at Q is a fraction OQ/OP of input cost at P for *any* input price vector. Second, input weak efficiency (IWE) is represented by IWE = OR/OP. If both elements of the observed input vector x are scaled down proportionally by the scalar OR/OP, the resulting input vector located at point R is technically efficient in the weak sense. It is clear that at R, the output vector u cannot be obtained, since R $\notin$ L(u). However by disposing of RT units of x_2, u is obtainable and T $\in$ L(u). Thus if R is available, and if the production unit can dispose of inputs (only input x_2 need be disposable in this case), then u is obtainable from R. Moreover, IWE = OR/OP also measures the cost saving that results from moving from point P to point T: input cost at T is a fraction OR/OP of input cost at P for *any* input price vector. Note that this cost interpretation assumes that inputs R are purchased and inputs T are employed, the disposed inputs RT being purchased and paid but not employed. If the disposed inputs need not be paid a slightly larger cost reduction arises. Third, input overall efficiency (IOE), again in the sense of Farrell, is represented by IOE = OS/OP. Of course, at S, u is not obtainable, since S $\notin$ L(u). But for the same input cost, W can be purchased, and W $\in$ L(u).

Moreover, since W minimizes the input cost of producing output vector u at input prices p (i.e., W $\in$ CM(u, p)), IOE also measures the cost saving resulting from moving from point P to point W. Unlike the two previous measures of cost saving, however, this overall measure of cost saving is input price dependent since CM(u, p) is input price dependent.

Based on these three primary measures, we can now derive both the congestion and the allocative measures. The usefulness of these two measures is discussed later; here we concentrate solely on their graphical representations. Input congestion (IC) is represented by IC = OR/OQ or equivalently, by IC = IWE/ITE. An input reduction, and a consequent cost saving, of ITE = OR/OQ could be realized if the technology was not input congested, after which RT units of the congesting input x_2 could be disposed of. The input allocative measure (IA) is represented by IA = OS/OR or equivalently by IA = IOE/IWE. A reallocation of inputs from R to W eliminates allocative or input price inefficiency, thereby reducing input cost to a fraction IA = OS/OR of its value at R. Finally, we note that the overall measure of efficiency is the product of the technical, congestion, and allocative measures

$$\mathrm{IOE} = \mathrm{ITE} \cdot \mathrm{IC} \cdot \mathrm{IA}, \tag{3.1.1}$$

or, since IC = IWE/ITE, the overall measure can be expressed as the product of the weak and allocative measures

$$\mathrm{IOE} = \mathrm{IWE} \cdot \mathrm{IA}. \tag{3.1.2}$$

3.2 The Farrell Input Measure of Technical Efficiency

Farrell originally defined his measure of technical efficiency relative to a single output technology satisfying strong disposability of inputs and constant returns to scale (i.e., linear homogeneity). In order to define a Farrell input measure in the context of a multiple output technology satisfying only properties (L.1–L.5), consider first the effective domain of the Farrell input measure F_i

$$D(F_i) := \{(u,x) : \exists \lambda \geqq 0 \text{ such that } \lambda x \in \mathrm{L}(u)\}. \tag{3.2.1}$$

Now define

Definition: The function $F_i : R^m_+ \times R^n_+ \to R_+ \cup \{+\infty\}$ defined by (3.2.2)

$$F_i\,(u,x) := \begin{cases} \min\{\lambda \geqq 0 : \lambda x \in \mathrm{L}(u)\}, & (u,x) \in D(F_i), \\ +\infty, & (u,x) \in \text{Complement}\, D(F_i), \end{cases}$$

is called the Farrell Input Measure of Technical Efficiency.

Thus for $(u, x) \in D(F_i)$ the Farrell measure computes the ratio of the smallest feasible radial contraction of an observed input vector to the observed input vector itself. Since $\mathrm{L}(u)$ is closed for each u, the "minimum" in definition (3.2.2) exists. Call this minimum λ°. Then if $\lambda^\circ < 1$, the production unit can produce output vector u with the radially smaller input vector $\lambda^\circ x \in \mathrm{Isoq}\ \mathrm{L}(u)$, and the observed input vector x is technically inefficient. If $\lambda^\circ > 1$, it must be the case that $x \notin \mathrm{L}(u)$, and λ° becomes the smallest radial expansion of x such that $\lambda^\circ x \in$ Isoq $L(u)$. In both cases Isoq $L(u)$ is the reference set used by the Farrell measure to compute the technical efficiency of $(u, x) \in D(F_i)$. For $(u, x) \notin D(F_i)$ no radial contraction or expansion of x can produce u, and $F_i\ (u, x) = +\infty$.

To see that definition (3.2.2) coincides with the Farrell measure discussed in section 3.1, consider Fig. 3–2. Clearly at point P, $(u, x) \in D(F_i)$. The distances OP and OQ can be represented as: $\mathrm{OP} = \|x\|$ and $\mathrm{OQ} = \|F_i(u, x)\cdot x\|$, respectively. Thus we have that

$$\mathrm{ITE} = \frac{\mathrm{OQ}}{\mathrm{OP}} = \frac{\|F_i(u, x)\cdot x\|}{\|x\|} = F_i(u, x), \qquad (3.2.3)$$

i.e., the Farrell input measure of technical efficiency defined by (3.2.2) coincides with the geometric illustration in section 3.1. Moreover, if the production unit faces input prices $p \in R^n_{++}$, then it is easy to see that

$$F_i(u,\ x) = \lambda^\circ = \frac{p(\lambda^\circ x)}{px} \qquad (3.2.4)$$

Thus $F_i(u, x)$ has a cost interpretation: it measures the ratio of input cost at

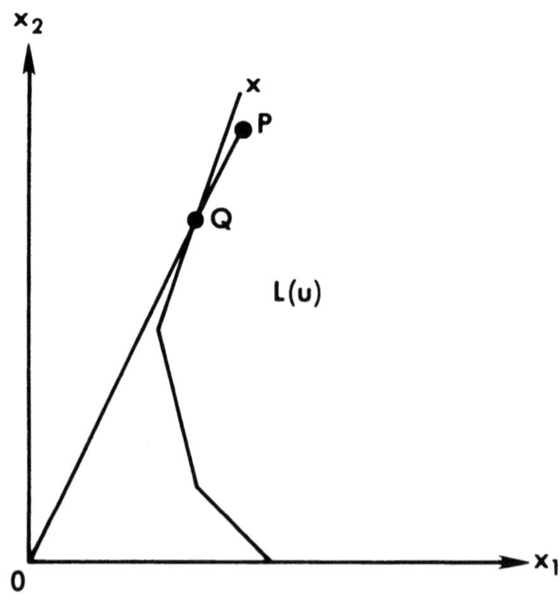

Figure 3-2

$\lambda^\circ x \in \text{Isoq } L(u)$ to observed input cost. And this ratio, $F_i(u, x) = \lambda^\circ$, is independent of input prices, as can be seen by substituting $q \neq p$ for p in equation (3.2.4).

The Farrell input measure of technical efficiency is the inverse of the distance function of the input sets L(u), a fact apparently first noted by Färe and Lovell (1978). This fact enables us to exploit the distance function in order to establish the properties of the Farrell input measure. Shephard (1970, chapter 9) has derived a number of properties of the distance function defined on a technology satisfying a set of axioms stronger than (L.1–L.5). Those properties of interest that survive the relaxation of the axiom system to (L.1–L.5) are adapted to yield the following properties of the Farrell input measure of technical efficiency.

Theorem: If L satisfies (L.1–L.5), then

$F_i.1$ $F_i(0, x) = 0, x \in R^n_+,$

$F_i.2$ $0 < F_i(u, x) < +\infty, u \geq 0, (x, u) \in D(F_i),$

$F_i.3$ $F_i(u, \lambda x) = \lambda^{-1} F_i(u, x), \lambda > 0, (x, u) \in D(F_i),$

$F_i.4$ $F_i(\theta u, x) \geqq F_i(u, x), \theta \geqq 1,$

$F_i.5$ $L(u) = \{x: 0 < F_i(u, x) \leqq 1\}, u \geq 0,$ if and only if inputs are weakly disposable,

$F_i.6$ $\text{Isoq } L(u) = \{x: F_i(u, x) = 1\}, u \geq 0.$ (3.2.5)

Proof: Property F_i. 1 follows from the condition L.1 that $L(0) = R^n_+$.

$F_i.2$: Since $u \geq 0$, $x \geq 0$ for $x \in L(u)$, see L.1. For $(u, x) \in D(F_i)$ there exists $\lambda \geqq 0$, such that $\lambda x \in L(u)$. Now since $u \geq 0 \Rightarrow x \geq 0$, $F_i(u, x) \in (0, +\infty)$.

$$\begin{aligned} F_i.3\text{: } F_i(u, \lambda x) &= \min\{\delta\text{: } \delta\lambda x \in L(u)\} \\ &= \min\{\lambda\lambda^{-1}\delta\text{: } \delta\lambda x \in L(u)\} \\ &= \lambda^{-1} \min\{\gamma\text{: } \gamma x \in L(u)\} \\ &= \lambda^{-1} F_i(u, x). \end{aligned}$$

$F_i.4$: Since outputs are weakly disposable, $L(\theta u) \subseteqq L(u)$ for $\theta \geqq 1$, property F_i. 4 holds.

$F_i.5$: Let $u \geq 0$ and $x \in L(u)$, then clearly $F_i(u, x) \leqq 1$. since $0 \notin L(u)$ for $u \geq 0$, it follows that $0 < F_i(u, x)$. Thus $L(u) \subseteqq \{x: 0 < F_i(u, x) \leqq 1\}$. Next, assume that $x \notin L(u)$. If there does not exist a $\lambda \geqq 0$ such that $\lambda x \in L(u)$, $F_i(u, x) = +\infty$. Thus assume there exists $\lambda \geqq 0$ such that $\lambda x \in L(u)$. Since inputs are weakly disposable, $\lambda > 1$, thus $\{x: 0 < F_i(u, x) \leqq 1\} = L(u)$. Conversely, assume $L(u) = \{x: 0 < F_i(u, x) \leqq 1\}$, $u \geq 0$. Let $x \in L(u)$, then we must show that $\lambda x \in L(u)$, $\lambda \geqq 1$, i.e., $0 < F_i(u, \lambda x) \leqq 1$. Since $x \in L(u)$,

$\lambda \geqq 1$, and using property $F_i.3$, $0 < F_i(u, x) \leqq \lambda/\lambda \Rightarrow 0 < \lambda^{-1} F_i(u, x) \leqq 1/\lambda \leqq 1 \Rightarrow 0 < F_i(u, \lambda x) \leqq 1$. Thus $\lambda x \in L(u)$ proving that inputs are weakly disposable.

$F_i.6$: If $x \in \text{Isoq } L(u)$, $u \geq 0$, then clearly $F_i(u, x) = 1$. If $x \notin L(u)$, then $F_i(u, x) > 1$ and if $x \in L(u)$ but $x \notin \text{Isoq } L(u)$, there is a $\lambda < 1$ such that $\lambda x \in L(u)$ thus $F_i(u, x) < 1$. Hence if $x \notin \text{Isoq } L(u)$, $u \geq 0$, then $F_i(u, x) \neq 1$, or equivalently, if $F_i(u, x) = 1$ then $x \in \text{Isoq } L(u)$. ■

Among the properties of the Farrell input measure of technical efficiency one should note that it is homogeneous of degree -1 in inputs, $F_i.3$, although it is only nondecreasing in outputs, $F_i.4$. This asymmetry arises because the input correspondence is not rquired to be linearly homogeneous. Also, the Farrell input measure of technical efficiency calls an input vector $x \in L(u)$ technically efficient in the production of $u \geq 0$ if and only if x belongs to the isoquant of $L(u)$, $F_i.6$. Moreover, property $F_i.5$ shows that the Farrell input measure of technical efficiency provides a complete characterization of the production technology as given by $L(u)$ if and only if inputs are weakly disposable.

Next we consider the properties of $F_i(u, x)$ implied by assuming different special structures of the input correspondence

Theorem: Let L satisfy (L.1–L.5), then

(1) $F_i(u, x) = \dfrac{F(u)}{F(u/\|u\|)} \cdot F_i(u/\|u\|, x)$ if and only if L is ray-homothetic,

(2) $F_i(u, x) = F(u) \cdot F_i(1, x)$ if and only if L is homothetic,

(3) $F_i(\theta u, x) = \theta^{A(u/\|u\|)} \cdot F_i(u, x)$, $\theta > 0$, if and only if L is ray-homogeneous,

(4) $F_i(\theta u, x) = \theta^{\alpha} \cdot F_i(u, x)$, $\theta > 0$, if and only if L is homogeneous of degree $+\alpha$. (3.2.6)

Proof: Let L be ray-homothetic, then

$$F_i(u, x) = \min \left\{ \lambda : \lambda x \in \frac{F(u)}{F(u/\|u\|)} \cdot L(u/\|u\|) \right\} \text{ (definition 2.4.1))}$$

$$= \min\left\{\lambda: \frac{F(u/\|u\|)}{F(u)}\lambda x \in L(u/\|u\|)\right\}$$

$$= \frac{F(u)}{F(u/\|u\|)} \cdot F_i(u/\|u\|, x).$$

Conversely assume (1) holds, then using $F_i.3$ and $F_i.5$ one has

$$\begin{aligned} L(u) &= \left\{x: 0 < \frac{F(u)}{F(u/\|u\|)} \cdot F_i(u/\|u\|, x) \leqq 1\right\} \\ &= \left\{x: 0 < F_i\left(u/\|u\|, x\frac{F(u/\|u\|)}{F(u)}\right) \leqq 1\right\} \\ &= \frac{F(u)}{F(u/\|u\|)} \cdot \{y: 0 < F_i(u/\|u\|, y) \leqq 1\} \\ &= \frac{F(u)}{F(u/\|u\|)} \cdot L(u/\|u\|). \end{aligned}$$

Similar arguments apply to show (2)–(4). ■

Thus, this theorem illustrates that different forms of separability of the Farrell measure are equivalent to the different special structures of the input correspondence.

3.3 The Weak Input Measure of Technical Efficiency

Recall that the Farrell input measure of technical efficiency calls an input vector $x \in L(u)$ technically efficient if and only if $x \in \text{Isoq } L(u)$. The weak input measure of technical efficiency, introduced by Färe and Grosskopf (1983b), calls an input vector $x \in L(u)$ technically efficient if and only if $x \in \text{WEff } L(u)$. Clearly the two measures may assign different efficiency values to the same input vector if $\text{Isoq } L(u) \neq \text{WEff } L(u)$. In order to define the weak input measure of technical efficiency in the context of an input correspondence satisfying properties (L.1–L.5), consider first its effective domain given by

$$D(W_i) := \{(u, x): \exists\, \lambda \geqq 0 \text{ such that } (\lambda K(x) \cap L(u)) \neq \emptyset\}, \tag{3.3.1}$$

where

$$\mathrm{K}(x) := \{y : 0 \leqq y \leqq x\}, \tag{3.3.2}$$

i.e., K(x) is the set of all nonnegative input vectors, less than or equal to x.

Definition: The function $W_i\colon\ R^m_+ \times R^n_+ \to R_+ \cup \{+\infty\}$ defined by (3.3.3)

$$W_i(u,x) := \begin{cases} \min\{\lambda \geqq 0 : (\lambda \mathrm{K}(x) \cap \mathrm{L}(u)) \neq \emptyset\},\ (u,x) \in D(W_i) \\ +\infty,\ (u,x) \in \text{Complement}\ D(W_i), \end{cases}$$

is called the Weak Input Measure of Technical Efficiency.

The weak input measure of technical efficiency can be explained with the assistance of Fig. 3–3. At point P, $(u, x) \in D(W_i)$ and $x \in \mathrm{L}(u)$. Construct a nonpositive orthant K(x) with origin at P, and slide it as far as possible down the ray OP through x under the condition that the resulting nonpositive orthant λK(x) has a nonempty intersection with L(u). λK(x) has

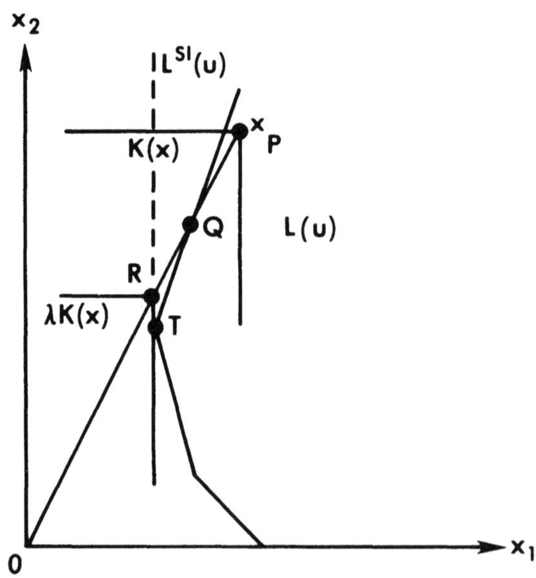

Figure 3-3

origin at R and intersection T with L(u). The weak input efficiency measure is $W_i(u, x) = \lambda$, where T $= \lambda$K(x) $\cap$ L(u), or equivalently $[\|W_i(u, x)\cdot x\|]/\|x\| =$ OR/OP. Thus $W_i(u, x) =$ IWE of section 3.1.

For $(u,x) \in D(W_i)$ and $x \in L^{SI}(u)$ the weak input measure computes the ratio of the smallest radial contraction of x, such that the radial contraction belongs to the weak efficient subset of $L^{SI}(u)$, to x itself. Assume for the moment that this minimum exists, and call it $\hat{\lambda}$. Then if $\hat{\lambda} < 1$ the production unit can produce output vector u with radially smaller input vector $\hat{\lambda}\, x$, disposing of congesting inputs as necessary and if possible, and the observed input vector x is technically inefficient. If $\hat{\lambda} > 1$ it follows that $x \notin L^{SI}(u)$ and $\hat{\lambda}$ becomes the smallest radial expansion of x such that $\hat{\lambda} x \in$ WEff $L^{SI}(u)$. In both cases WEff $L^{SI}(u)$ is the reference set used by the weak measure to compute the technical efficiency of $(u,x) \in D(W_i)$. For $(u,x) \notin D(W_i)$ no radial contraction or expansion of x belongs to WEff $L^{SI}(u)$, and $W_i(u,x) = +\infty$.

Prior to stating the properties which are satisfied by the weak input measure of technical efficiency, we need to prove that the minimum in definition (3.3.3) exists and is not merely an infimum.

Theorem: The function $W_i(u,x)$ is well-defined. (3.3.4)

Proof: Let $(u,x) \in D(W_i)$. We need to show that there exists a $\lambda \geqq 0$ which minimizes $\{\lambda \geqq 0\colon (\lambda K(x) \cap L(u)) \neq \emptyset\}$. Since $(u,x) \in D(W_i)$, there is a $\bar{\lambda}$ such that $(\bar{\lambda}K(x) \cap L(u)) \neq \emptyset$. The intersection $(\bar{\lambda}K(x) \cap L(u))$ is compact since $\bar{\lambda}K(x)$ is compact and since by property L.4, L(u) is closed. Consider next the family of sets: $F\colon= \{(\lambda K(x) \cap L(u))\colon 0 \leqq \lambda \leqq \bar{\lambda}, (\lambda K(x) \cap L(u)) \neq \emptyset\}$. Every $(\lambda K(x) \cap L(u)) \in F$ is closed and F has the finite intersection property. Thus $\bigcap_F (\lambda K(x) \cap L(u)) \neq \emptyset$. Let $\hat{\lambda} = \inf\{\lambda \geqq 0\colon 0 \leqq \lambda \leqq \bar{\lambda}, (\lambda K(x) \cap L(u)) \neq \emptyset\}$, then $(\hat{\lambda}K(x) \cap L(u)) = \bigcap_F (\lambda K(x) \cap L(u)) \neq \emptyset$. Thus $\hat{\lambda} = \min\{\lambda \geqq 0\colon (\lambda K(x) \cap L(u)) \neq \emptyset\}$. ■

Since this minimum exists, we can provide a cost interpretation for $W_i(u, x)$. Call the minimum $\hat{\lambda}$ and let the production unit face input prices $p \in R^n_{++}$. Then it follows that

$$W_i(u,x) = \hat{\lambda} = p(\hat{\lambda}x)/px, \qquad (3.3.5)$$

and so $W_i(u,x)$ measures the ratio of input cost at $\hat{\lambda}\, x \in$ WEff $L^{SI}(u)$ to observed input cost. This ratio is independent of input prices.

We can now state the properties of the weak input measure of technical efficiency. As will become evident, the name "weak input measure" is derived from property $W_i.6$.

Theorem: If L satisfies (L.1–L.5), then (3.3.6)

$W_i.1$ $W_i(0, x) = 0, x \in R^n_+$,

$W_i.2$ $0 < W_i(u, x) < +\infty, (u, x) \in D(W_i)$,

$W_i.3$ $W_i(u, \lambda x) = \lambda^{-1} W_i(u, x), \lambda > 0, (u, x) \in D(W_i)$,

$W_i.4$ $W_i(\theta u, x) \geqq W_i(u, x), \theta \geqq 1$,

$W_i.5$ $L(u) \subsetneqq \{x: 0 < W_i(u, x) \leqq 1\}, u \geq 0$,

$W_i.6$ $\text{WEff } L(u) = \{x: x \in L(u), W_i(u, x) = 1\}, u \geq 0$.

Proof: Property $W_i.1$ follows from condition L.1 that $L(0) = R^n_+$.

$W_i.2$: Since $u \geq 0$, $x \geq 0$ for $x \in L(u)$. For $(u, x) \in D(W_i)$, there exists a $\lambda \geqq 0$ such that $\lambda x \in L(u)$. Thus, since $u \geq 0 \Rightarrow x \geq 0$, $W_i(u,x) \in (0, +\infty)$.

$W_i.3$: Note that $K(\lambda x) = \lambda K(x)$, $\lambda > 0$. Thus $W_i(u, \lambda x) = \min\{\delta \geqq 0: (\delta K(\lambda x) \cap L(u)) \neq \emptyset\} = \min\{\delta \geqq 0: (\delta\lambda K(x) \cap L(u)) \neq \emptyset\} = \lambda^{-1} \min\{\delta\lambda \geqq 0: (\delta\lambda K(x) \cap L(u)) \neq \emptyset\} = \lambda^{-1} W_i(u, x)$.

$W_i.4$: Since outputs are weakly disposable (i.e., L.5 holds), $L(\theta u) \subsetneqq L(u)$ for $\theta \geqq 1$. Thus property $W_i.4$ follows.

$W_i.5$: Let $u \geq 0$ and let $x \in L(u)$. Then $0 < W_i(u, x) < +\infty$. Moreover, since $x \in L(u)$, $W_i(u, x) \leqq 1$. Thus, $L(u) \subsetneqq \{x: 0 < W_i(u, x) \leqq 1\}$.

$W_i.6$: Since in general, $\text{WEff } L(u) \subsetneqq L(u)$, it follows from property $W_i.5$ that $\text{WEff } L(u) \subsetneqq \{x: 0 < W_i(u, x) \leqq 1\}$, $u \geq 0$. Let $x \in L(u)$ and assume $0 < W_i(u, x) < 1$. Then $(W_i(u, x) \cdot K(x) \cap L(u)) \neq \emptyset$. Thus there exists a y, $y \in (W_i(u, x) \cdot K(x) \cap L(u))$ such that $y \overset{*}{<} x$. Hence, $x \notin \text{WEff } L(u)$. Therefore, $\text{WEff } L(u) = \{x: x \in L(u), W_i(u, x) = 1\}$. ■

We note that properties $W_i.1$–$W_i.4$ of the weak input measure coincide with properties $F_i.1$–$F_i.4$ of the Farrell input measure, aside from the possibly different effective domains of the two measures. However the weak input measure calls an input vector $x \in L(u)$ technically efficient if and only if $x \in \text{WEff} L(u)$, ($W_i.6$), and this property clearly differs from the corresponding property $F_i.6$ of the Farrell input measure. Property $W_i.5$ also differs from the corresponding property $F_i.5$ of the Farrell input measure. We now prove that the weak input measure $W_i(u,x)$ completely characterizes the production technology as given by the input correspondence if and only if inputs are strongly disposable.

Theorem: Let L satisfy (L.1–L.5). $L(u) = \{x: 0 < W_i(u,x) \leqq 1\}$, $u \geq 0$ if and only if inputs are strongly disposable, i.e., L.3.S holds. (3.3.7)

Proof: From property W_i.5 above, we have that $L(u) \subseteqq \{x: 0 < W_i(u,x) \leqq 1\}$. Next, let inputs be strongly disposable and assume that $x \notin L(u)$. Then $(K(x) \cap L(u)) = \emptyset$ and $(\lambda K(x) \cap L(u)) = \emptyset$ for all $\lambda \leqq 1$. Thus if $(\bar{\lambda}K(x) \cap L(u)) \neq \emptyset, \bar{\lambda} > 1$. This shows that $L(u) \supseteqq \{x: 0 < W_i(u,x) \leqq 1\}$. Conversely, assume that $L(u) = \{x: 0 < W_i(u,x) \leqq 1\}, u \geq 0$. Let $x \in L(u)$, then we have to show that if $y \geqq x, y \in L(u)$, i.e., $0 < W_i(u,y) \leqq 1$. $x \in L(u)$ implies that $(W_i(u,x)\cdot K(x) \cap L(u)) \neq \emptyset$. Since $y \geqq x$, $K(y) \supseteqq K(x)$, thus $(W_i(u,x)\cdot K(y) \cap L(u)) \neq \emptyset$. Hence, $W_i(u,y) \leqq W_i(u,x)$ and $0 < W_i(u,y) \leqq 1$, showing that $y \in L(u)$. ■

Theorem (3.3.7) yields the following corollary, which strengthens property W_i.6.

Corollary: If inputs are strongly disposable then WEff $L(u) = \{x: W_i(u,x) = 1\}, u \geq 0$. (3.3.8)

The proof is obvious and thus omitted.

Properties F_i.5 and W_i.5 indicate that since in general Isoq $L(u) \neq$ WEff $L(u)$, the Farrell input measure of technical efficiency and the weak input measure of technical efficiency may not yield the same value, but they can be ordered. From their respective definitions it is clear that for $x \in L(u)$,

$$F_i(u,x) \geqq W_i(u,x). \tag{3.3.9}$$

The next theorem gives a necessary and sufficient condition for the two measures to be equal.

Theorem: If L satisfies (L.1–L.5), then $F_i(u,x) = W_i(u,x)$ for all $(u,x) \in R^m_+ \times R^n_+$ if and only if inputs are strongly disposable, i.e., L.3.S holds. (3.3.10)

Proof: If $F_i(u,x) = W_i(u,x)$, it follows from properties F_i.5, W_i.5, and theorem (3.3.7) that inputs are strongly disposable. To prove the converse, one notes that, in general, $D(F_i) \subseteqq D(W_i)$. If inputs are strongly disposable we need to show that $D(F_i) = D(W_i)$. Let $(u,x) \in D(W_i)$, then we need to show that there is a $\lambda \geqq 0$ such that $\lambda x \in L(u)$. Since $(u,x) \in D(W_i)$, there is a $\bar{\lambda} \geqq 0$ such that $(\bar{\lambda}K(x) \cap L(u)) \neq \emptyset$. Assume $\bar{\lambda}x \notin L(u)$ and let $y \in$

$(\bar{\lambda}K(x) \cap L(u))$. Then $y \leq \bar{\lambda}x$ and $y \in L(u)$. This contradicts strong disposability of inputs. Thus $D(F_i) = D(W_i)$ and $F_i(u,x) = W_i(u,x)$ for $(u, x) \in$ Complement $D(F_i)$. Properties $F_i.1$ and $W_i.1$ show that $F_i(0, x) = W_i(0, x), x \in R^n_+$. Thus assume $u \geq 0$ and $(x, u) \in D(F_i) = D(W_i)$. Then $(W_i(u, x) \cdot K(x) \cap L(u)) \neq \emptyset$, and it is sufficient to show that $(W_i(u,x) \cdot x) \in (W_i(u,x) \cdot K(x) \cap L(u))$, since then $F_i(u,x) = W_i(u,x)$. Assume therefore that $(W_i(u, x) \cdot x) \notin (W_i(u, x) \cdot K(x) \cap L(u))$. Then there exists a $y \in (W_i(u, x) \cdot K(x) \cap L(u))$, i.e., $y \leq W_i(u, x) \cdot x$ and $y \in L(u)$, which contradicts strong disposability of inputs. ■

This theorem will prove very useful (see section 3.7) in the actual measurement of weak input efficiency. It is worth noting, however, that the theorem states "for all (u,x)." It is of course possible for $F_i(u,x) = W_i(u,x)$ *for some* (u,x) in the absence of strong disposability of inputs. In Fig. 3–4 strong disposability fails, and $F_i(u,x) > W_i(u,x)$, yet $F_i(u,y) = W_i(u,y)$ because input vector y does not congest the technology at output vector u, whereas input vector x does.

We end this section by showing properties of the weak input measure of technical efficiency inherited from different special structures on the parent input correspondence.

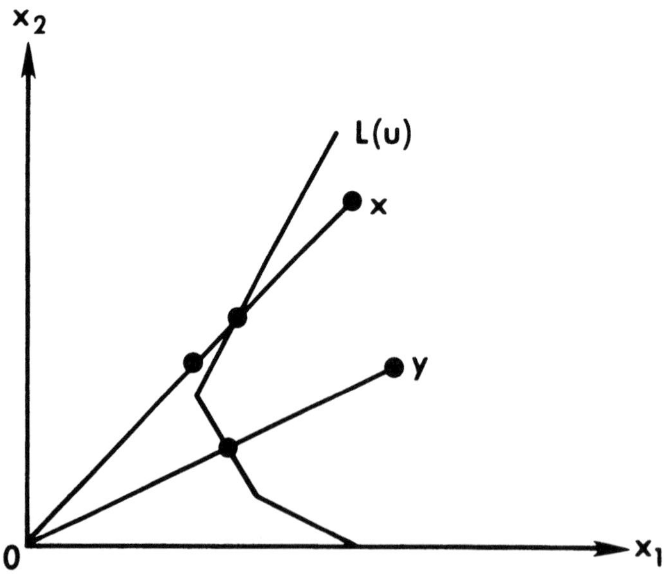

Figure 3-4

Theorem: Let L satisfy (L.1–L.5), then (3.3.11)

(1) $W_i(u, x) = \dfrac{F(u)}{F(u/\|u\|)} \cdot W_i(u/\|u\|, x)$ if L is ray-homothetic,

(2) $W_i(u, x) = F(u) \cdot W_i(1, x)$ if L is homothetic,

(3) $W_i(\theta u, x) = \theta^{A(u/\|u\|)} \cdot W_i(u, x)$, $\theta > 0$, if L is ray-homogeneous,

(4) $W_i(\theta u, x) = \theta^{\alpha} \cdot W_i(u, x)$, $\theta > 0$ if L is homogeneous of degree $+\alpha$.

If, in addition, L satisfies L.3.S, (1)–(4) are necessary and sufficient conditions.

Proof: Let L be ray-homothetic, then

$$W_i(u, x) = \min\left\{\lambda \geqq 0 : \lambda x \in \frac{F(u)}{F(u/\|u\|)} \cdot L(u/\|u\|)\right\}$$

(definition (2.4.1))

$$= \min\left\{\lambda \geqq 0 : \frac{F(u/\|u\|)}{F(u)} \cdot \lambda x \in L(u/\|u\|)\right\}$$

$$= \frac{F(u)}{F(u/\|u\|)} \cdot W_i(u/\|u\|, x).$$

Similar arguments apply to show (2)–(4). Next, assume that inputs are strongly disposable, i.e., L.3.S holds. If

$$W_i(u, x) = \frac{F(u)}{F(u/\|u\|)} \cdot W_i(u/\|u\|, x)$$

we must show that the input correspondence is ray-homothetic. Since L.3.S applies, by theorem (3.3.7) we can write

$$L(u) = \left\{ x : 0 < \frac{F(u)}{F(u/\|u\|)} \cdot W_i(u/\|u\|, x) \leqq 1 \right\}.$$

The result follows upon application of property $W_i.3$. Similar arguments can be used for the other special structures. ■

3.4 The Overall Input Efficiency Measure

The overall input efficiency measure was introduced by Farrell (1957), and extended by Eichhorn (1978a,b) to indicate the extent to which the production unit succeeds, by adjusting its input vector in light of the input prices it faces, in minimizing the cost of producing a certain output vector. Since these adjustments can combine a radial shrinkage of the input vector with a change in the input mix, it follows that the overall input efficiency measure has both technical and non-technical (i.e., allocative) components, and thus is input price-dependent.

In order to define the overall input efficiency measure in the context of an input correspondence L satisfying properties (L.1–L.5), we need the following notions. Let

$$H_i^-(x, p) := \{y : py \leqq px\} \tag{3.4.1}$$

be the lower halfspace generated by (x, p), $p \in R^n_{++}$. We observe the following properties of $H_i^-(x, p)$

$$\begin{aligned} &H_i^-.1\ H_i^-(\lambda x, p) = \lambda H_i^-(x, p),\ \lambda > 0, \\ &H_i^-.2\ H_i^-(x, \lambda p) = H_i^-(x, p),\ \lambda > 0. \end{aligned} \tag{3.4.2}$$

Both properties follow directly from the definition of $H_i^-(x,p)$. Secondly, the effective domain of the overall input efficiency measure is given by

$$D(O_i) := \{(u, x, p) : \exists\, \lambda \geqq 0 \text{ such that } \lambda H_i^-(x, p) \cap \mathrm{L}(u) \neq \emptyset\}. \tag{3.4.3}$$

Now define

Definition: The function W_i^o: $R^m_+ \times R^n_+ \to R_+ \cup \{+\infty\}$ defined by (3.4.4)

$$O_i(u, x, p) := \begin{cases} \min\{\lambda \geqq 0 : (\lambda H_i^-(x, p) \cap L(u)) \neq \emptyset\}, \\ \quad (u, x, p) \in D(O_i), \\ +\infty,\ (u, x, p) \in \text{Complement } D(O_i), \end{cases}$$

is called the Overall Input Efficiency Measure.

Since input prices are taken to be strictly positive in defining $O_i(u,x,p)$, it follows (as in theorem (3.3.4)) that the overall input efficiency measure is well-defined. To illustrate the overall input efficiency measure, consider Fig. 3–5. For $x \in L(u)$, $p \in R^n_{++}$, the lower halfspace generated by (x, p) is labeled $H_i^-(x, p)$. The overall input efficiency measure $O_i(u, x, p)$ pushes $H_i^-(x, p)$ as far as possible down the ray OP under the condition that the translated lower halfspace $H_i^-(x, p)$ has a nonempty intersection with $L(u)$. Thus $O_i(u, x, p) = \lambda = OS/OP$. Moreover, since $OS/OP = \|O_i(u,x,p) \cdot x\|/\|x\|$ it follows that $O_i(u,x,p) =$ IOE of section 3.1. Thus $O_i(u, x, p)$ measures the cost saving available to the production unit by adjusting inputs from $x \in L(u)$ at point P to point W $\in CM(u,p)$. If $x \notin L(u)$ then $O_i(u, x, p)$ measures the change in cost, which can be either positive or negative, incurred by adjusting inputs from $x \notin L(u)$ to point W $\in CM(u,p)$. In both cases $CM(u,p)$ is the reference set used by the overall measure of efficiency.

For the actual computation of the overall input efficiency measure a second interpretation of $O_i(u,x,p)$ is useful, namely

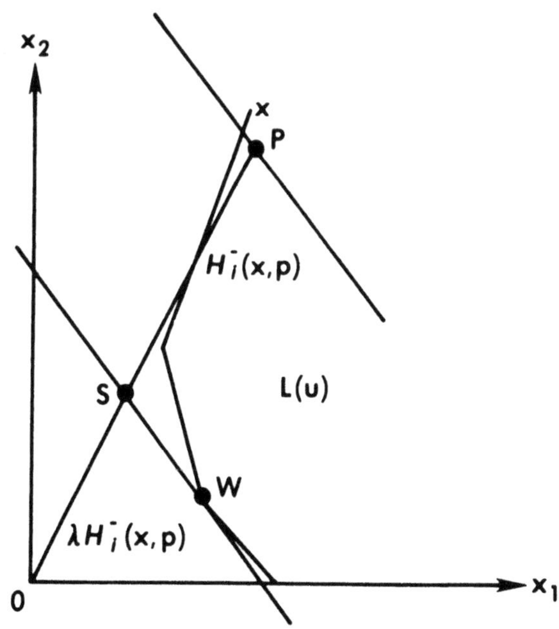

Figure 3-5

Theorem: $O_i(u,x,p) = Q(u,p)/px$. (3.4.5)

Proof: Let $y \in (O_i(u,x,p) \cdot H_i^-(x,p) \cap L(u))$, then $y \in L(u)$ and since $O_i(u,x,p)$ is a minimum, $py = O_i(u,x,p) \cdot px$. Recall (2.2.27) defining $Q(u,p)$ as $\inf\{px : x \in L(u)\}$. Now assume $py < Q(u,p)$, but then $y \notin L(u)$ contradicting the above. Thus assume $py > Q(u,p)$, but then $\{z : pz \leqq py\} \supset \{z : pz \leqq Q(u,p)\}$ and since the two sets are parallel, $O_i(u,x,p)$ cannot be a minimum. Thus, $py = Q(u,p)$ and since $py = O_i(u,x,p) \cdot px$, $O_i(u,x,p) = Q(u,p)/px$. ■

This theorem shows that the overall input efficiency measure is the quotient between the minimum cost $Q(u,p)$ and the actual cost, px.

Before stating the properties of the overall input efficiency measure, we need to define what is meant by overall input efficiency.

Definition: An input vector $x \in L(u)$ is Overall Input Efficient for prices $p \in R^n_{++}$ if $x \in CM(u,p)$. (3.4.6)

The properties of $O_i(u,x,p)$ are given in the following theorem.

Theorem: Let L satisfy (L.1–L.5), then (3.4.7)

O_i.1 $O_i(0,x,p) = 0$, $(x,p) \in R^n_+ \times R^n{}_{++}$,

O_i.2 $0 < O_i(u,x,p) < +\infty$, $(u,x,p) \in D(O_i)$,

O_i.3 $O_i(u,\lambda x,p) = \lambda^{-1} O_i(u,x,p)$, $\lambda > 0$, $(u,x,p) \in D(O_i)$,

O_i.4 $O_i(\theta u,x,p) \geqq O_i(u,x,p)$, $\theta \geqq 1$,

O_i.5 $O_i(u,x,\lambda p) = O_i(u,x,p)$, $\lambda > 0$,

O_i.6 For $x \in L(u)$, $O_i(u,x,p) = 1$ if and only if x is overall input efficient for the price vector p.

Proof: Properties O_i.1–O_i.4 are easily proved, following the ideas outlined in the proofs of theorems (3.2.5) and (3.3.6). Property O_i.5 is a direct consequence of property H_i^-.2. O_i.6: Let $x \in L(u)$ and $O_i(u,x,p) = 1$. Then by theorem (3.4.5), $Q(u,p) = px$. Thus $x \in CM(u,p)$. Conversely, assume $x \in CM(u,p)$. Then $x \in L(u)$ and $px = Q(u,p)$, thus by theorem (3.4.5) $O_i(u,x,p) = 1$. ■

We note that properties $O_i.1$–$O_i.4$ are analogous to properties $F_i.1$–$F_i.4$ and $W_i.1$–$W_i.4$, taking account of the additional arguments of O_i and the possibly different effective domain of O_i. Also, property $O_i.5$ implies that the overall input efficiency measure, although it is input price-dependent, depends only upon relative prices, i.e., $O_i(u, x, p) = O_i(u, x, p/\|p\|)$. This follows from $O_i.5$ by choosing $\lambda = 1/\|p\|$. Finally, property $O_i.6$ shows that $O_i(u, x, p) = 1$ if and only if $x \in \mathrm{CM}(u, p)$; see definition (3.4.6).

To conclude this section we show what separability properties the overall input efficiency measure inherits from the special input structures discussed in section 2.4.

Theorem: Let L satisfy (L.1–L.5), then (3.4.8)

(1) $O_i(u, x, p) = \dfrac{\mathrm{F}(u)}{\mathrm{F}(u/\|u\|)} \cdot O_i(u/\|u\|, x, p)$ if L is ray-homothetic,

(2) $O_i(u, x, p) = \mathrm{F}(u) \cdot O_i(1, x, p)$ if L is homothetic,

(3) $O_i(\theta u, x, p) = \theta^{\mathrm{A}(u/\|u\|)} \cdot O_i(u, x, p)$ if L is ray-homogeneous,

(4) $O_i(\theta u, x, p) = \theta^{\alpha} \cdot O_i(u, x, p)$ if L is homogeneous of degree $+\alpha$.

The proof of this theorem follows that of theorem (3.3.11).

3.5 The Input Congestion Measure

Prior to introducing a measure of input congestion along the lines proposed in section 3.1, we first need a formal definition of what we mean by input congestion. Introduce therefore

Definition: The production technology is input congested if for some $u \geq 0$ and $y \in \mathrm{L}(u)$, there exists an $x \geq y$ such that $x \in \mathrm{L}(\theta u)$, $0 \leqq \theta < 1$, $x \notin \mathrm{L}(u)$. (3.5.1)

This definition is a generalization of MOL-congestion (Färe and Svensson, 1980), and is consistent with the generally accepted notion that input congestion occurs whenever increasing some input(s) decreases output, or conversely, when by decreasing some input(s) output may be increased. The input vector $x \in L(\theta u)$, $0 \leqq \theta < 1$, is said to be congesting if by decreasing x to y, output can be increased to u. To measure this type of input congestion we also need the notion of an input congestion-free technology so that we have a reference technology.

Definition: The technology is Input Congestion-Free if it is not input congested. (3.5.2)

The following theorem gives a complete characterization of an input congestion-free technology.

Theorem: Let L satisfy (L.1–L.5). The technology is input congestion-free if and only if inputs are strongly disposable, i.e., L.3.5 holds. (3.5.3)

Proof: Assume inputs are strongly disposable, then for $x \geqq y \in L(u), u \geq 0$, $x \in L(u)$. By weak disposability of outputs, $x \in L(\theta u)$, $0 \leqq \theta < 1$. Thus the technology is input congestion-free. Conversely, assume inputs are not strongly disposable, then there exists an $x \geq y$ and $y \in L(u), u \geq 0$, such that $x \notin L(u)$. Since $L(0) = R^n_+$ (see L.1), and $L(\theta u) \subseteqq L(u)$ for $\theta \geqq 1, x \in L(\theta u)$ for some $\theta \in [0, 1)$. ■

Given a technology L satisfying (L.1–L.5), a unique minimal input congestion-free technology L^{SI} can be derived from L, using equation (2.1.4), by means of

$$L^{SI}(u) := L(u) + R^n_+ = \{z: z = x + y,\ x \in L(u),\ y \in R^n_+\}. \qquad (3.5.4)$$

This new technology satisfies (L.1–L.5) and L.3.S by theorem (2.1.5), and thus by theorem (3.5.3) it is input congestion-free.

To measure input congestion radially, we need to determine by how much an input vector can be radially reduced to reach the closest input congestion-free technology from the congested technology. Such an input congestion measure can be derived from the Farrell input efficiency and the weak input efficiency measures.

Definition: For $x \in L(u)$, $u \geq 0$, the Input Congestion Measure is $C_i(u, x) := W_i(u, x)/F_i(u, x)$. (3.5.5)

The definition clearly indicates why we refer to $C_i(u, x)$ as a "derived" measure. In terms of Fig. 3–6, the input congestion measure is given by $C_i(u, x) = \text{OR/OP} \div \text{OQ/OP} = \text{OR/OQ} = W_i(u, x)/F_i(u, x)$. It follows that $C_i(u, x) = \text{OR/OQ} = \text{IC}$ of section 3.1. $C_i(u, x)$ measures the proportional reduction in inputs from the isoquant of the parent technology to the weak efficient subset of the corresponding input congestion-free technology. Although R $\notin$ L(u), disposal of RT units of x_2 generates T $\in$ L(u).

We know from sections 3.2 and 3.3 that both $F_i(u, x)$ and $W_i(u, x)$ have a cost interpretation, so it follows from definition (3.5.5) that the input congestion measure $C_i(u, x)$ also has a cost interpretation. To show this, in Fig. 3–6 let the point Q be $\lambda^\circ x$ and let the point R be $\hat{\lambda}x$, where λ° and $\hat{\lambda}$ are defined in equations (3.2.4) and (3.2.5). Also let the firm face input prices $p \in R^n_{++}$. Then it follows directly from definition (3.5.5) that

$$C_i(u, x) = \frac{\hat{\lambda}}{\lambda^\circ} = \frac{p(\hat{\lambda}x)}{px} \div \frac{p(\lambda^\circ x)}{px} = \frac{p(\hat{\lambda}x)}{p(\lambda^\circ x)}. \qquad (3.5.6)$$

Thus $C_i(u, x)$ measures the ratio of input cost at $\hat{\lambda}x \in$ WEff L(u) to input cost at $\lambda^\circ x \in$ Isoq L(u).

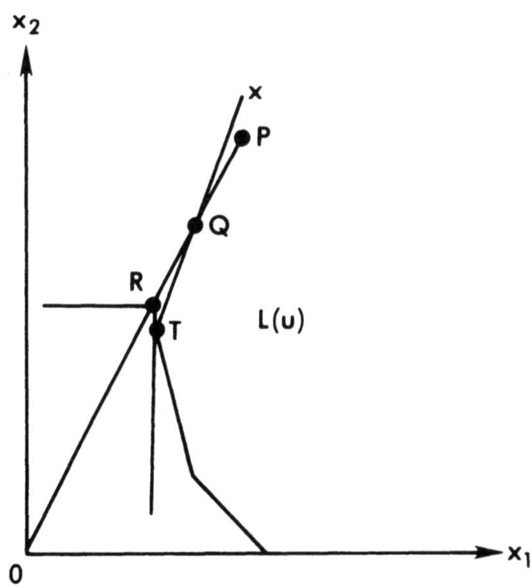

Figure 3-6

The properties of the input congestion measure are given by the following theorem

Theorem: If L satisfies (L.1–L.5), then (3.5.7)

C_i.1 $0 < C_i(u, x) \leqq 1$,

C_i.2 $C_i(u, x) = 1$ if and only if x is not congesting for u,

C_i.3 $C_i(u, \lambda x) = C_i(u, x), \lambda > 0$.

Proof: Property C_i.1 follows from properties F_i.2, W_i.2 and corollary (3.3.8), noting that $x \in L(u)$.
Property C_i.2 holds since if $x \in L(u), F_i(u, x) = W_i(u, x)$ if and only if $x \in$ WEff $L(u)$, i.e., if and only if x is not congesting for u.
Property C_i.3 follows from properties F_i.3 and W_i.3. ■

It is of interest to note that property C_i.3 implies that

$$C_i(u, x) = C_i(u, x/\|x\|), \tag{3.5.8}$$

i.e., the input congestion measure is a function of the input mix rather than of the size of input.

In order to determine which subvector of inputs creates congestion, a partial weak input measure of technical efficiency is introduced.

Let $x \in L(u)$, be written as $x = (x_\alpha, x_\beta)$ where $\alpha \cup \beta = \{1, 2, \ldots, n\}$ and $\alpha \cap \beta = \emptyset$. Now consider

$$K(x(\alpha)) := \{y: 0 \leqq y_\alpha \leqq x_\alpha, y_\beta = x_\beta\}, \tag{3.5.9}$$

and

$$D(W_i^\alpha) := \{(u, x): \exists \lambda \geqq 0 \text{ such that } (\lambda K(x(\alpha)) \cap L(u)) \neq \emptyset\}. \tag{3.5.10}$$

Definition: The function $W_i^\alpha: R_+^m \times R_+^n \to R_+ \cup \{+\infty\}$ defined by (3.5.11)

$$W_i^\alpha(u, x) := \begin{cases} \min\{\lambda \geqq 0: (\lambda K(x(\alpha)) \cap L(u)) \neq \emptyset\}. \\ \quad (u, x) \in D(W_i^\alpha), \\ +\infty, (u, x) \in \text{Complement } D(W_i^\alpha), \end{cases}$$

is called the Partial Weak Input Measure of Technical Efficiency.

Clearly, if $\alpha = \{1, 2, \ldots, n\}$, $W_i^\alpha(u,x) = W_i(u,x)$. However, $W_i^\alpha(u,x)$ may equal $W_i(u, x)$ even for $\alpha \neq \{1, 2, \ldots, n\}$, and it follows directly that congestion is created by the subsets of inputs $\{1, 2, \ldots, n\}$ for which $W_i^\alpha(u,x) = W_i(u,x)$ whenever $W_i(u,x) \neq F_i(u,x)$. To identify the specific input vector(s) creating congestion, compare $W_i^\alpha(u,x)$ with $W_i(u,x)$ for each subvector $\alpha \subsetneqq \{1, 2, \ldots, n\}$.

If the input structure is ray-homothetic or homothetic, respectively, then the input congestion measure depends on output mix or is independent of output, respectively

$$C_i(u,x) = \frac{W_i(u/\|u\|, x)}{F_i(u/\|u\|, x)} = C_i\left(\frac{u}{\|u\|}, x\right), \qquad (3.5.12)$$

$$C_i(u,x) = \frac{W_i(1,x)}{F_i(1,x)} = C_i(1,x).$$

These properties of the input congestion measure under ray-homotheticity and homotheticity are direct consequences of theorems (3.2.6) and (3.3.11).

3.6 The Allocative Input Efficiency Measure

The second derived input efficiency measure is now examined. This measure, the allocative input efficiency measure, was introduced by Farrell (1957) to gauge input mix error relative to the input prices faced by the production unit. That this measure is a derived measure is apparent from the following

Definition: For $x \in L(u)$, $u \geq 0$, the Allocative Input Efficiency Measure is given by $A_i(u, x, p) := [O_i(u, x, p)/W_i(u,x)]$. (3.6.1)

To illustrate the allocative input efficiency measure, consider Fig. 3–7. Here the input price plane Z–Z′ faced by the firm intersects L(u) at W, and the translated (along ray OP) nonpositive orthant intersects L(u) at T. Using definition (3.4.4) of $O_i(u,x,p)$ and definition (3.3.3) of $W_i(u,x)$, it follows from definition (3.6.1) that $A_i(u, x, p)$ = (OS/OP)/(OR/OP) = OS/OR. Clearly, OS/OR = IA of section 3.1. Thus the allocative input efficiency measure $A_i(u, x, p)$ measures the minimal ray distance from the input

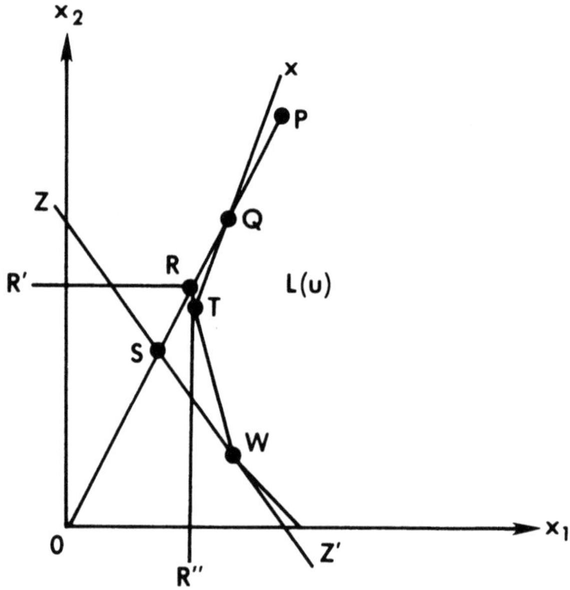

Figure 3-7

congestion-free technology to the hyperplane yielding the minimum cost of producing output u at input prices p.

Since $O_i(u, x, p)$ and $W_i(u, x)$ both have cost interpretations, so does $A_i(u, x, p)$. Using theorem (3.4.5) and equation (3.3.5) together with definition (3.6.1), we have

$$A_i(u, x, p) = \frac{Q(u, p)}{px} \div \frac{p(\hat{\lambda}x)}{px} = \frac{Q(u, p)}{p(\hat{\lambda}x)}. \tag{3.6.2}$$

Thus $A_i(u, x, p)$ measures the ratio of the minimum input cost required to produce u to the input cost at $\hat{\lambda}x \in$ WEff L(u).

Before listing the properties of the allocative input efficiency measure, we first provide a formal definition of Farrell's notion of allocative efficiency.

Definition: An input vector $x \in$ L(u), $u \geq 0$, is Allocatively Efficient for $p \in R^n_{++}$ if there exists a $\lambda \in (0, 1]$ such that λx $\in$ CM(u, p). (3.6.3)

The properties of the allocative input efficiency measure are summarized in

Theorem: For $x \in L(u)$, $u \geq 0$, $A_i(u, x, p)$ has the properties (3.6.4)

$A_i.1$ $0 < A_i(u, x, p) \leqq 1$,

$A_i.2$ $A_i(u, x, p) = 1$ if and only if x is allocatively efficient for $p \in R^n_{++}$,

$A_i.3$ $A_i(u, \lambda x, p) = A_i(u, x, p), \lambda > 0$,

$A_i.4$ $A_i(u, x, \lambda p) = A_i(u, x, p), \lambda > 0$.

Proof: Property $A_i.1$ follows from properties $W_i 5$, $O_i.2$ and that $x \in L(u)$.

$A_i.2$: Assume $x \in L(u)$, $u \geq 0$, is allocatively efficient for p. Then there exists a $\lambda \in (0, 1]$ such that $\lambda x \in CM(u, p)$. Thus, $W_i(u, x) \cdot x \in CM(u, p)$ and $A_i(u, x, p) \cdot x \in CM(u, p)$. Both $W_i(u, x) \cdot x$ and $A_i(u, x, p) \cdot x$ belong to the Isoq $L(u)$, hence $W_i(u, x) = O_i(u, x, p)$. Therefore $A_i(u, x, p) = 1$. Conversely, assume $A_i(u, x, p) = 1$, then $W_i(u, x) = A_i(u, x, p)$. Hence $O_i(u, x, p) \cdot x = W_i(u, x) \cdot x$. Since $x \in L(u)$, $u \geq 0$, it follows that $0 < O_i(u, x, p) \leqq 1$. Thus we only have to show that $O_i(u, x, p) \cdot x \in CM(u, p)$. We first show that $O_i(u, x, p) \cdot x = W_i(u, x) \cdot x \in L(u)$. Since $p \in R^n_{++}$, $W_i(u, x) \cdot K(x) \cap \{y: py = px\} \cdot O_i(u, x, p) = W_i(u, x) \cdot x$. If $W_i(u, x) \cdot x \notin L(u)$, then since $K(x) \subset H_i^-(x, p)$, note $p \in R^n_{++}$, $W_i(u, x) \cdot K(x) \cap L(u) = \emptyset$, a contradiction. Thus $W_i(u,x) \cdot x = O_i(u,x,p) \cdot x \in L(u)$. Finally, since by theorem (3.4.5), $O_i(u,x,p) = [Q(u,p)/px]$, $O_i(u,x,p) \cdot x \in CM(u,p)$.

$A_i.3$: Follows from properties $W_i.3$ and $O_i.3$.

$A_i.4$: Follows from property $O_i.5$. ■

If the input structure is ray-homothetic or homothetic, then

$$\begin{cases} A_i(u,x,p) = \dfrac{O_i[(u/\|u\|), x, p]}{W_i[(u/\|u\|), x]} = A_i\left(\dfrac{u}{\|u\|}, x, p\right), \\[2ex] A_i(u,x,p) = \dfrac{O_i(1,x,p)}{W_i(1,x)} = A_i(1,x,p), \end{cases} \tag{3.6.5}$$

respectively.

Finally, we note that the multiplicative decompositions stated in (3.1.1) and (3.1.2) now take the form

$$O_i(u,x,p) = F_i(u,x) \cdot C_i(u,x) \cdot A_i(u,x,p) \qquad (3.6.6)$$

and

$$O_i(u,x,p) = W_i(u,x) \cdot A_i(u,x,p). \qquad (3.6.7)$$

3.7 Linear Programming Example

The input efficiency measures derived and characterized in the previous sections can, of course, be used in empirical work. In this section we construct a linear programming example and calculate $F_i(u,x)$, $W_i(u,x)$, and $O_i(u,x,p)$. In addition, we calculate the derived measures, $A_i(u,x,p)$ and $C_i(u,x)$.

We begin by constructing the input correspondence, $L(u)$, from the observed data. As in section 2.4, let m_{ij} represent the output per unit intensity of the jth good from the ith activity or firm, and n_{ij} represent the input per unit intensity of the jth input in the ith activity or firm. The corresponding matrices are denoted by M and N, where M is of order (k,m), i.e., k activities or firms and m outputs and N is of order (k,n), i.e., k activities or firms and n inputs. As shown in section 2.4, we can now write the input correspondence for a technology with weak disposability of inputs and outputs as

$$L^W(u) = \{x: \mu \cdot z \cdot M = u, z \cdot N = \delta \cdot x; \mu, \delta \in (0, 1], z \in R^k_+\}. \qquad (3.7.1)$$

where z is the intensity vector. This correspondence tells us all the input vectors that can be used to produce a given output level, u, given the weakly disposable technology.

The Farrell input measure of technical efficiency, $F_i(u,x)$, can now be derived relative to the weakly disposable technology described in (3.7.1). Specifically, to calculate $F_i(u,x)$ for a firm (activity) (u°, x°), we have the following linear programming problem

$$\min \lambda$$

subject to

$$\mu \cdot z \cdot M = u^\circ$$

$$z \cdot N = \lambda \cdot \delta \cdot x^\circ$$

$\mu, \delta \in (0, 1]$

$\lambda \in R_+, z \in R^k_+.$ (3.7.2)

To derive the weak input measure of technical efficiency, $W_i(u, x)$, we make use of theorem (3.3.10) which states that the Farrell and weak efficiency measures are identical if and only if the technology satisfies strong disposability of inputs. Thus we need to specify a strongly rather than weakly disposable technology. As in section 2.4 define

$$L^S(u) = \{x: z \cdot M \geqq u, z \cdot N \leqq x, z \in R^k_+\} \quad (3.7.3)$$

which imposes strong disposability of both inputs and outputs.[1] To calculate $W_i(u, x)$ for a firm or activity (u°, x°), we merely modify the linear programming problem (3.7.2) to take account of the strongly disposable technology specified in (3.7.3) as follows

$\min \lambda$

subject to

$z \cdot M \geqq u^\circ$

$z \cdot N \leqq \lambda \cdot x^\circ$

$z \in R^k_+$

$\lambda \in R_+.$ (3.7.4)

The last primary measure to be calculated is the overall input efficiency measure, $O_i(u,x,p)$. To calculate $O_i(u,x,p)$ we make use of theorem (3.4.5) which states that $O_i(u,x,p) = Q(u,p)/px$. Thus, $O_i(u,x,p)$ can be derived from the simple linear programming problem of finding the minimum cost given the technology specified in (3.7.3) and positive prices. Then $O_i(u, x, p)$ is calculated by dividing the solution to the cost minimizing problem, $Q(u,p)$, by actual costs in a given firm, i.e., px°. The cost minimization problem can be written as

$\min px$

subject to

$z \cdot M \geqq u^\circ$

$$z \cdot N \leqq x^{\circ}$$

$$z \in R^{k}_{+}, p \in R^{n}_{+}. \tag{3.7.5}$$

Now consider the following numerical example (summarized in Table 3–1) which we shall use to calculate the primary and derived measures of input efficiency.

Table 3-1

	Output	*Inputs*	
Firm	(u)	(x_1)	(x_2)
1	2	1	2
2	2	2	2
3	2	2	1
4	2	1	3
5	2	1	4
6	2	3	1.25
7	2	4	1.25

Table 3-2

Firm	$F_i(u,x)$	$W_i(u,x)$	$O_i(u,x,p)$	$C_i(u,x)$	$A_i(u,x,p)$
1	1.00	1.00	1.00	1.00	1.00
2	.75	.75	.75	1.00	1.00
3	1.00	1.00	1.00	1.00	1.00
4	1.00	1.00	.75	1.00	.75
5	1.00	1.00	.60	1.00	.60
6	.86	.80	.71	.93	.89
7	1.00	.80	.57	.80	.71

In this example there are seven firms (or activities), each producing two units of output with two inputs, x_1 and x_2. These are plotted in Fig. 3–8. For the Farrell input measure of technical efficiency, the linear program (3.7.2) constructs the boundary of the weakly disposable technology as the line segments 54137. Clearly, points 2 and 6 are Farrell input "inefficient." Under strong disposability of inputs, the boundary of $L^S(u)$ is constructed as 5413 and the broken line extending from 3 parallel to the x_1 axis, and points 2, 6 and 7 are all weakly inefficient.

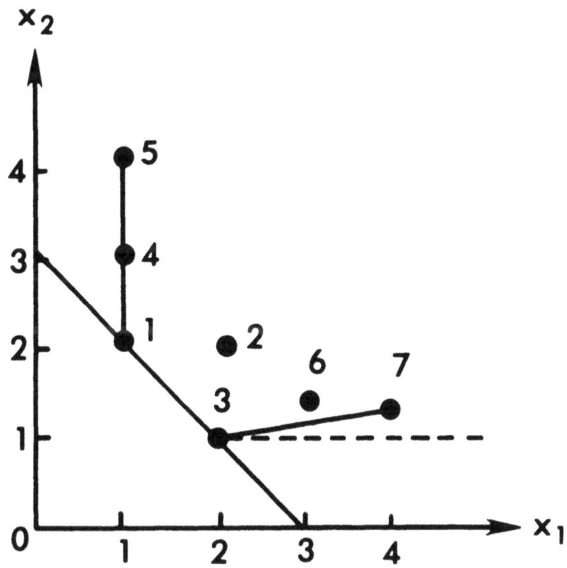

Figure 3-8

In order to calculate the overall measure, we assume that the price of x_1 is one and that the price of x_2 is one. In Fig. 3–8, the cost minimizing hyperplane contains the line segment between points 1 and 3.

The results of applying the linear programs to the data in Table 3–1 are presented in Table 3–2. In addition, the calculated or derived measures, $C_i(u, x)$ and $A_i(u, x, p)$ are included. From (3.5.4), $C_i(u, x)$ is calculated as $W_i(u,x)/F_i(u,x)$, and from (3.6.1), $A_i(u,x,p)$ is calculated as $O_i(u,x,p)/W_i(u,x)$.

Finally, it is easy to see, using the method described in section 3.5, that the first factor creates congestion for firms 6 and 7.

Notes

1. Since u is fixed to define $L^S(u)$, strong disposability of outputs does not alter the basic structure.

4 RADIAL OUTPUT EFFICIENCY MEASURES

4.0 Introduction

In chapter 3 we modeled the technology of a production unit with an input correspondence $u \rightarrow L(u) \subseteqq R^n_+$, and we developed various measures of the efficiency with which inputs are used to produce a certain output vector $u \in R^m_+$. Three of these measures are technical, and so are input price-independent, while one is allocative and input price-dependent. Thus the overall measure of input efficiency is also input price-dependent, having the cost minimizing set $CM(u, p)$ as its reference set, and so the behavioral assumption underlying the construction of the overall measure of input efficiency is one of minimizing input cost in the production of a certain output vector.

In some circumstances, however, it may be more plausible to view the production unit as seeking to maximize output revenue obtainable from a certain input vector. This is the approach taken in this chapter. We model the technology of a production unit with an output correspondence $x \rightarrow P(x) \subseteqq R^m_+$, and we develop various measures of the efficiency with which outputs are produced from a certain input vector $x \in R^n_+$. As in chapter 3, three of these measures are technical, and so are output price-independent, while one is allocative and output price-dependent. The overall measure of output efficiency is output price-dependent also, having the revenue maximizing set RM(x, r) as its reference set. All five measures of output efficiency are radial in the sense that the search for larger (i.e., more efficient) feasible output vectors is constrained to equiproportionately larger feasible output vectors against which to measure the efficiency of an observed output vector. The radial nature of these output efficiency measures has the advantage of providing a revenue interpretation for each, since equiproportionate output increases translate directly into corresponding revenue increases at fixed output prices.

In section 4.1 we provide an intuitive geometric interpretation of each of the five output efficiency measures for an output correspondence P satisfying properties (P.1–P.5).

In sections 4.2–4.4 we develop somewhat more rigorously the three primary measures of output efficiency, the Farrell technical measure, the weak technical measure, and the overall measure. In section 4.5 we obtain a derived measure of output loss due to lack of output disposability, a measure that is analogous to the measure of input congestion developed in section 3.5 of chapter 3. In section 4.6 we obtain a derived measure of output allocative efficiency. Like the overall measure of output efficiency, the measure of output allocative efficiency is output price-dependent. All five of these measures generalize and extend the results of Färe and Grosskopf (1983a).

Section 4.7 concludes the chapter with a linear programming example designed to illustrate the calculation of each of the five measures of output efficiency.

4.1 Radial Output Efficiency Measures

It is true that either the input correspondence or the output correspondence completely characterizes a production technology, since they are inverses of each other. However, if inputs are used in an efficient manner, this does not imply that the produced output vector is efficient. Nor is the converse true. In sections 2.2 and 2.3 of chapter 2, examples were introduced showing that $x \in \text{Isoq L}(u) \not\Rightarrow u \in \text{Isoq P}(x)$ and $u \in \text{Isoq P}(x) \not\Rightarrow x \in \text{Isoq L}(u)$. These examples are intended to show that the various forms of input efficiency do not imply, nor are they implied by, the corresponding forms of output efficiency. It is therefore important to introduce output efficiency measures analogous to the input efficiency measures discussed in chapter 3.

The five output efficiency measures discussed in this chapter consist of three primary measures and two derived measures. All five measures can be illustrated with the help of Fig. 4–1. In Fig. 4–1 point P denotes an output vector u produced with input vector x, where u belongs to the interior of the output set P(x), which is bounded by the line segments $\overline{\text{OABCDO}}$. The set R′–R–R″ is the nonnegative orthant radially translated along a ray from the origin through point P, as far away from the origin as possible so long as it maintains a nonempty intersection with P(x). This intersection is labeled point B. The line Z–Z′ is a price plane representing the output prices $r \in R^m_+$, $r \neq 0$, faced by the production unit.

The revenue maximizing intersection of Z–Z′ with P(x) is labeled point C.

The three primary measures of output efficiency can now be identified. The Farrell output measure of technical efficiency (OTE) is represented by OTE = OQ/OP. Thus OTE measures the maximum proportional increase in both elements of the observed output vector such that the scaled output vector, located at Q, remains feasible. Note that the point Q belongs to the isoquant of P(x). Moreover, OTE also measures the revenue increase that results from expanding from point P to point Q: output revenue at Q is a multiple OQ/OP of output revenue at P for *any* output price vector. Second, the weak output measure of technical efficiency (OWE) is represented by

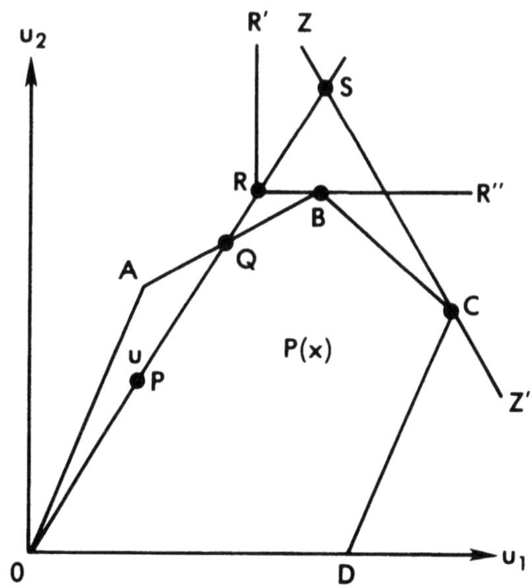

Figure 4–1

OWE = OR/OP. If both elements of the observed output vector located at P are scaled up proportionally by the scalar OR/OP, the resulting output vector located at point R $\in$ WEff $P^{SO}(x)$ is technically efficient in the weak sense. Of course the output vector R cannot be produced by the given input vector x, since R $\notin$ P(x). However the output vector located at point B is producible, and by disposing of BR units of u_1, R is obtainable. Note also that OWE = OR/OP measures the revenue increase that results from expanding production from point P to point R: output revenue at R is a multiple OR/OP of output revenue at P for *any* output price vector. This revenue interpretation requires that the excess outputs (BR units of u_1) be disposable at zero net cost. The third measure, the overall output efficiency measure (OOE), is represented by OOE = OS/OP. Again, output S cannot be produced from inputs x, since S $\notin$ P(x). But point C $\in$ P(x) is producible from inputs x, and the revenues received at C and S are the same. Moreover, since point C maximizes the output revenue obtainable from input vector x at output prices r (i.e. C $\in$ RM(x, r)), OOE also measures the revenue increase resulting from expanding production from point P to point C. since RM(x, r) is output price-dependent, so is OOE.

From these three primary measures, we can derive two additional measures, namely (1) the measure of loss of output due to lack of output disposability (OC), and (2) the output allocative measure (OA). As can be seen from Fig. 4–1, OC = OR/OQ = OWE/OTE measures the loss of output (along the ray through P) due to a lack of output disposability. If outputs were strongly disposable, an output increase and consequent revenue increase of OC = OR/OQ could be realized by producing at point B and disposing of BR units of u_1. The allocative output measure is defined as OA = OS/OR = OOE/OWE. A reallocation of outputs from R to C eliminates allocative (or output price) inefficiency, thereby increasing output revenue by a multiple OA = OS/OR of its value at R.

Finally, we note that the overall output measure is the product of the technical measure, the measure of lost output due to lack of disposability, and the allocative measure. Thus we have

$$\text{OOE} = \text{OTE} \cdot \text{OC} \cdot \text{OA}, \tag{4.1.1}$$

or, since OC = OWE/OTE, the overall measure also can be expressed as the product of the weak and allocative measures

$$\text{OOE} = \text{OWE} \cdot \text{OA}. \tag{4.1.2}$$

4.2 The Farrell Output Measure of Technical Efficiency

In his original paper, Farrell (1957) introduced both an input and an output measure of technical efficiency under strong regularity conditions on the technology of a production unit producing a single output. In order to generalize his output measure to the multiproduct case with technology satisfying only conditions (P.1–P.5), we begin by specifying the effective domain of F_o, the Farrell output measure of technical efficiency

$$D(F_o) := \{(x, u) \colon \exists\, \theta \geqq 0 \text{ such that } \theta u \in \mathrm{P}(x)\}. \qquad (4.2.1)$$

Now define

Definition: The function $F_o\colon R_+^n \times R_+^m \to R_+ \cup \{+\infty\}$ defined by (4.2.2)

$$F_o(x, u) := \begin{cases} \max\{\theta \geqq 0 \colon \theta u \in \mathrm{P}(x)\}, & (x, u) \in D(F_o), \\ +\infty, & (x, u) \in \text{Complement } D(F_o), \end{cases}$$

is called the Farrell Output Measure of Technical Efficiency.

To illustrate the Farrell output measure of technical efficiency, consider Fig. 4–2, where the output set P(x) represents an output correspondence P satisfying (P.1–P.5). The distances OP $= \|u\|$ and OQ $= \|F_o(x, u) \cdot u\|$, thus we have

$$\mathrm{OTE} = \frac{\mathrm{OQ}}{\mathrm{OP}} = \frac{\|F_o(x, u) \cdot u\|}{\|u\|} = F_o(x, u), \qquad (4.2.3)$$

where $F_o(x, u)$ clearly coincides with OTE of section 4.1.

The Farrell output measure of technical efficiency measures the maximal proportional increase in output possible given the technology and the input vector x. In Fig. 4–2 this is the measure of how far one can push u proportionately to the northeast and yet remain in P(x). Since P(x) is a compact set (P.2 and P.4), definition (4.2.2) is permissable in the sense that the maximum exists. Call this maximum θ°. Then if $\theta^\circ > 1$ the production unit can produce radially larger output vector $\theta^\circ u \in \mathrm{Isoq}\ \mathrm{P}(x)$, and the

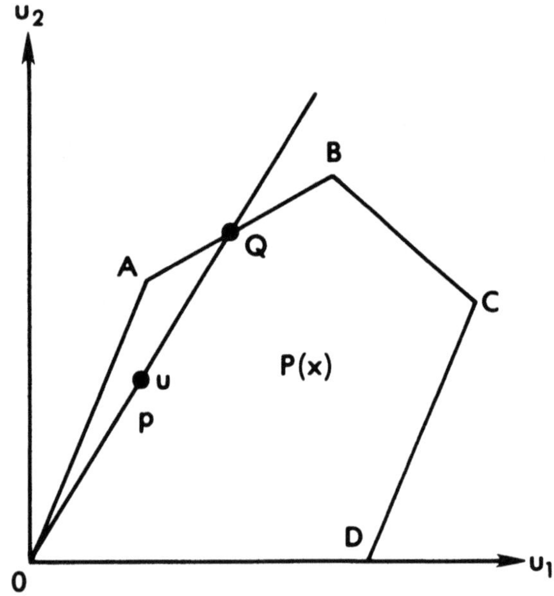

Figure 4-2

observed output vector u is technically inefficient. If $\theta^\circ < 1$ then $u \notin \mathrm{P}(x)$, and θ° is the smallest radial contraction of u such that $\theta^\circ u \in \mathrm{Isoq}\ \mathrm{P}(x)$. In both cases, Isoq P($x$) is the reference set used by the Farrell output measure to gauge the technical efficiency of $(x, u) \in D(F_o)$. For $(x, u) \notin D(F_o)$ no radial expansion or contraction of u can be produced by x, and $F_o = +\infty$. We note finally that definition (4.2.2) differs slightly from the one used in Färe and Lovell (1978).

If the production unit faces output prices $r \in R^m_+$, $r \neq 0$, then

$$F_o(x,\ u) = \theta^\circ = \frac{\mathrm{r}(\theta^\circ u)}{ru}, \tag{4.2.4}$$

and so the Farrell output measure of technical efficiency has a revenue interpretation. $F_o(x,\ u)$ measures the ratio of output revenue at $\theta^\circ u \in \mathrm{Isoq}$ $\mathrm{P}(x)$ to observed output revenue at $u \in \mathrm{P}(x)$. This ratio is independent of output prices, as can be seen by substituting $s \neq r$ for r in equation (4.2.4).

The properties of the Farrell output measure of technical efficiency are summarized in the following theorem. Since $F_o(x, u)$ is the inverse of the distance function of the output sets P(x), the relevant properties of the latter as given in Shephard (1970, chapter 9) need only be modified to accommodate our axiom system (P.1–P.5).

Theorem: If P satisfies (P.1–P.5), then (4.2.5)

F_o.1 $F_o(0, u) = +\infty$,

F_o.2 $0 < F_o(x, u) < +\infty$, $u \geq 0$, $(x, u) \in D(F_o)$,

F_o.3 $F_o(x, \theta u) = \theta^{-1} F_o(x, u)$, $\theta > 0$,
$(x, u) \in D(F_o)$,

F_o.4 $F_o(\lambda x, u) \geqq F_o(x, u)$, $\lambda \geqq 1$,

F_o.5 $\mathrm{P}(x) = \{u\colon F_o(x, u) \geqq 1\}$, $\mathrm{P}(x) \neq \{0\}$, if and only if outputs are weakly disposable,

F_o.6 $\mathrm{Isoq\ P}(x) = \{u\colon F_o(x, u) = 1\}$, $x \geq 0$,
$\mathrm{P}(x) \neq \{0\}$.

Proof: Property F_o.1 follows from condition P.1 that P(0) = {0}.

F_o.2: This property follows directly from definition (4.2.2).

$$\begin{aligned} F_o.3\colon F_o(x, \theta u) &= \max\{\delta\colon \delta\theta u \in \mathrm{P}(x)\} \\ &= \max\{\theta\delta\theta^{-1}\colon \delta\theta u \in \mathrm{P}(x)\} \\ &= \theta^{-1}\max\{\mu\colon \mu u \in \mathrm{P}(x)\} \\ &= \theta^{-1}F_o(x, u). \end{aligned}$$

F_o.4: Since inputs are weakly disposable, $\mathrm{P}(\lambda x) \supseteqq \mathrm{P}(x)$ for $\lambda \geqq 1$, thus F_o.4 follows.

F_o.5: Let $u \in \mathrm{P}(x)$, $u \neq 0$, then clearly, $F_o(x, u) \geqq 1$. Thus $\mathrm{P}(x) \subseteqq \{u\colon F_o(x, u) \geqq 1\}$. Next assume $u \notin \mathrm{P}(x)$, $\mathrm{P}(x) \neq \{0\}$. If there does not exist a $\theta \geqq 0$ such that $\theta u \in \mathrm{P}(x)$, $F_o(x, u) = +\infty$. Thus assume there exists a $\theta \geqq 0$ such that $\theta u \in \mathrm{P}(x)$. Since outputs are weakly disposable, $\theta < 1$, thus $\{u\colon F_o(x, u) \geqq 1\} \subseteqq \mathrm{P}(x)$. Conversely, assume that $\mathrm{P}(x) = \{u\colon F_o(x, u) \geqq 1\}$. Let $u \in \mathrm{P}(x) \neq \{0\}$, then we need to show that $\theta u \in \mathrm{P}(x)$ for $0 < \theta \leqq 1$. This is equivalent to showing that $F_o(x, \theta u) \geqq 1$. Since $u \in \mathrm{P}(x)$, one can write $F_o(x, u) \geqq \theta\theta^{-1} = 1$. Property F_o.3 implies that $F_o(x, \theta u) \geqq \theta^{-1} \geqq 1$. Thus $\theta u \in \mathrm{P}(x)$.

F_o.6: If $u \in \mathrm{Isoq\ P}(x)$ and $\mathrm{P}(x) \neq \{0\}$, then clearly, $F_o(x, u) = 1$. If $u \notin \mathrm{P}(x)$, then $F_o(x, u) < 1$ and if $u \in \mathrm{P}(x)$ but $u \notin \mathrm{Isoq\ P}(x)$, then there exists a $\theta > 1$, such that $\theta u \in \mathrm{P}(x)$. Thus $F_o(x, u) > 1$. Hence if $u \notin \mathrm{Isoq\ P}(x)$, then $F_o(x, u) \neq 1$, or equivalently, if $F_o(x, u) = 1$ then $u \in \mathrm{Isoq\ P}(x)$. ■

Among the properties of $F_o(x, u)$, one should note that it is homogeneous of degree -1 in outputs (F_o.3), but only nondecreasing in inputs (F_o.4). This asymmetry arises because the output correspondence is not required to be linearly homogeneous. Property F_o.5 shows that $F_o(x, u)$ can provide a complete characterization of the technology, provided outputs are weakly disposable. Property F_o.6 shows that an output vector is technically efficient in accordance with $F_o(x, u)$, if and only if $u \in \text{Isoq } P(x)$. That is, the Farrell output measure measures technical efficiency relative to the output isoquant.

Next, we show properties of the Farrell output measure of technical efficiency inherited from different special structures on the output correspondence

Theorem: If P satisfies (P.1–P.5), then (4.2.6)

(1) $F_o(x, u) = \dfrac{G(x)}{G(x/\|x\|)} \cdot F_o\left(\dfrac{x}{\|x\|}, u\right)$ if and only if P is ray-homothetic,

(2) $F_o(x, u) = G(x) \cdot F_o(1, u)$ if and only if P is homothetic,

(3) $F_o(\lambda x, u) = \lambda^{B(x/\|x\|)} \cdot F_o(x, u)$ if and only if P is ray-homogeneous, $\lambda > 0$.

(4) $F_o(\lambda x, u) = \lambda^{\beta} \cdot F_o(x, u)$ if and only if P is homogeneous of degree $+\beta$.

Proof: Let P be ray-homothetic, then

(definition (2.4.5))

$$F_o(x, u) = \max\left\{\theta\colon \theta u \in \frac{G(x)}{G(x/\|x\|)} \cdot P\left(\frac{x}{\|x\|}\right)\right\}$$

$$= \max\left\{\theta\colon \frac{G(x/\|x\|)}{G(x)} \cdot \theta u \in P\left(\frac{x}{\|x\|}\right)\right\}$$

$$= \frac{G(x)}{G(x/\|x\|)} \cdot F_o\left(\frac{x}{\|x\|}, u\right).$$

Conversely, assume (1) holds, then using F_o.3 and F_o.5 one has

$$P(x) = \{u: \frac{G(x)}{G(x/\|x\|)} \cdot F_o\left(\frac{x}{\|x\|}, u\right) \geqq 1\}$$

$$= \{u: F_o\left(\frac{x}{\|x\|}, \frac{G(x/\|x\|)}{G(x)} \cdot u\right) \geqq 1\}$$

$$= \frac{G(x)}{G(x/\|x\|)} \cdot P\left(\frac{x}{\|x\|}\right).$$

Similar arguments apply to show (2)–(4). ■

4.3 The Weak Output Measure of Technical Efficiency

Recall from the previous section that the Farrell output measure of technical efficiency calls $u \in P(x)$ technically efficient if and only if $u \in$ Isoq P(x). The weak output measure of technical efficiency, introduced by Färe and Grosskopf (1983a), is more stringent in its requirements in that it calls $u \in P(x)$ technically efficient if and only if $u \in$ WEff P(x). Hence the two measures may assign different efficiency values to the same output vector if WEff P(x) $\neq$ Isoq P(x).

To define this radial output efficiency measure for an output correspondence satisfying (P.1–P.5), consider the effective domain of W_o, the weak output measure of technical efficiency

$$D(W_o) := \{(x, u): \exists \theta \geqq 0 \text{ such that } \theta M(u) \cap P(x) \neq \emptyset\}, \tag{4.3.1}$$

where

$$M(u) := \{v: v \geqq u\}, \tag{4.3.2}$$

i.e., M(u) is the set of output vectors at least as large as u, or the nonnegative orthant with origin translated to u.

Definition: The function $W_o: R^n_+ \times R^m_+ \to R_+ \cup \{+\infty\}$ defined by (4.3.3)

$$W_o(x, u) := \begin{cases} \max\{\theta \geqq 0 : (\theta M(u) \cap P(x)) \neq \emptyset\}, \\ \quad (x, u) \in D(W_o), \\ +\infty, (x, u) \in \text{Complement } D(W_o), \end{cases}$$

is called the Weak Output Measure of Technical Efficiency.

To illustrate the weak output measure of technical efficiency, consider Fig. 4–3, representing an output correspondence P which satisfies (P.1–P.5). P(x) is given by $\overline{OABCDO}$, and for $u \in P(x)$, M(u) is the translated nonnegative orthant. The weak output measure of technical efficiency pushes M(u) as far out from the origin as possible along the ray through P under the condition that $\theta M(u) \cap P(x)$ is nonempty. $\theta M(u)$ has origin at point R and intersection with P(x) at point B. To see that $W_o(x, u)$ coincides with the weak output measure of section 4.1, we observe that OP = $\|u\|$ and OR = $\|W_o(x, u) \cdot u\|$. Thus,

$$\text{OWE} = \text{OR/OP} = \frac{\|W_o(x, u) \cdot u\|}{\|u\|} = W_o(x, u). \quad (4.3.4)$$

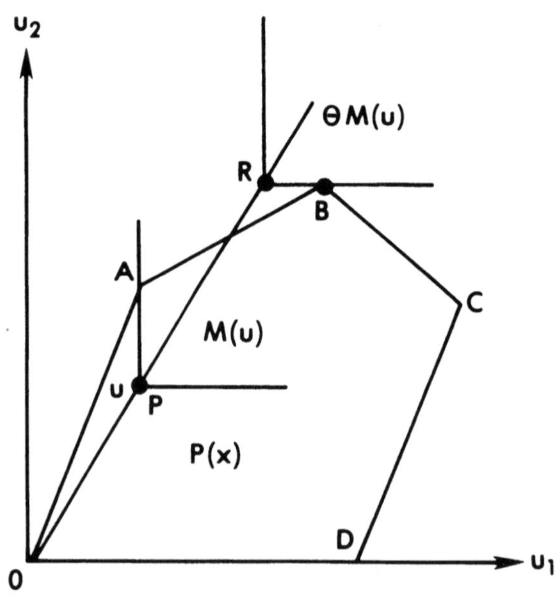

Figure 4-3

For $(x, u) \in D(W_o)$ and $u \in P^{SO}(x)$ the weak output measure computes the ratio of the largest radial expansion of u, such that the radial expansion belongs to WEff $P^{SO}(x)$, to u itself. Assume that this maximum exists, and call it $\hat{\theta}$. If $\hat{\theta} > 1$ the production unit can produce radially larger output vector $\hat{\theta}\, u \in$ WEff $P^{SO}(x)$ from input vector x by producing at point B and, if possible, by disposing of the excess output (BR units of u_1 in Fig. 4–3). If $\hat{\theta} < 1$ then $u \notin P^{SO}(x)$ and $\hat{\theta}$ is the minimum radial contraction of u such that $\hat{\theta}\, u \in$ WEff $P^{SO}(x)$. In both cases WEff P(x) is the reference set used by the weak measure to compute the technical efficiency of $(x, u) \in D(W_o)$. For $(x, u) \notin D(W_o)$ no radial expansion or contraction of u belongs to WEff P(x), and $W_o(x, u) = +\infty$.

Before stating the properties that $W_o(x, u)$ satisfies, we need to show that this measure is well-defined, i.e., that the maximum in definition (4.3.3) exists.

Theorem: The function $W_o(x, u)$ is well-defined. (4.3.5)

Proof: Let $(x, u) \in D(W_o)$. We need to show that there exists a $\theta \geqq 0$ which maximizes $\{\theta \geqq 0\colon (\theta \mathrm{M}(u) \cap \mathrm{P}(x)) \neq \emptyset\}$. Since $(x, u) \in D(W_o)$, there is a $\bar{\theta}$ such that $(\bar{\theta}\mathrm{M}(u) \cap \mathrm{P}(x)) \neq \emptyset$. The intersection $(\bar{\theta}\mathrm{M}(u) \cap \mathrm{P}(x))$ is compact, since M(u) is closed and P(x) is compact (P.2 and P.4 hold). Consider the family of sets $F := \{(\theta\mathrm{M}(u) \cap \mathrm{P}(x))\colon \theta \geqq \bar{\theta}, (\theta\mathrm{M}(u) \cap \mathrm{P}(x)) \neq \emptyset\}$. Every $(\theta\mathrm{M}(u) \cap \mathrm{P}(x)) \in F$ is closed and F has the finite intersection property, thus $\bigcap_F (\theta\mathrm{M}(u) \cap \mathrm{P}(x)) \neq \emptyset$. Let $\hat{\theta} = \sup\{\theta \geqq 0\colon \theta \geqq \bar{\theta}, (\theta\mathrm{M}(u) \cap \mathrm{P}(x)) \neq \emptyset\}$, then $(\hat{\theta}\mathrm{M}(u) \cap \mathrm{P}(x)) = \bigcap_F(\theta\mathrm{M}(u) \cap \mathrm{P}(x)) \neq \emptyset$. Thus $\hat{\theta} = \max\{\theta \geqq 0\colon (\theta\mathrm{M}(u) \cap \mathrm{P}(x)) \neq \emptyset\}$. ■

Since the maximum exists, we can provide a revenue interpretation for $W_o(x, u)$. Let the maximum be $\hat{\theta}$, and let the production unit face output prices $r \in R^m_+$, $r \neq 0$. Then

$$W_o(x, u) = \hat{\theta} = \frac{r(\hat{\theta}u)}{ru}, \qquad (4.3.6)$$

and so $W_o(u, x)$ measures the ratio of output revenue at $\hat{\theta}u \in$ WEff $P^{SO}(x)$ to actual output revenue at $u \in$ P(x). This ratio is independent of output prices.

The properties that $W_o(x, u)$ satisfies are summarized in the next theorem.

Theorem: If P satisfies (P.1–P.5), then (4.3.7)

$W_o.1$ $W_o(0, u) = +\infty$,

$W_o.2$ $0 < W_o(x, u) < +\infty$, $u \geq 0$, $(x, u) \in D(W_o)$,

$W_o.3$ $W_o(x, \theta u) = \theta^{-1} W_o(x, u)$, $\theta > 0$, $(x, u) \in D(W_o)$,

$W_o.4$ $W_o(\lambda x, u) \geqq W_o(x, u)$, $\lambda \geqq 1$,

$W_o.5$ $\mathrm{P}(x) \subsetneqq \{u: W_o(x, u) \geqq 1\}$, $\mathrm{P}(x) \neq \{0\}$,

$W_o.6$ $\mathrm{WEff\ P}(x) = \{u: u \in \mathrm{P}(x), W_o(x, u) = 1\}$.

Proof: Property $W_o.1$ follows from Property P.1.

$W_o.2$: This property follows from the definition of $W_o(x, u)$.

$W_o.3$: Note that $\mathrm{M}(\theta u) = \theta \mathrm{M}(u)$. Thus,

$$\begin{aligned} W_o(x, \theta u) &= \max\{\delta \geqq 0: (\delta \mathrm{M}(\theta u) \cap \mathrm{P}(x)) \neq \emptyset\} \\ &= \max\{\theta\delta\theta^{-1} \geqq 0: (\delta\theta \mathrm{M}(u) \cap \mathrm{P}(x)) \neq \emptyset\} \\ &= \theta^{-1} W_o(x, u). \end{aligned}$$

$W_o.4$: This property follows from weak disposability of inputs, i.e., $\mathrm{P}(\lambda x) \supseteqq \mathrm{P}(x)$.

$W_o.5$: Let $u \in \mathrm{P}(x)$, $\mathrm{P}(x) \neq \{0\}$, then clearly, $W_o(x, u) \geqq 1$.

$W_o.6$: Since by property $W_o.5$, $\mathrm{P}(x) \subsetneqq \{u: W_o(x, u) \geqq 1\}$, $\mathrm{WEff\ P}(x) \subsetneqq \{u: W_o(x, u) \geqq 1\}$. Let $u \in \mathrm{P}(x)$ and $W_o(x, u) > 1$. Then $W_o(x, u) \cdot \mathrm{M}(u) \cap \mathrm{P}(x) \neq \emptyset$. Thus, there exists a v, $v \in (W_o(x, u) \cdot \mathrm{M}(u) \cap \mathrm{P}(x))$ such that $v \overset{*}{>} u$. Thus $u \notin \mathrm{WEff\ P}(x)$. Therefore, $\mathrm{WEff\ P}(x) = \{u: u \in \mathrm{P}(x), W_o(x, u) = 1\}$. ■

Properties $W_o.1$–$W_o.4$ of the weak output measure of technical efficiency coincide with properties $F_o.1$–$F_o.4$ of the Farrell output measure of technical efficiency, apart from the possible different effective domains, and so they have the same interpretation. However, the weak output measure of technical efficiency calls an output vector $u \in \mathrm{P}(x)$ technically efficient if and only if $u \in \mathrm{WEff\ P}(x)$, $(W_o.6)$, a more restrictive property than $F_o.6$. Property $W_o.5$ also differs from property $F_o.5$. However, if in addition to (P.1–P.5) it is also assumed that the output correspondence P satisfies strong disposability of outputs, i.e., P.5.S, then we also have

Theorem: Let P satisfy (P.1–P.5). $\mathrm{P}(x) = \{u: W_o(x, u) \geqq 1\}$,

$P(x) \neq \{0\}$, if and only if outputs are strongly disposable (i.e., P.5.S holds). (4.3.8)

Proof: By property W_o.5, $P(x) \subseteq \{u: W_o(x,u) \geqq 1\}$. Now, assume outputs are strongly disposable and assume $u \notin P(x)$. Then $(M(u) \cap P(x)) = \emptyset$ and $(\theta M(u) \cap P(x)) = \emptyset$ for all $\theta \geqq 1$. Thus $u \notin \{u: W_o(x,u) \geqq 1\}$, showing that $P(x) = \{u: W_o(x,u) \geqq 1\}$. Conversely, assume $P(x) = \{u: W_o(x,u) \geqq 1\}$. Let $u \in P(x)$, $P(x) \neq \{0\}$, then we need to show that $v \in P(x)$ if $0 \leqq v \leqq u$, i.e., that $W_o(x,v) \geqq 1$. $u \in P(x)$ implies that $(W_o(x,u) \cdot M(u) \cap P(x)) \neq \emptyset$. Since $v \leqq u$, $M(v) \supseteqq M(u)$, thus $(W_o(x, u) \cdot M(u) \cap P(x)) \neq \emptyset$. Hence $W_o(x, v) \geqq W_o(x, u)$ showing that $v \in P(x)$. ■

This theorem shows that if the weak output measure of technical efficiency is a complete characterization of the output set $P(x)$,then and only then are outputs strongly disposable. Theorem (4.3.8) also yields the following corollary, which strengthens property W_o.6

Corollary: If outputs are strongly disposable, then
WEff $P(x) = \{u: W_o(x, u) = 1\}$, $P(x) \neq \{0\}$. (4.3.9)

The proof is obvious.

The properties F_o.5 and W_o.5 indicate that since Isoq $P(x)$ and WEff $P(x)$ are not in general the same, the Farrell output and the weak output measure of technical efficiency will in turn generally yield different values. From their definitions it is clear that

$$F_o(x, u) \leqq W_o(x, u). \tag{4.3.10}$$

The next theorem gives a necessary and sufficient condition under which the two measures will be equal.

Theorem: If P satisfies (P.1–P.5), then $F_o(x,u) = W_o(x,u)$ for all $(x, u) \in R^n_+ \times R^m_+$ if and only if outputs are strongly disposable. (4.3.11)

Proof: If $F_o(x, u) = W_o(x, u)$ for all (x, u), then it follows from properties F_o.5, W_o.5, and theorem (4.3.8) that outputs are strongly disposable. To prove the converse, one notes that in general, $D(F_o) \subseteq D(W_o)$. If outputs are strongly disposable we have to show that $D(F_o) = D(W_o)$. Let $(x, u) \in D(W_o)$, then we need to show that there is a $\theta \geqq 0$ such that $\theta u \in P(x)$. Since $(x, u) \in D(W_o)$, there is a $\bar{\theta} \geqq 0$ such that $(\bar{\theta} M(u) \cap P(x)) \neq \emptyset$. Assume that $\theta u \notin P(x)$ and let $v \in (\bar{\theta} M(u) \cap P(x))$. Then $v \geqq \bar{\theta} u$ and $v \in P(x)$. This contradicts strong disposability of outputs. Thus $D(F_o) = D(W_o)$ and $F_o(x, u) = W_o(x,u)$ for all $(x,u) \in$ Complement $D(F_o)$. Next let $u \geq 0$ with (x,u)

$\in D(F_o) = D(W_o)$. Then $(W_o(x, u) \cdot \mathrm{M}(u) \cap \mathrm{P}(x)) \neq \emptyset$, and it is sufficient to show that $W_o(x, u) \cdot u \in (W_o(x, u) \cdot \mathrm{M}(u) \cap \mathrm{P}(x))$, since then $F_o(x, u) = W_o(x, u)$. Assume therefore that $W_o(x, u) \cdot u \notin (W_o(x, u) \cdot \mathrm{M}(u) \cap \mathrm{P}(x))$. Then there exists a $v \in (W_o(x, u) \cdot \mathrm{M}(u) \cap \mathrm{P}(x))$, i.e., $v \geq W_o(x, u) \cdot u$ and $v \in \mathrm{P}(x)$, which contradicts strong disposability of outputs. ■

This theorem plays an important role in section 4.7, where we show how to compute weak output efficiency using simple linear programming techniques. We note that the theorem states "for all (x, u)", and this does not prevent $F_o(x, u) = W_o(x, u)$ *for some* (x, u) in the absence of strong disposability of outputs.

Finally, we show properties of the weak output efficiency measure of technical efficiency induced by different special output structures.

Theorem: Let P satisfy (P.1–P.5), then (4.3.12)

(1) $W_o(x, u) = \dfrac{G(x)}{G(x/\|x\|)} \cdot W_o\left(\dfrac{x}{\|x\|}, u\right)$ if P is ray-homothetic,

(2) $W_o(x, u) = G(x) \cdot W_o(1, u)$ if P is homothetic,

(3) $W_o(\lambda x, u) = \lambda^{B(x/\|x\|)} \cdot W_o(x, u)$ if P is ray-homogeneous, $\lambda > 0$,

(4) $W_o(\lambda x, u) = \lambda^{\beta} \cdot W_o(x, u)$ if P is homogeneous of degree $+\beta$.

If P satisfies P.5.S as well as (P.1–P.5), then (1)–(4) are necessary and sufficient conditions.

Proof: Let P be ray-homothetic, then

$$W_o(x, u) = \max\left\{\theta \geqq 0 \colon \theta u \in \frac{G(x)}{G(x/\|x\|)} \cdot \mathrm{P}\left(\frac{x}{\|x\|}\right)\right\}$$

(definition (2.4.5))

$$= \max\left\{\theta \geqq 0 \colon \frac{G(x/\|x\|)}{G(x)} \cdot \theta u \in \mathrm{P}\left(\frac{x}{\|x\|}\right)\right\}$$

$$= \frac{G(x)}{G(x/\|x\|)} \cdot W_o\left(\frac{x}{\|x\|}, u\right).$$

Similar arguments apply to show (2)–(4). Next, assume that outputs are strongly disposable. If (1) holds, then by theorem (4.3.8) we have

$$P(x) = \left\{ u: \frac{G(x)}{G(x/\|x\|)} \cdot W_o\left(\frac{x}{\|x\|}, u\right) \geqq 1 \right\},$$

hence by applying property $W_o.3$, we get

$$P(x) = \frac{G(x)}{G(x/\|x\|)} \cdot \left\{ v: W_o\left(\frac{x}{\|x\|}, v\right) \geqq 1 \right\},$$

i.e.,

$$P(x) = \frac{G(x)}{G(x/\|x\|)} \cdot P(x/\|x\|). \quad \blacksquare$$

4.4 The Overall Output Efficiency Measure

Any measure of overall output efficiency must respect input availability and technological constraints, as do measures of output technical efficiency, but it must also consider output prices. A measure of overall output efficiency therefore has both technical and allocative components. To define an overall output efficiency measure for a technology satisfying (P.1–P.5), we first need to introduce the upper halfspace

$$H_o^+(u, r) := \{v: rv \geqq ru\}. \tag{4.4.1}$$

Here we assume that the output prices $r \in R_+^m$, but $r \neq 0$. The upper halfspace $H_o^+(u, r)$ has the following two properties

$$H_o^+.1 \ H_o^+(\theta u, r) = \theta H_o^+(u, r), \ \theta > 0,$$
$$H_o^+.2 \ H_o^+(u, \lambda r) = H_o^+(u, r), \ \lambda > 0. \tag{4.4.2}$$

Both properties are direct consequences of (4.4.1). Next we use this upper halfspace to define the effective domain of the overall output efficiency measure O_o

$$D(O_o) := \{(x, u): \exists\ \theta \geqq 0 \text{ such that } (\theta H_o^+(u, r) \cap P(x)) \neq \emptyset\}. \tag{4.4.3}$$

Now define

Definition: The function $O_o: R^n_+ \times R^m_+ \times (R^m_+ \setminus \{0\}) \to R_+ \cup \{+\infty\}$ defined by (4.4.4)

$$O_o(x, u, r) := \begin{cases} \max\{\theta \geqq 0: (\theta H_o^+(u, r) \cap \mathrm{P}(x)) \neq \emptyset\}, \\ \quad (x, u) \in D(O_o), \\ +\infty, \ (x, u) \in \text{Complement } D(O_o), \end{cases}$$

is called the Overall Output Efficiency Measure.

Since the output set $\mathrm{P}(x)$ is compact (P.2 and P.4), the overall output efficiency measure is well-defined for all $r \in (R^m_+ \setminus \{0\})$. This measure is illustrated with the help of Fig. 4–4. For $u \in \mathrm{P}(x)$ the upper halfspace generated by (u, r) is labeled $H_o^+(u, r)$. The overall output efficiency measure $O_o(x, u, r)$ pushes $H_o^+(u, r)$ as far out from the origin as possible along the ray through P under the condition that $H_o^+(u, r)$ has a nonempty intersection with $\mathrm{P}(x)$. Thus $O_o(x, u, r) = \theta = \mathrm{OS/OP}$, or, equivalently $\|O_o(x, u, r) \cdot u\|/\|u\| = O_o(x, u, r)$, showing that $O_o(x, u, r) = \mathrm{OOE}$ of section 4.1. Furthermore,

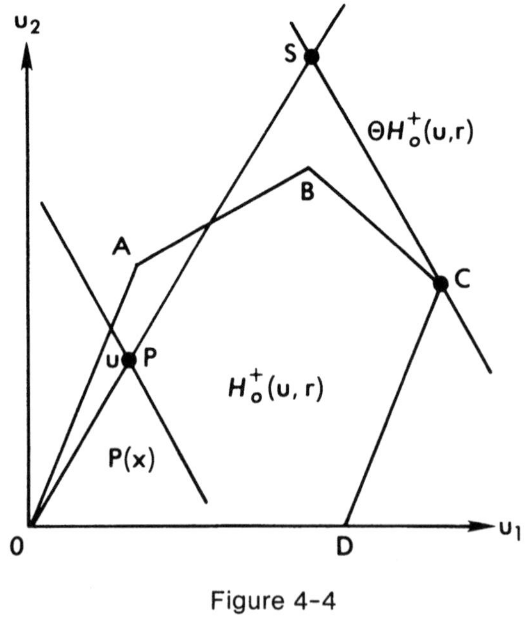

Figure 4-4

$O_o(x, u, r)$ measures the revenue gain available to the production unit by adjusting outputs from $u \in P(x)$ at point P to point $C \in RM(x, r)$. If $u \notin P(x)$ then $O_o(x, u, r)$ measures the change in revenue, which may be either positive or negative, accruing to the production unit by adjusting outputs from $u \notin P(x)$ to point $C \in RM(x, r)$. In either case the reference set for $O_o(x, u, r)$ is $RM(x, r)$.

The next theorem will prove to be extremely useful in simplifying the calculation of overall output efficiency:

Theorem: $O_o(x, u, r) = [R(x, r)/ru], ru > 0.$ (4.4.5)

Proof: Let $v \in (O_o(x, u, r) \cdot H_o^+(u, r) \cap P(x))$, then $v \in P(x)$ and since $O_o(x, u, r)$ is a maximum, $rv = O_o(x, u, r) \cdot ru$. Recall definition (2.2.29) of $R(x, v)$. Now assume $rv < R(x, r)$, but then $v \notin P(x)$, which is a contradiction. Thus assume $rv > R(x, r)$, but then $\{w: rw \geqq rv\} \subset \{w: rw \geqq R(x, r)\}$ and, since the two sets are parallel, $O_o(x, u, r)$ cannot be a maximum. Thus, $rv = R(x, r)$, and, since $rv = O_o(x, u, r) \cdot ru$, $O_o(x, u, r) = R(x, r)/ru$. ∎

This theorem shows that the overall output efficiency measure can be calculated as the quotient between maximum revenue, $R(x, r)$, and actual revenue, ru.

In order to state the properties that $O_o(x, u, r)$ satisfies, we first need to introduce a definition of overall output efficiency.

Definition: An output vector $u \in P(x)$ is Overall Output Efficient for prices $r \in (R_+^m \setminus \{0\})$ if $u \in RM(x, r)$. (4.4.6)

The properties that the overall output efficiency measure satisfies are collected in the next theorem.

Theorem: Let P satisfy (P.1–P.5), then (4.4.7)

$O_o.1$ $O_o(0, u, r) = +\infty, (u, r) \in R_+^m \times (R_+^m \setminus \{0\}),$

$O_o.2$ $0 < O_o(x, u, r) < +\infty, u \geq 0,$
$(x, u) \in D(O_o),$

$O_o.3$ $O_o(x, \theta u, r) = \theta^{-1} O_o(x, u, r), \theta > 0,$
$(x, u) \in D(O_o),$

$O_o.4$ $O_o(\lambda x, u, r) \geqq O_o(x, u, r), \lambda \geqq 1,$

$O_o.5$ $O_o(x, u, \theta r) = O_o(x, u, r), \theta > 0$,

$O_o.6$ For $u \in \mathrm{P}(x)$, $\mathrm{P}(x) \neq \{0\}$, $O_o(x, u, r) = 1$ if and only if u is overall output efficient for the price vector r.

Proof: Properties $O_o.1$–$O_o.4$ are proved in the same way as the first four properties in theorems (4.2.5) and (4.3.7).

Property $O_o.5$ follows from the fact that $H_o^+(u, \theta r) = H_o^+(u, r), \theta > 0$.

Property $O_o.6$ follows from theorem (4.4.5) and the definition of O_o. ■

We note that properties ($O_o.1$–$O_o.4$) are analogous to properties ($F_o.1$–$F_o.4$) and ($W_o.1$–$W_o.4$), taking account of the additional arguments of O_o and the possibly different effective domain of O_o. Also, property $O_o.5$ tells us that the overall output efficiency measure depends only on relative prices, i.e., $O_o(x, u, r) = O_o(x, u, r/\|r\|)$. Property $O_o.6$ states that $O_o(x, u, r) = 1$ if and only if the output vector $u \in \mathrm{P}(x)$ is overall output efficient for r.

We conclude this section by listing properties of the overall output efficiency measure inherited from special output structures.

Theorem: Let P satisfy (P.1–P.5), then (4.4.8)

(1) $O_o(x, u, r) = \dfrac{\mathrm{G}(x)}{\mathrm{G}(x/\|x\|)} \cdot O_o\left(\dfrac{x}{\|x\|}, u, r\right)$ if P is ray-homothetic,

(2) $O_o(x, u, r) = \mathrm{G}(x) \cdot O_o(1, u, r)$ if P is homothetic,

(3) $O_o(\lambda x, u, r) = \lambda^{\mathrm{B}(x/\|x\|)} \cdot O_o(x, u, r)$ if P is ray-homogeneous, $\lambda > 0$,

(4) $O_o(\lambda x, u, r) = \lambda^{\beta} \cdot O_o(x, u, r)$ if P is homogeneous of degree $+\beta$.

The proofs follow those used in proving theorems (4.2.6) and (4.3.12), and are omitted.

4.5 Measuring Output Loss due to Lack of Disposability

In general, one cannot assume that outputs are strongly disposable since the technology may produce bads as well as goods, where, for example, the bads may not be freely disposable due to government regulations. In such cases, the Farrell output and the weak output measures of technical efficiency can obviously differ (see equation (4.3.10)). Since the two measures yield the same value for each $(x, u) \in R^n_+ \times R^m_+$ if and only if the production technology exhibits strong disposability of outputs (theorem (4.3.11)), the amount by which the two measures diverge under weak output disposability is an appropriate measure of output loss due to lack of output disposability. As an example, the loss of output due to regulations restricting emissions could be measured by the difference between F_o and W_o.

Formally, introduce

Definition: For $u \in P(x)$, $P(x) \neq \{0\}$, the Measure of Output Loss Due to Lack of Output Disposability is $C_o(x, u) := W_o(x, u)/F_o(x, u)$. (4.5.1)

In terms of Fig. 4–5, $C_o(x, u) = (OR/OP) \div (OQ/OP) = (OR/OQ)$. Thus, $C_o(x, u) = OC$ of section 4.1, and measures the proportional loss in output due to lack of output disposability. In Fig. 4–5, if outputs were

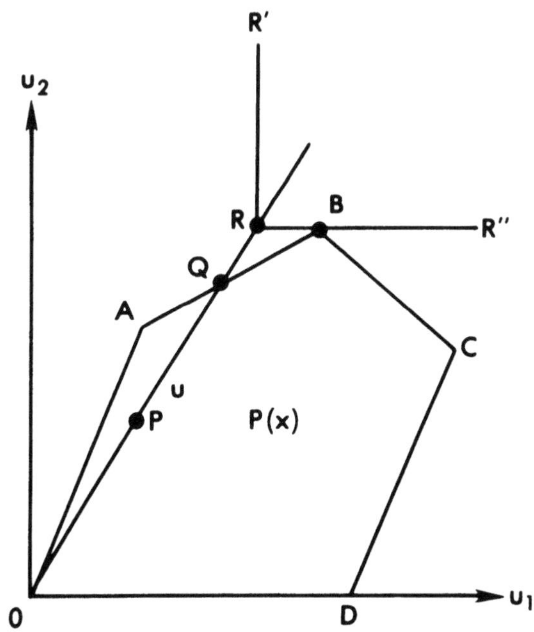

Figure 4-5

strongly disposable, then R would be obtainable with the input vector x. However, without strong disposability, only Q is obtainable.

Since both $W_o(u, x)$ and $F_o(x, u)$ have a revenue interpretation, it follows from definition (4.5.1) that $C_o(x, u)$ also has a revenue interpretation. To show this, in Fig. 4–5 let the point Q be $\theta^\circ u$ and let the point R be $\hat{\theta} u$, where θ° and $\hat{\theta}$ are defined in equations (4.2.4) and (4.3.6). Also, let the production unit face output prices $r \in (R^m_+ \backslash \{0\})$. Then it follows from definition (4.5.1) that

$$C_o(x, u) = \frac{\hat{\theta}}{\theta^\circ} = \frac{r(\hat{\theta} u)}{ru} \div \frac{r(\theta^\circ u)}{ru} = \frac{r(\hat{\theta} u)}{r(\theta^\circ u)}, \tag{4.5.2}$$

and so $C_o(x, u)$ measures the ratio of output revenue at $\hat{\theta} u \in$ WEff P(x) to output revenue at $\theta^\circ u \in$ Isoq P(x).

This measure of output loss due to a lack of output disposability has the following properties

Theorem: If P satisfies (P.1–P.5), then (4.5.3)

$C_o.1$ $C_o(x, u) \geqq 1$,

$C_o.2$ $C_o(x, u) = 1$ if and only if output cannot be proportionally increased along $\{v\colon v = \theta u, \theta \geqq 0\}$ by allowing strong disposability,

$C_o.3$ $C_o(x, \theta u) = C_o(x, u)$, $\theta > 0$.

Proof: All three properties are direct consequences of the properties of F_o and W_o. See the proofs of theorems (4.2.5) and (4.3.7). ■

It is worth noting that from property $C_o.3$ it follows that $C_o(x, u) = C_o(x, u/\|u\|)$, i.e., the measure C_o depends only on the output mix rather than on the size of outputs.

In order to find the subvector of outputs that obstruct production of the others, a partial weak output measure of technical efficiency is introduced. Let $u \in$ P(x), be written as $u = (u_\alpha, u_\beta)$, where $\alpha \cup \beta = \{1, 2, \ldots, m\}$ and $\alpha \cap \beta = \emptyset$. Now consider

$$\text{M}(u(\alpha))\colon = \{v\colon v_\alpha \geqq u_\alpha,\ v_\beta = u_\beta\} \tag{4.5.4}$$

and

$$D(W_o^\alpha)\colon = \{(x, u)\colon \quad \theta \geqq 0 \text{ such that } (\theta \text{M}(u(\alpha)) \cap \text{P}(x)) \neq \emptyset\}. \tag{4.5.5}$$

Definition: The function $W_o^\alpha: R_+^n \times R_+^m \to R_+ \cup \{+\infty\}$ defined by (4.5.6)

$$W_o^\alpha(x, u) := \begin{cases} \max\{\theta \geqq 0: (\theta M(u(\alpha)) \cap P(x)) \neq \emptyset\} \\ \quad (x, u) \in D(W_o^\alpha), \\ +\infty, \ (x, u) \in \text{Complement } D(W_o^\alpha), \end{cases}$$

is called the Partial Weak Output Measure of Technical Efficiency.

It is clear that if $\alpha = \{1, 2, \ldots, m\}, W_o^\alpha(x, u) = W_o^\alpha(x, u)$. It is also clear that if $W_o(x, u) \neq F_o(x, u)$, the output vectors α such that $W_o^\alpha(x, u) = W_o(x, u)$, are those that obstruct output. In order to identify the specific output(s) that obstruct production, we need to compare $W_o^\alpha(x, u)$ with $W_o(x, u)$ for all $\alpha \subsetneqq \{1, 2, \ldots, m\}$. If $W_o^\alpha(x, u) = W_o(x, u)$ then the outputs u_β are not congesting. If $W_o^\alpha(x, u) \neq W_o(x, u)$, then the outputs u_β are congesting. If the output structure is ray-homothetic or homothetic, respectively, then the measure of output loss due to lack of output disposability takes the following special forms

$$\begin{cases} C_o(x, u) = \dfrac{W_o[(x/\|x\|), u]}{F_o[(x/\|x\|), u]} = C_o\left(\dfrac{x}{\|x\|}, u\right), \\ \\ C_o(x, u) = \dfrac{W_o(1, u)}{F_o(1, u)} = C_o(1, u). \end{cases} \tag{4.5.7}$$

These properties are direct consequences of theorems (4.2.6) and (4.3.12).

4.6 The Allocative Output Efficiency Measure

The second derived output efficiency measure is now introduced. It is essentially a measure of output mix error in light of the output prices faced by the firm. A formal definition which makes apparent the derived nature of this measure is provided by

Definition: For $u \in P(x)$, $P(x) \neq \{0\}$, the Allocative Output Efficiency Measure is given by $A_o(x, u, r) = O_o(x, u, r)/W_o(x, u)$. (4.6.1)

The allocative output efficiency measure indicates the maximal ray distance from the strongly disposable output technology to the hyperplane yielding maximum revenue. In Fig. 4–6 this is represented by OS/OR. It is clear that $A_o(x, u, r) = \text{OS/OR} = \text{OA}$ of section 4.1.

Since $O_o(x, u, r)$ and $W_o(x, u)$ both have revenue interpretations, so does $A_o(x, u, r)$. Using theorem (4.4.5) and equation (4.3.6) together with definition (4.6.1), we have

$$A_o(x, u, r) = \frac{R(x, r)}{ru} \div \frac{r(\hat{\theta} u)}{ru} = \frac{R(x, r)}{r(\hat{\theta} u)}, \tag{4.6.2}$$

and so $A_o(x, u, r)$ measures the ratio of maximum output revenue obtainable from x at output prices r to the output revenue obtainable at $\hat{\theta} u \in \text{WEff } P(x)$.

Before stating the properties that the allocative output efficiency measure satisfies, we first provide a formal definition of output allocative efficiency.

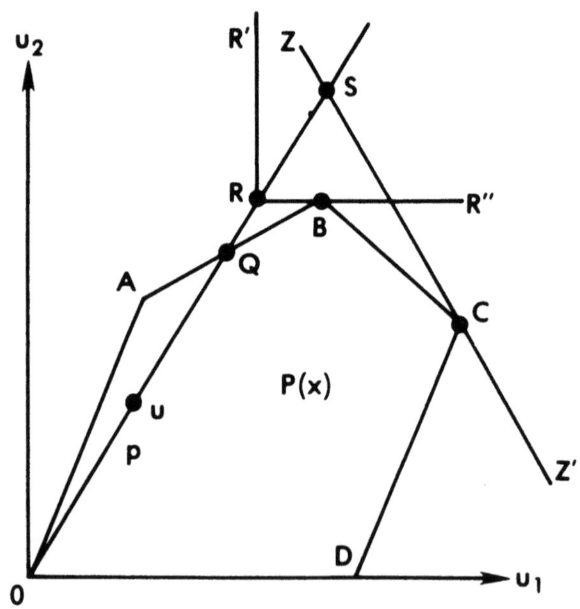

Figure 4-6

Definition: An output vector $u \in \mathrm{P}(x)$, $\mathrm{P}(x) \neq \{0\}$, is Allocatively Efficient for $r \in (R^m_+ \setminus \{0\})$ if there exists a $\theta \geqq 1$, such that $\theta u \in \mathrm{RM}(x, r)$. (4.6.3)

The following properties hold for the allocative output measure.

Theorem: For $u \in \mathrm{P}(x)$, $\mathrm{P}(x) \neq \{0\}$, $A_o(x, u, r)$ has the properties (4.6.4)

$A_o.1$ $A_o(x, u, r) \geqq 1$,

$A_o.2$ $A_o(x, u, r) = 1$ if and only if u is allocatively efficient for $r \in R^m_{++}$,

$A_o.3$ $A_o(x, \theta u, r) = A_o(x, u, r)$, $\theta > 0$,

$A_o.4$ $A_o(x, u, \theta r) = A_o(x, u, r)$, $\theta > 0$.

Proof: Properties $A_o.1$, $A_o.3$ and $A_o.4$ follow directly from the definition of A_o and the properties of O_o and W_o. To show that $A_o.2$ holds, assume $u \in \mathrm{P}(x)$, $\mathrm{P}(x) \neq \{0\}$ is allocatively efficient for r. Then there is a $\theta \geqq 1$, such that $\theta u \in \mathrm{RM}(x, r)$. Thus, $W_o(x, u) \cdot u$ and $O_o(x, u, r) \cdot u$ belong to $\mathrm{RM}(x, r)$. Also, $W_o(x, u) \cdot u$ and $O_o(x, u, r) \cdot u$ belong to Isoq $\mathrm{P}(x)$, thus $W_o(x, u) = O_o(x, u, r)$. Therefore, $A_o(x, u, r) = 1$. Conversely, assume $A_o(x, u, r) = 1$ then $W_o(x, u) = O_o(x, u, r)$. Hence $W_o(x, u) \cdot u = O_o(x, u, r) \cdot u$. Since $u \in \mathrm{P}(x)$, $\mathrm{P}(x) \neq \{0\}$, $O_o(x, u, r) \geqq 1$. Thus we only need to show that $O_o(x, u, r) \cdot u \in \mathrm{RM}(x, r)$. It is first shown that $O_o(x, u, r) \cdot u = W_o(x, u) \cdot u \in \mathrm{P}(x)$. Since $r \in R^m_{++}$, $W_o(x, u) \cdot \mathrm{M}(u) \cap \{v : rv = ru\} \cdot O_o(x, u, r) = W_o(x, u) \cdot u$. If $W_o(x, u) \cdot u \notin \mathrm{P}(x)$, then since $\mathrm{M}(u) \subset H_o^+(u, r)$, $W_o(x, u) \cdot \mathrm{M}(u) \cap \mathrm{P}(x) = \emptyset$ a contradiction. Thus $W_o(x, u) \cdot u = O_o(x, u, r) \cdot u \in \mathrm{P}(x)$. Since by theorem (4.4.5), $O_o(x, u, r) = \mathrm{R}(x, r)/ru$, $O_o(x, u, r) \cdot u \in \mathrm{RM}(x, r)$. ■

If the output structure is ray-homothetic or homothetic, respectively, then the allocative output measure becomes

$$A_o(x, u, r) = \frac{O_o[(x/\|x\|), u, r]}{W_o[(x/\|x\|), u, r]} = A_o\left(\frac{x}{\|x\|}, u, r\right),$$

$$A_o(x, u, r) = \frac{O_o(1, u, r)}{W_o(1, u, r)} = A_o(1, u, r). \tag{4.6.5}$$

As a final point, note that the overall output efficiency measure has the following multiplicative decompositions

$$O_o(x, u, r) = F_o(x, u) \cdot C_o(x, u) \cdot A_o(x, u, r), \qquad (4.6.6)$$

and

$$O_o(x, u, r) = W_o(x, u) \cdot A_o(x, u, r). \qquad (4.6.7)$$

4.7 Calculating Output Efficiency: A Linear Programming Example

In this section we calculate the three primary output efficiency measures $F_o(x, u)$, $W_o(x, u)$, $O_o(x, u, r)$ as well as the two derived output efficiency measures $C_o(x, u)$ and $A_o(x, u, r)$ based on the data presented in Table 4–1. In this example there are seven firms each producing the two (joint) outputs u_1 and u_2 using one input x_1.

As in chapter 3, we describe the technology by the matrices M (with m outputs and k activities or firms) and N (with n inputs and k activities or firms). Specifically, (following Shephard (1970)) we construct the weakly disposable output correspondence as:

$$\mathrm{P}^{\mathrm{W}}(x) = \{u : \mu \cdot z \cdot \mathrm{M} = u,\ z \cdot \mathrm{N} = \delta \cdot x,\ \delta, \mu \in (0, 1],\ z \in R^k_+\}. \qquad (4.7.1)$$

Table 4-1

	Outputs		Input
Firm	(u_1)	(u_2)	(x_1)
1	2	5	5
2	3	5	5
3	4	6	5
4	5	4	5
5	6	5	5
6	6	4	5
7	6	2	5

As shown by Shephard, $P^W(x)$ satisfies (P.1–P.5), is a convex set, and is homogeneous of degree +1. We can now calculate the Farrell output measure of technical efficiency for a firm or activity (x°, u°) relative to the weakly disposable output technology specified in (4.7.1). Using definition (4.2.2) of $F_o(x, u)$, we have the following programming problem

$$\begin{aligned} &\max \theta \\ &\text{subject to} \\ &\mu \cdot z \cdot M = \theta \cdot u^\circ \\ &z \cdot N = \delta \cdot x^\circ \\ &\delta, \mu \in (0, 1] \\ &z \in R^k_+ \end{aligned} \tag{4.7.2}$$

which can be transformed into the following linear form

$$\begin{aligned} &\max \theta \\ &\text{subject to} \\ &\gamma \cdot M = \theta \cdot u^\circ \\ &\gamma \cdot N = \sigma \cdot x^\circ \\ &\gamma \in R^k_+ \\ &\sigma \in (0, 1] \end{aligned} \tag{4.7.3}$$

where $\gamma = \mu \cdot z$ and $\sigma = \mu \cdot \delta$.

In order to calculate the weak output measure of technical efficiency, $W_o(x, u)$, we exploit theorem (4.3.11), which states that $F_o(x, u)$ and $W_o(x, u)$ are identical if and only if outputs are strongly disposable. Thus we need only impose strong disposability of outputs on the technology, and calculate $F_o(x, u)$ relative to that technology to obtain $W_o(x, u)$.

We follow Shephard (1970) in specifying the strongly disposable output correspondence as

$$P^S(x) = \{u: z \cdot M \geqq u, z \cdot N \leqq x, z \in R^k_+\}. \tag{4.7.4}$$

This correspondence tells us how much output can be produced using x and assuming strong disposability of outputs. The following linear program (also equivalent to that used by Charnes, Cooper, and Rhodes (1978)) can be used to calculate $W_o(x, u)$

$$\begin{aligned}
&\max \theta \\
&\text{subject to} \\
&z \cdot M \geqq \theta \cdot u^{\circ} \\
&z \cdot N \leqq x^{\circ} \\
&z \in R^k_+.
\end{aligned} \tag{4.7.5}$$

We note in passing that, for the single output case, (4.7.5) is also equivalent to the programming problem used by Burley (1980), namely (in our notation)

$$\begin{aligned}
&\max z \cdot M \\
&\text{subject to} \\
&z \cdot N \leqq x^{\circ} \\
&z \in R^k_+.
\end{aligned} \tag{4.7.6}$$

That (4.7.5) and (4.7.6) are equivalent is easily seen by letting $\theta = (z \cdot M)/u^{\circ}$.

In order to calculate the overall output efficiency measure $O_o(x, u, r)$, we first find maximum revenue, $R(x, r)$ given ouput prices ($r_1 = 2, r_2 = 1$) and fixed inputs, x°. Using theorem (4.4.5), we can then calculate $O_o(x, u, r)$ as the ratio of $R(x, r)$ and actual revenues ru. Maximum revenue $R(x, r)$ for an observation (x°, u°) can be derived by solving the following linear programming problem

$$\begin{aligned}
&\max ru \\
&\text{subject to} \\
&z \cdot M \geqq u^{\circ} \\
&z \cdot N \leqq x^{\circ} \\
&z \in R^k_+.
\end{aligned} \tag{4.7.7}$$

The derived output efficiency measures, $C_o(x, u)$ and $A_o(x, u, r)$, are calculated from the primary output efficiency measures. Specifically, $C_o(x,$

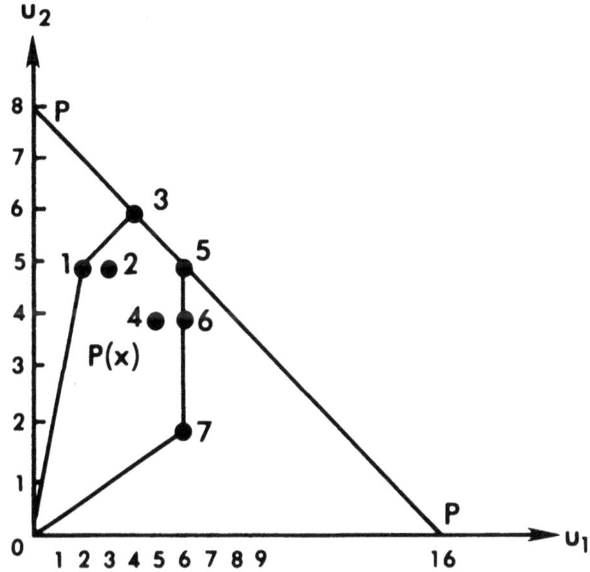

Figure 4-7

$u) = W_o(x, u)/F_o(x, u)$ and $A_o(x, u, r) = O_o(x, u, r)/W_o(x, u)$ from definitions (4.5.1) and (4.6.1), respectively.

These five output efficiency measures are calculated for the data in Table 4–1. As is evident from Fig. 4–7, firms 1, 3, 5, 6, and 7 are all Farrell efficient, i.e., are on the Isoq P(x).

Given output prices $r_1 = 2$ and $r_2 = 1$, firms 3 and 5 are overall efficient. The values of the five output efficiency measures are summarized in Table 4–2. It is also clear from section 4.5 that output u_1 is the one that hinders production for firms 1 and 2.

Table 4-2

Firm	$F_o(x, u)$	$W_o(x, u)$	$O_o(x, u, r)$	$C_o(x, u)$	$A_o(x, u, r)$
1	1.00	1.20	1.33	1.20	1.11
2	1.14	1.20	1.24	1.08	1.03
3	1.00	1.00	1.00	1.00	1.00
4	1.20	1.20	1.24	1.00	1.03
5	1.00	1.00	1.00	1.00	1.00
6	1.00	1.00	1.14	1.00	1.14
7	1.00	1.00	1.60	1.00	1.60

5 HYPERBOLIC GRAPH EFFICIENCY MEASURES

5.0 Introduction

In chapter 3 we developed a series of measures of the efficiency with which a production unit uses variable inputs to produce a given output vector. These measures are appropriate under a behavioral assumption of constrained cost minimization. In chapter 4 we developed an analogous series of measures of the efficiency with which a production unit produces variable outputs from a given input vector. These measures are appropriate under a behavioral assumption of constrained revenue maximization. In this chapter we drop the assumption that either outputs or inputs are given, and develop a similar series of measures of the efficiency with which a production unit uses variable inputs to produce variable outputs. That is, the production unit is assumed to be able to freely adjust all inputs and all outputs, subject only to the constraints imposed by the production technology. These measures are appropriate under a behavioral assumption of profit maximization. Since all inputs and all outputs are freely variable, we model technology with the graph rather than with the input correspondence or the output correspondence.

The efficiency measures developed in chapters 3 and 4 were all radial, in that they sought the maximum possible proportional reduction in all inputs consistent with the input correspondence, or the maximum proportional increase in all outputs consistent with the output correspondence. The analogous efficiency measures developed in this chapter seek the maximum proportional change in all variables (increase for outputs, decrease for inputs) consistent with the technology as represented by its graph. Although these measures are straightforward combinations of the two series of measures developed earlier, they are not radial, or even linear, in input-output space. They are hyperbolic.

The efficiency measures developed in chapters 3 and 4 were consistent with cost minimizing and revenue maximizing behavior, and had appealing cost and revenue interpretations. The efficiency measures developed in this chapter are consistent with profit maximizing behavior, but they enjoy no such analogous profit interpretation. They do have, simultaneously, a revenue and a cost interpretation, but these properties do not translate into a profit interpretation.

In section 5.1 we offer an intuitive introduction to the five graph efficiency measures, three of which are primary and two of which are derived. In sections 5.2–5.6 we examine each measure more rigorously. In section 5.7 we suggest a natural extension of the measures proposed in sections 5.2–5.6. The suggestion is not pursued to its conclusion; we leave that task to interested readers. The suggested extension does, however, provide a convenient introduction to the nonradial efficiency measures discussed in chapter 7. Section 5.8 concludes the chapter with a linear programming exercise designed to illustrate the calculation of each of the graph efficiency measures.

5.1 Hyperbolic Graph Efficiency Measures

The radial input and output measures of efficiency discussed in the two previous chapters are defined under the conditions that outputs or inputs are fixed, respectively. To allow for simultaneous variations in outputs and inputs, graph measures of efficiency are introduced in this chapter. The graph measures differ markedly from the input and output measures, which were both radial (i.e., measured relative to a ray through the origin) in nature. Although zero belongs to the graph, the rays through the origin used as the base for the input and output measures of efficiency are not a natural base when measuring efficiency in input-output space. Instead, paths (which are not rays) are used to "scale" inputs and outputs for the graph measures.

These paths are referred to as "hyperbolic" in reference to the single input, single output case in which the scaling path is a hyperbola.

The distinction among input, output, and graph measures of efficiency can be illustrated with the assistance of Fig. 5–1. Here we assume a single-input, single-output technology, and for simplicity we focus solely on Farrell-type measures of technical efficiency. Consider production plan $(x, u) \in GR$ at point P, a plan that is plainly technically inefficient. The Farrell input measure of technical efficiency seeks a maximum input reduction consistent with continued production of the same output, and so compares (x^i, u) at point Q^i with (x, u) at point P. The Farrell output measure of technical efficiency seeks a maximum output expansion consistent with continued usage of the same input, and so compares (x, u^o) at point Q^o with (x, u) at point P. The Farrell graph measure of technical efficiency presented in section 5.2 seeks the maximum equiproportionate input reduction and output expansion, and so compares (x^g, u^g) at point Q^g with (x, u) at point P.

In addition to a Farrell-type graph measure of technical efficiency, two other primary measures are discussed below, namely the weak graph measure of technical efficiency and the overall graph efficiency measure. From these three measures two others will be derived and discussed, namely

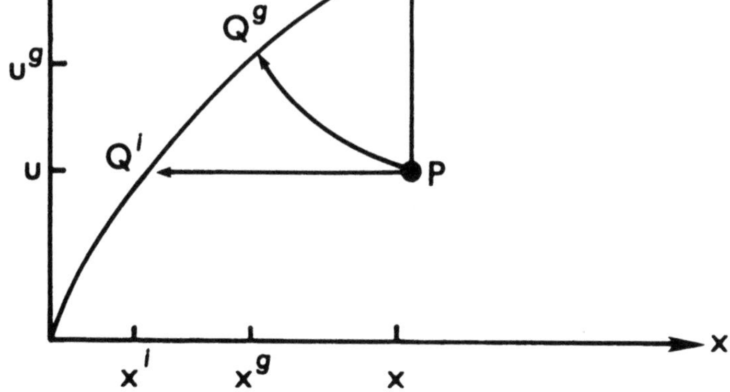

Figure 5-1

the measure of lost outputs and inputs due to lack of disposability, and the allocative graph measure. It will also be shown that the overall efficiency measure has two different multiplicative decompositions.

5.2 The Farrell Graph Measure of Technical Efficiency

Although Farrell (1957) did not introduce graph measures as we define them, they are a natural extension of his ideas. We therefore attribute the first of these measures to Farrell.

In order to define a Farrell graph measure of technical efficiency for a technology satisfying properties (GR.1–GR.5), we first define the effective domain of the measure as

$$D(F_g) := \{(x, u) : \exists\, \lambda \geqq 0 \text{ such that } (\lambda x, \lambda^{-1} u) \in GR\}. \tag{5.2.1}$$

Now define

Definition: The function $F_g: R_+^n \times R_+^m \rightarrow R_+ \cup \{+\infty\}$ defined by (5.2.2)

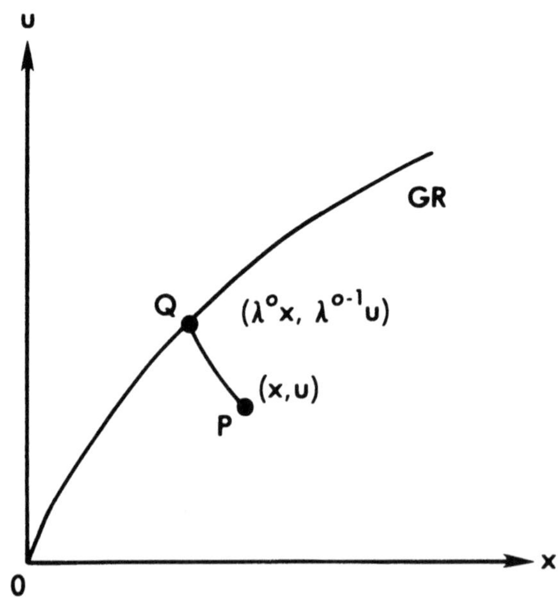

Figure 5-2

$$F_g(x, u) := \begin{cases} \min\{\lambda \geqq 0: (\lambda x, \lambda^{-1}u) \in \text{GR}\}, (x, u) \in D(F_g), \\ +\infty, (x, u) \in \text{Complement } D(F_g), \end{cases}$$

is called the Farrell Graph Measure of Technical Efficiency.

From definition (5.2.2) and property GR.2 it is clear that the Farrell graph measure of technical efficiency is well-defined, and so the minimum is attained whenever $(x, u) \in D(F_g)$. To illustrate the definition, consider Fig. 5–2. Since $(x, u) \in$ GR, the smallest nonnegative scalar λ such that $(\lambda x, \lambda^{-1}u) \in$ GR is contained in the isoquant of the graph is the Farrell graph measure of technical efficiency. Call this minimum λ°. If $\lambda^\circ < 1$ then λ° measures the maximum equiproportionate deflation of all inputs and inflation of all outputs that remains technically feasible. If $\lambda^\circ > 1$ then (x, u) must not belong to the graph, and λ° measures the maximum equiproportionate inflation of all inputs and deflation of all outputs such that technical feasibility is attained. In either case the path from (x, u) to $(\lambda^\circ x, (\lambda^\circ)^{-1} u)$ is hyperbolic. Finally if $(x, u) \notin D(F_g)$ then no equiproportionate contraction (expansion) of inputs and expansion (contraction) of outputs is technically feasible, and $F_g(x, u) = +\infty$.

If the production unit faces output prices $r \in (R^m_+ \backslash \{0\})$ and input prices $p \in R^n_{++}$, we can provide a value interpretation for $F_g(x, u)$.

$$F_g(x, u) = \lambda^\circ = \frac{ru}{(r(\lambda^\circ)^{-1}u)} = \frac{p(\lambda^\circ x)}{px} \neq \frac{ru - px}{(r(\lambda^\circ)^{-1}u) - p(\lambda^\circ x)} . \quad (5.2.3)$$

Thus $F_g(x, u)$ measures simultaneously the ratio of output revenue at u to output revenue at $((\lambda^\circ)^{-1}u)$ and the ratio of input cost at $(\lambda^\circ x)$ to input cost at x. But it does *not* measure the ratio of profit at (x, u) to profit at $(\lambda^\circ x, (\lambda^\circ)^{-1}u)$. Thus $F_g(x, u)$ does not have a profit interpretation, and this is in sharp contrast to the cost and revenue interpretations attached to $F_i(u, x)$ and $F_o(x, u)$, respectively.

The properties of the Farrell graph measure are summarized in the following theorem.

Theorem: If GR satisfies (GR.1–GR.5), then (5.2.4)

$F_g.1$ $F_g(0, 0) = 0$,

$F_g.2$ $0 < F_g(x, u) < +\infty, u \geq 0, (x, u) \in D(F_g)$,

$F_g.3$ $F_g(\theta x, \theta^{-1}u) = \theta^{-1}F_g(x, u), \theta > 0, (x, u) \in D(F_g)$,

F_g.4 $F_g(\lambda x, u) \leqq F_g(x, u), \lambda \geqq 1$,

F_g.5 $F_g(x, \theta u) \leqq F_g(x, u), \theta \in [0, 1]$,

F_g.6 $\text{GR} = \{(x, u): 0 < F_g(x, u) \leqq 1\}, u \geq 0$, if and only if inputs and outputs are weakly disposable,

F_g.7 $\text{Isoq GR} = \{(x, u): F_g(x, u) = 1\}, u \geq 0$.

Proof: Property F_g.1 follows from Property GR.1.

F_g.2: This property follows directly from the definition of F_g.

F_g.3:
$$\begin{aligned} F_g(\theta x, \theta^{-1}u) &= \min\{\lambda: (\lambda\theta x, \lambda^{-1}\theta^{-1}u) \in \text{GR}\} \\ &= \min\{\theta\lambda\theta^{-1}: (\lambda\theta x, \lambda^{-1}\theta^{-1}u) \in \text{GR}\} \\ &= \theta^{-1}\min\{\delta: (\delta x, \delta^{-1}u) \in \text{GR}\} \\ &= \theta^{-1}F_g(x, u). \end{aligned}$$

F_g.4: Follows from property GR.3 and definition (5.2.2).

F_g.5: Follows from the definition of F_g and property GR.5.

F_g.6: Let $(x, u) \in \text{GR}$, $u \geq 0$, then clearly, $F_g(x, u) \in (0, 1]$. Thus $\text{GR} \subseteqq \{(x, u): 0 < F_g(x, u) \leqq 1\}$. Next assume $(x, u) \notin \text{GR}$, $u \geq 0$. If there does not exist a $\lambda \geqq 0$ such that $(\lambda x, \lambda^{-1}u) \in \text{GR}$, $F_g(x, u) = +\infty$. Thus assume that there is a $\lambda^\circ \geqq 0$ such that $(\lambda^\circ x, (\lambda^\circ)^{-1}u) \in \text{GR}$. Since inputs and outputs are weakly disposable, $\lambda^\circ > 1$. Thus, $\{(x, u): 0 < F_g(x, u) \leqq 1\} \subseteqq \text{GR}$. Conversely, assume $\text{GR} = \{(x, u): 0 < F_g(x, u) \leqq 1\}$, $u \geq 0$. Let $(x, u) \in \text{GR}$ and we have to show that $(\lambda x, u) \in \text{GR}$, $\lambda \geqq 1$ and $(x, \theta u) \in \text{GR}$, $\theta \in [0, 1]$. It is thus sufficient to show that $F_g(\lambda x, u) \leqq F_g(x, u)$, $\lambda \geqq 1$ and that $F_g(x, \theta u) \leqq F_g(x, u)$, $\theta \in (0, 1]$. These conditions follow directly from properties F_g.2 and F_g.4.

F_g.7: From property F_g.6 we know that $\text{Isoq GR} \subseteqq \{(x, u): 0 < F_g(x, u) \leqq 1\}$, $u \geq 0$. Now if $(x, u) \in \text{GR}$, but $(x, u) \notin \text{Isoq GR}$, then by the definition of the isoquant of the graph (definition (2.5.2)), there is a $\lambda < 1$ such that $(\lambda x, \lambda^{-1}u) \in \text{GR}$, thus $F_g(x, u) < 1$. Therefore, since if $(x, u) \notin \text{GR}$, $F_g(x, u) > 1$, and $\text{Isoq GR} = \{(x, u): F_g(x, u) = 1\}$. ■

Among the properties of F_g we note first that F_g is almost homogeneous of degree -1 and $+1$ in inputs and outputs, respectively (property F_g.3). Second, we note that F_g is nonincreasing in inputs (F_g.4) and nondecreasing in outputs (F_g.5). Property F_g.6 shows that F_g completely characterizes the technology if and only if both inputs and outputs are weakly disposable. Finally, property F_g.7 shows that F_g calls an input-output vector technically efficient if and only if it belongs to the graph isoquant.

5.3 The Weak Graph Measure of Technical Efficiency

In order to define a weak technical efficiency measure on the graph of a technology satisfying properties (GR.1–GR.5) we need to introduce the following sets

$$K(x) := \{y: y \leqq x\} \text{ and } M(u) := \{v: v \geqq u\}, \qquad (5.3.1)$$

$$D(W_g) := \{(x, u): \exists\, \lambda \geqq 0 \text{ such that } (K(\lambda x) \times M(\lambda^{-1}u) \cap GR \neq \emptyset\}, \qquad (5.3.2)$$

i.e., $D(W_g)$ is the effective domain of the weak graph measure W_g, where $K(x)$ is the set of input vectors less than or equal to x, and $M(u)$ is the set of output vectors greater than or equal to u. Now define

Definition: The function W_g: $R^n_+ \times R^m_+ \rightarrow R_+ \cup \{+\infty\}$ defined by (5.3.3)

$$W_g(x, u) := \begin{cases} \min\{\lambda \geqq 0: (K(\lambda x) \times M(\lambda^{-1}u)) \cap GR \neq \emptyset\}, \\ \quad (x, u) \in D(W_g), \\ +\infty, (x, u) \in \text{Complement } D(W_g), \end{cases}$$

is called the Weak Graph Measure of Technical Efficiency.

An illustration of this measure is given in Fig. 5–3. For $(x, u) \in GR$, the weak graph measure of technical efficiency pushes the set $(K(x) \times M(u))$ as far away from (x, u) as possible along the hyperbolic path PR under the condition that $(K(\lambda x) \times M(\lambda^{-1}u))$ has a nonempty intersection with the graph.

Due to the fact that Figs. 5–2 and 5–3 are two-dimensional, there appears to be no distinction between the Farrell graph measure of Fig. 5–2 and the weak graph measure of Fig. 5–3. Indeed, for a single-input, single-output technology satisfying (GR.1–GR.5) there is no distinction between the Farrell and weak graph measures. However for a multiple-input, multiple-output technology satisfying (GR.1–GR.5) there is a distinction between the two measures, and this distinction will become evident as we progress.

Next, we will show that the weak graph measure is appropriately defined

Theorem: The function $W_g(x, u)$ is well-defined. (5.3.4)

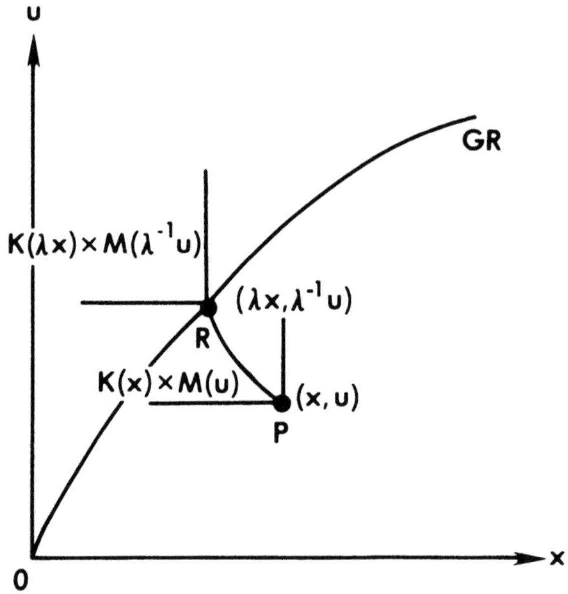

Figure 5-3

Proof: Let $(x, u) \in D(W_g)$. We need to show that there exists a $\lambda \geqq 0$ which minimizes $\{\lambda \geqq 0$: $(K(\lambda x) \times M(\lambda^{-1}u)) \cap GR \neq \emptyset\}$. Since $(x, u) \in D(W_g)$, $\exists \bar{\lambda} \geqq 0$ such that $(K(\bar{\lambda} x) \times M(\bar{\lambda}^{-1}u)) \cap GR \neq \emptyset$. The intersection $(K\bar{\lambda} x) \times M(\bar{\lambda}^{-1}u)) \cap GR$ is compact since property GR.2 holds. Consider next the family of sets: $F := \{(K(\lambda x) \times M(\lambda^{-1}u)) \cap GR$: $0 \leqq \lambda < \bar{\lambda}$, $(K(\lambda x) \times M(\lambda^{-1}u)) \cap GR \neq \emptyset\}$. Every element in F is closed and F has the finite intersection property. Thus $\bigcap_F (K(\lambda x) \times M(\lambda^{-1}u)) \cap GR \neq \emptyset$. Let $\hat{\lambda} = \inf\{\lambda \geqq 0$: $0 \leqq \lambda \leqq \bar{\lambda}$, $(K(\lambda x) \times M(\lambda^{-1}u)) \cap GR \neq \emptyset$, then $(K(\hat{\lambda} x) \times M(\hat{\lambda}^{-1}u)) \cap GR = \bigcap_F (K(\lambda x) \times M(\lambda^{-1}u)) \cap GR \neq \emptyset$. Thus $\hat{\lambda} = \min\{\lambda \geqq 0$: $(K(\lambda x) \times M(\lambda^{-1}u)) \cap GR \neq \emptyset\}$. ■

Even though there exists a $\hat{\lambda} \geqq 0$ that minimizes $W_g(x, u)$, there is still no profit interpretation attached to $\hat{\lambda}$, aside from the fact that profit at $(\hat{\lambda} x, \hat{\lambda}^{-1}u)$ is not less than profit at (x, u). See the discussion following equation (5.2.3) in section 5.2 for details.

We can now state the properties which the weak graph measure of technical efficiency satisfies

Theorem: If GR satisfies (GR.1–GR.5), then (5.3.5)

W_g.1 $W_g(0, 0) = 0$,

W_g.2 $0 < W_g(x, u) < +\infty, u \geq 0, (x, u) \in D(W_g)$,

W_g.3 $W_g(\theta x, \theta^{-1}u) = \theta^{-1}W_g(x, u), (x, u) \in D(W_g)$,

W_g.4 $W_g(\lambda x, u) \leqq W_g(x, u), \lambda \geqq 1$,

W_g.5 $W_g(x, \theta u) \leqq W_g(x, u), \theta \in [0, 1]$,

W_g.6 $\text{GR} \subseteqq \{(x, u): 0 < W_g(x, u) \leqq 1\}, u \geq 0$,

W_g.7 $\text{WEff GR} = \{(x, u): (x, u) \in \text{GR}, W_g(x, u) = 1\}, u \geq 0$.

Proof: Property W_g.1 follows from $0 \in \text{GR}$.

W_g.2: Follows from the definition of W_g.

W_g.3:
$$\begin{aligned} W_g(\theta x, \theta^{-1}u) &= \min\{\lambda \geqq 0: (\text{K}(\theta\lambda x) \times \text{M}(\theta^{-1}\lambda^{-1}u)) \cap \text{GR} \neq \emptyset\} \\ &= \min\{\theta\lambda\theta^{-1} \geqq 0: (\text{K}(\theta\lambda x) \times \text{M}(\theta^{-1}\lambda^{-1}u)) \cap \text{GR} \neq \emptyset\} \\ &= \theta^{-1}\min\{\delta \geqq 0: (\text{K}(\delta x) \times \text{M}(\delta^{-1}u)) \cap \text{GR} \neq \emptyset\} \\ &= \theta^{-1} W_g(x, u). \end{aligned}$$

W_g.4: Follows from property GR.3 and the definition of W_g.

W_g.5: Follows from property GR.5 and the definition of W_g.

W_g.6: Let $(x, u) \in \text{GR}$, $u \geq 0$, then $x \geq 0$. Thus, $W_g(x, u) > 0$. Since $u \geq 0$, $x \geq 0$, $(x, u) \in D(W_g)$. Therefore, since $u \geq 0$, $x \geq 0$, and $(x, u) \in \text{GR}$, $W_g(x, u) \leqq 1$.

W_g.7: In general, WEff GR $\subseteqq$ GR, thus by W_g.6, WEff GR $\subseteqq \{(x, u): 0 < W_g(x, u) \leqq 1\}, u \geq 0$. Let $(x, u) \in \text{GR}$ and assume $W_g(x, u) < 1$. Then $(\text{K}(W_g(x, u)\cdot x) \times \text{M}((W_g(x, u))^{-1}\cdot u)) \cap \text{GR} \neq \emptyset$. Thus there is a $(y, v) \in (\text{K}(W_g(x, u)\cdot x) \times \text{M}((W_g(x, u))^{-1}\cdot u)) \cap \text{GR}$ such that $(y, -v) \overset{*}{<} (x, -u)$. Hence $(x, u) \notin$ WEff GR. Therefore, WEff GR $= \{(x, u): (x, u) \in \text{GR}, W_g(x, u) = 1\}$. ■

Among the properties of the weak graph measure of technical efficiency, we note that properties (W_g.1–W_g.5) parallel properties (F_g.1–F_g.5) in content and interpretation, apart from the possibly different effective domains of the two measures. Property W_g.7 states that W_g calls an input-output vector in GR technically efficient if and only if the vector belongs to the weak efficient subset of GR. It is properties $W_g.7$ and $F_g.7$ which distinguish the weak graph measure of technical efficiency from the Farrell graph measure of technical efficiency.

Next we show that the weak graph measure of technical efficiency completely characterizes the technology if and only if inputs and outputs are strongly disposable.

Theorem: Let GR satisfy (GR.1–GR.5). $\text{GR} = \{(x, u): 0 < W_g(x, u) \leqq 1\}$, $u \geq 0$, if and only if inputs and outputs are strongly disposable, i.e., GR.6 holds. (5.3.6)

Proof: From property $W_g.6$ we have that $\text{GR} \subseteqq \{(x, u): 0 < W_g(x, u) \leqq 1\}$. Let inputs and outputs be strongly disposable and assume that $(x, u) \notin \text{GR}$. Then $(\text{K}(x) \times \text{M}(u)) \cap \text{GR} = \emptyset$ and $(\text{K}(\lambda x) \times \text{M}(\lambda^{-1}u)) \cap \text{GR} = \emptyset$ for all $\lambda \leqq 1$. Thus if $(\text{K}(\bar{\lambda} x) \times \text{M}(\bar{\lambda}^{-1}u)) \cap \text{GR} \neq \emptyset$, $\bar{\lambda} > 1$. This shows that $\text{GR} \supseteqq \{(x, u): 0 < W_g(x, u) \leqq 1\}$, $u \geq 0$. Conversely, assume that $\text{GR} = \{(x, u): 0 < W_g(x, u) \leqq 1\}$, $u \geq 0$. Let $(x, u) \in \text{GR}$, then we need to show that if $(y, -v) \geqq (x, -u)$, then $(y, v) \in \text{GR}$, or equivalently, $0 < W_g(y, v) \leqq 1$, $(x, u) \in \text{GR}$ implies that $(\text{K}(W_g(x, u) \cdot x) \times \text{M}((W_g(x, u))^{-1} \cdot u)) \cap \text{GR} \neq \emptyset$. Since $(y, -v) \geqq (x, -u)$, $y \geqq x$ and $u \geqq v$, thus $\text{K}(y) \supseteqq \text{K}(x)$ and $\text{M}(v) \supseteqq \text{M}(u)$, thus $(\text{K}(W_g(x, u) \cdot y) \times \text{M}((W_g(x, u))^{-1} \cdot v)) \cap \text{GR} = \emptyset$. Hence, $W_g(y, v) \leqq W_g(x, u)$ and $0 < W_g(y, v) \leqq 1$, showing that $(y, v) \in \text{GR}$. ■

This theorem yields the following corollary, which strengthens property $W_g.7$.

Corollary: If (GR.1–GR.6) hold, then $\text{WEff GR} = \{(x, u): W_g(x, u) = 1\}$. (5.3.7)

The proof is immediate and therefore is omitted.

Since in general, Isoq GR ≠ WEff GR, the Farrell graph measure and the weak graph measure also in general yield different values. From their respective definitions, it is clear that for $(x, u) \in \text{GR}$

$$F_g(x, u) \geqq W_g(x, u). \tag{5.3.8}$$

To illustrate the relationship between F_g and W_g, consider Fig. 5–4. Here we model a two-input, single-output technology whose graph satisfies properties (GR.1–GR.5). In particular, weak disposability of inputs holds (GR.3), but strong disposability of inputs does not hold. The failure of strong disposability of inputs is illustrated by the fact that $(x_1/x_2) > (x_1/x_2)^*$ causes

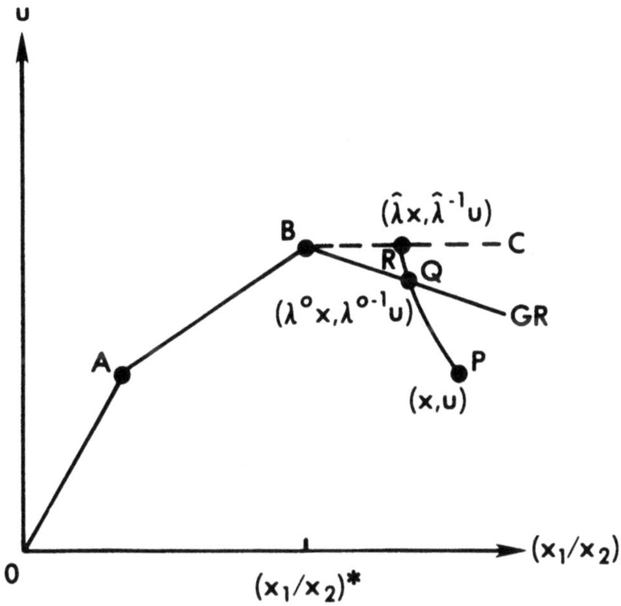

Figure 5-4

a decline in u for any fixed value of x_2. Suppose we observe $(x, u) \in \text{GR}$ at point P in a region where strong disposability of inputs does not hold. The Farrell graph measure of technical efficiency pushes the production unit back along the hyperbolic path from (x, u) at P to $(\lambda^\circ x, (\lambda^\circ)^{-1}u)$ at Q in Isoq GR, and so $F_g(x, u) = \lambda^\circ$. The weak graph measure of technical efficiency pushes the production unit back along the same hyperbolic path from (x, u) at P to $(\hat{\lambda}x, \hat{\lambda}^{-1}u)$ at R on the strongly disposable technology OABC. Although point R does not belong to GR, the set $(K(\hat{\lambda}x) \times M(\hat{\lambda}^{-1}u))$ with origin at R does have a nonempty intersection with GR, at point B. Hence $W_g(x, u) = \hat{\lambda}$. Note also that $\lambda^\circ > \hat{\lambda}$, and so F_g calls (x, u) more technically efficient than does W_g, as is required by equation (5.3.8).

In the next theorem a necessary and sufficient condition for the two measures to be equal is established.

Theorem: $F_g(x, u) = W_g(x, u)$ for all $(x, u) \in R^n_+ \times R^m_+$ if and only if inputs and outputs are strongly disposable, i.e., GR.6 holds. (5.3.9)

Proof: If $F_g(x, u) = W_g(x, u)$ for all $(x, u) \in R^n_+ \times R^m_+$, it follows from properties $F_g.6$, $W_g.6$, and theorem (5.3.6) that inputs and outputs are strongly disposable, i.e., GR.6 holds. To prove the converse, we note that $D(F_g) \subseteqq D(W_g)$. If GR.6 holds, we need to show that $D(F_g) = D(W_g)$. Let $(x, u) \in D(W_g)$, then we need to show that there is a $\lambda \geqq 0$ such that $(\lambda x, \lambda^{-1}u) \in \text{GR}$. Since $(x, u) \in D(W_g)$, there exists a $\bar{\lambda}$ such that $(\text{K}(\bar{\lambda}x) \times \text{M}(\bar{\lambda}^{-1}u)) \cap \text{GR} \neq \emptyset$. Assume $(\bar{\lambda}x, \bar{\lambda}^{-1}u) \notin \text{GR}$ and let $(y, v) \in (\text{K}(\bar{\lambda}x) \times \text{M}(\bar{\lambda}^{-1}u)) \cap \text{GR}$. Then $(y, -v) \leqq (\bar{\lambda}x, -\bar{\lambda}^{-1}u)$ and $(y, v) \in \text{GR}$. This contradicts GR.6, thus $D(F_g) = D(W_g)$. From properties $F_g.1$ and $W_g.1$, it is now sufficient to assume that $u \geq 0$, $(x, u) \in D(F_g) = D(W_g)$, then $(\text{K}(W_g(x, u)\cdot x) \times \text{M}((W_g(x, u))^{-1}\cdot u)) \cap \text{GR} \neq \emptyset$, and it it sufficient to show that $(W_g(x, u)\cdot x, (W_g(x, u))^{-1}\cdot u) \in (\text{K}(W_g(x, u)\cdot x) \times (\text{M}(W_g(x, u))^{-1}\cdot u)) \cap \text{GR}$, since then $F_g(x, u) = W_g(x, u)$. Assume therefore that $(W_g(x, u)\cdot x, (W_g(x, u))^{-1}\cdot u) \notin (\text{K}(W_g(x, u)\cdot x) \times \text{M}((W_g(x, u))^{-1}\cdot u)) \cap \text{GR}$. But then there exists a $(y, v) \in (\text{K}(W_g(x, u)\cdot x) \times \text{M}((W_g(x, u))^{-1}\cdot u)) \cap \text{GR}$, i.e., $(y, -v) \leq (W_g(x, u)\cdot x, -(W_g(x, u))^{-1}\cdot u)$ and $(y, v) \in \text{GR}$. This contradicts GR.6. ■

This theorem will prove useful in section 5.8, where graph efficiency is calculated.

5.4 The Overall Graph Efficiency Measure

The Farrell and weak graph efficiency measures are measures of technical efficiency only, and both are price-independent. The overall graph efficiency measure introduced here measures more than just technical efficiency, and is price-dependent. In order to define an overall graph measure of efficiency in the context of a technology satisfying properties (GR.1–GR.5), we need the following notion

$$H^+_g(x, u, p, r) := \{(y, v): rv - py \geqq ru - px\}, \qquad (5.4.1)$$

i.e., the upper halfspace generated by $(x, u, p, r) \in R^n_+ \times R^m_+ \times R^n_{++} \times (R^m_+ \backslash \{0\})$. We note that (5.4.1) has the following property

$$H^+_g(x, u, p, r) = H^+_g(x, u, \lambda p, \lambda r), \lambda > 0. \qquad (5.4.2)$$

Furthermore, we need to define the effective domain of O_g, the overall graph efficiency measure, namely

$D(O_g):=\{(x,u): \exists\, \lambda \geqq 0 \text{ such that } (H_g^+(\lambda x, \lambda^{-1}u, p, r) \cap \mathrm{GR}) \neq \emptyset\}.$ (5.4.3)

We are now ready to introduce

Definition: The function $O_g: R_+^n \times R_+^m \times R_{++}^n \times (R_+^m \backslash \{0\}) \rightarrow R_+ \cup \{+\infty\}$ defined by (5.4.4)

$$O_g(x,u,p,r):=\begin{cases} \inf\{\lambda \geqq 0: (H_g^+(\lambda x, \lambda^{-1}u, p, r) \cap \mathrm{GR}) \neq \emptyset\},\ (x,u) \in D(O_g), \\ +\infty,\ (x,u) \in \text{Complement } D(O_g), \end{cases}$$

is called the Overall Graph Efficiency Measure.

In this definition an infimum is used since, even when $(x, u) \in D(O_g)$, there need not exist a minimizing λ. This can be seen by choosing the graph $\mathrm{GR}=\{(x, u): u \leqq x^2, x \in R_+\}$. This graph satisfies (GR.1–GR.5), but for $r=p=1$, $\inf\{\lambda \geqq 0: (H_g^+(\lambda x, \lambda^{-1}u, p, r) \cap \mathrm{GR}) \neq \emptyset\}=0$, but no $\lambda \geqq 0$ is a minimum. To further illustrate this point we may rewrite the infimum expression as

$$\begin{aligned} &\inf\{\lambda \geqq 0: (H_g^+(\lambda x, \lambda^{-1}u, p, r) \cap \mathrm{GR}) \neq \emptyset\} \\ &= \inf\{\delta^{-1} \geqq 0: (H_g^+(\delta^{-1}x, \delta u, p, r) \cap \mathrm{GR}) \neq \emptyset\} \\ &= \sup\{\delta \geqq 0: (H_g^+(\delta^{-1}x, \delta u, p, r) \cap \mathrm{GR}) \neq \emptyset\}. \end{aligned} \quad (5.4.5)$$

From this expression, (and again assuming that $r=p=1$), the supremum is $+\infty$, thus no δ maximizes the expression, or in terms of (5.4.4), no λ minimizes the expression.

To further illustrate the overall graph measure, consider Fig. 5–5. $H_g^+(x, u, p, r)$ is the upper halfspace generated by (x, u, p, r), where $(x, u) \in \mathrm{GR}$ at point P. The overall graph efficiency measure pushes (x, u) as far as possible out along the hyperbolic path PQS, under the condition that the resulting upper halfspace $H_g^+(\lambda x, \lambda^{-1} u, p, r)$ has a nonempty intersection with GR. This intersection occurs at point T, and $\mathrm{T} \in \Pi\mathrm{M}(r, p)$, a point to which we shall return. In the actual computation of the overall graph efficiency measure, the following theorem is useful.

Theorem: If $O_g(x,u,p,r)>0$ is a minimum, $(O_g(x,u,p,r))^2 \cdot px + O_g(x,u,p,r) \cdot \pi(r,p) = ru.$ (5.4.6)

Proof: Let $(y, v) \in (H_g^+(O_g(x,u,p,r) \cdot x, (O_g(x,u,p,r))^{-1} \cdot u, p, r) \cap \mathrm{GR})$, then $(y, v) \in \mathrm{GR}$ and since $O_g(x,u,p,r)$ is a minimum, $rv - py = (O_g(x,u,$

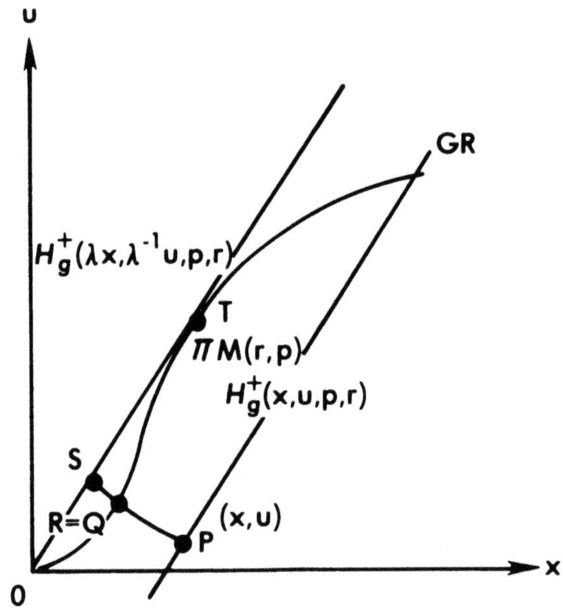

Figure 5-5

$p, r))^{-1} \cdot ru - O_g(x,u,p,r) \cdot px$. Now, assume $rv - py > \pi(r,p)$, then $(y,v) \notin$ GR. Thus, assume that $rv - py < \pi(r,p)$, then $\{(z,w): rw - pz \geqq rv - py\} \supset \{(z,w): rw - pz \geqq \pi(r,p)\}$, and since the two sets are parallel, $O_g(x,u,p,r)$ cannot be a minimum. Thus, $rv - py = \pi(r,p)$. Therefore, $(O_g(x,u,p,r))^{-1} \cdot ru - O_g(x,u,p,r) \cdot px = \pi(r,p)$ and hence, $(O_g(x,u,p,r))^2 \cdot px + O_g(x,u,p,r) \cdot \pi(r,p) = ru$. ■

To state the properties that the overall graph measure satisfies, we first need

Definition: An input-output vector $(x, u) \in$ GR is Overall Graph Efficient for $(p, r) \in R^n_{++} \times (R^m_+ \setminus \{0\})$ if $(x, u) \in \Pi M(r, p)$. (5.4.7)

In Fig. 5–5, $\Pi M(r,p)$ occurs at point T.

The overall graph efficiency measure has the following properties

Theorem: Let GR satisfy (GR.1–GR.5), then (5.4.8)

$O_g.1$ $O_g(0, 0, p, r) = 0$, $(p, r) \in R^n_{++} \times (R^m_+ \backslash \{0\})$,

$O_g.2$ $O_g(\lambda x, \lambda^{-1} u, p, r) = \lambda^{-1} O_g(x, u, p, r)$, $\lambda > 0$, whenever $O_g(x, u, p, r)$ is a minimum,

$O_g.3$ $O_g(\lambda x, u, p, r) \leqq O_g(x, u, p, r)$, $\lambda \geqq 1$,

$O_g.4$ $O_g(x, \theta u, p, r) \leqq O_g(x, u, p, r)$, $\theta \in [0, 1]$,

$O_g.5$ $O_g(x, u, \lambda p, \lambda r) = O_g(x, u, p, r)$, $\lambda > 0$,

$O_g.6$ For $(x, u) \in \text{GR}$, $O_g(x, u, p, r) = 1$ if and only if (x, u) is overall graph efficient for $(p, r) \in R^n_{++} \times (R^m_+ \backslash \{0\})$.

Proof: The first four properties can be proved, following arguments similar to those used to prove theorem (5.3.5). Property $O_g.5$ holds, since property (5.4.2) for H_g^+ is valid. To show that $O_g.6$ applies, let $(x, u) \in \text{GR}$, and assume that $O_g(x, u, p, r) = 1$. Then by theorem (5.4.6), $\pi(r, p) = ru - px$. Thus $(x, u) \in \Pi\text{M}(r, p)$. Conversely, assume $(x, u) \in \Pi\text{M}(r, p)$, then $(x, u) \in \text{GR}$ and $\pi(r, p) = ru - px$. Then by theorem (5.4.6), $O_g(x, u, p, r) = 1$. Finally, we note that by taking $\lambda = 1/\|(p, r)\|$, it follows from $O_g.5$, that the overall graph measure depends solely on relative prices, i.e., $O_g(x, u, (p, r)/\|(p, r\|)$. ■

5.5 Measuring Input-Output Loss Due to Lack of Disposability

We have argued that, in general, one cannot assume that inputs and outputs are strongly disposable, and the axiom structure (GR.1–GR.5) does not assume strong disposability of either inputs or outputs. In the absence of strong disposability, theorem (5.3.9) states that a difference between the Farrell and weak graph measures of technical efficiency can occur. Fig. 5–4 illustrates this difference when strong disposability of inputs does not hold. It follows, then, that any difference between the Farrell and weak graph measures of technical efficiency indicates the presence of input waste and/or output loss attributable to a lack of strong disposability of inputs and/or outputs. This suggests the following measure of input-output loss due to a lack of strong disposability.

Definition: For $(x, u) \in \text{GR}$, $u \geq 0$, the Measure of Input-Output Loss Due to Lack of Disposability is given by $C_g(x, u) := W_g(x, u)/F_g(x, u)$. (5.5.1)

In Fig. 5–4 above, the measure of input-output loss due to a lack of input disposability is given by the distance along the hyperbolic path PQR between Q and R, or by the ratio $(\hat{\lambda}/\lambda^{\circ})$. This derived efficiency measure satisfies the following properties

Theorem: If GR satisfies (GR.1–GR.5), then (5.5.2)

C_g.1 $0 < C_g(x, u) \leqq 1$,

C_g.2 $C_g(x, u) = 1$ if and only if inputs cannot be proportionally decreased at the same time as outputs are proportionally increased along $\{(x, u):(x, u) = (\lambda y, \lambda^{-1} v), \lambda \geqq 0\}$, by allowing GR.6 to hold,

C_g.3 $C_g(\lambda x, \lambda^{-1} u) = C_g(x, u), \lambda > 0$.

Proof: All three properties follow directly from the definition of C_g and from the properties of F_g and W_g. ■

We note that by taking $\lambda = (\|(x, u)\|)$

$$C_g(x, u) = C_g(\|(x, u)\| \cdot x, [u/\|(x, u)\|]). \qquad (5.5.3)$$

From the procedures outlined in sections 3.5 and 4.5, it is clear that they jointly can be used to determine which input-output subvector causes output loss. Simultaneous application of the two procedures is straightforward and omitted.

5.6 The Allocative Graph Efficiency Measure

The allocative input efficiency measure $A_i(u, x, p)$ introduced in section 3.6 measures input mix error relative to the input prices faced by the production unit. The allocative output efficiency measure $A_o(x, u, r)$ introduced in section 4.6 measures output mix error relative to the output prices faced by the production unit. However, even if $A_i(u, x, p) = A_o(x, u, r) = 1$ the production unit can commit an allocative error, by using too much (too little) input to produce too much (too little) output in light of the input and output prices it faces. This possibility points to the need for a more general measure of allocative efficiency when both inputs and outputs are variable. The second derived graph efficiency measure, the allocative graph efficiency measure, serves this purpose.

Definition: For $(x, u) \in \text{GR}$, $u \geq 0$, the Allocative Graph Efficiency Measure is defined by (5.6.1)

$$A_g(x, u, p, r) := \frac{O_g(x, u, p, r)}{W_g(x, u)}.$$

To determine what is meant by allocative efficiency in the sense of the graph, define

Definition: An input-output vector $(x, u) \in \text{GR}$, $u \geq 0$, is Allocatively Efficient for $(p, r) \in R^n_{++} \times (R^m_+ \backslash \{0\})$, if there exists a $\lambda \in (0, 1]$ such that $(\lambda x, \lambda^{-1} u) \in \Pi\text{M}(r, p)$. (5.6.2)

The allocative graph efficiency measure is illustrated in Fig. 5–6. Consider first the input-output vector (x, u) at point P. The overall efficiency of this vector is given by the distance along the hyperbolic path from P to S, while the weak (= Farrell) efficiency of this vector is given by the distance along the hyperbolic path from P to R (=Q). Hence the allocative graph efficiency measure for this input-output vector $A_g(x, u, p, r) < 1$. Alternatively, by definition (5.6.2), since there exists no $\lambda \in (0, 1]$ such that $(\lambda x, \lambda^{-1} u) \in \Pi\text{M}(r, p)$ at point T, this input-output vector is not allocatively efficient. Moreover, the weak (= Farrell) efficient input-output vector located at point R (= Q) is not allocatively efficient either. Like the original vector at point P, it uses too few inputs to produce too few outputs in light of the input and output prices faced by the production unit. Next, consider another input-output vector (x', u') at point P′, and note that $(x', u') > (x, u)$. Both the overall graph efficiency and the weak (= Farrell) graph efficiency of this vector are given by the distance along the hyperbolic path from P′ to T. Hence the allocative graph efficiency measure of this input-output vector $A_g(x', u', p, r) = 1$.

The properties of the allocative graph measure are summarized in the following theorem

Theorem: For $(x, u) \in \text{GR}$, $u \geq 0$, $(p, r) \in R^n_{++} \times (R^m_+ \backslash \{0\})$, the allocative graph measure has the following properties (5.6.3)

$A_g.1$ $0 < A_g(x, u, p, r) \leqq 1$,

$A_g.2$ $A_g(x, u, p, r) = 1$ if and only if (x, u) is allocatively efficient for $(p, r) \in R^n_{++} \times R^m_+ \backslash \{0\}$,

$A_g.3$ $A_g(\lambda x, \lambda^{-1}u, p, r) = A_g(x, u, p, r), \lambda > 0,$

$A_g.4$ $A_g(x, u, \lambda p, \lambda r) = A_g(x, u, p, r), \lambda > 0.$

Proof: Property $A_g.1$ follows from properties $W_g.6$ and the fact that if $(x, u) \in \text{GR}$, then for $(p, r) \in R^n_{++} \times R^m_+\backslash\{0\}$, $O_g(x, u, p, r) \leqq 1$.

$A_g.2$: Assume $(x, u) \in \text{GR}$, $u \geq 0$, is allocatively efficient for (p, r). Then there is a $\lambda \in (0, 1]$, such that $(\lambda x, \lambda^{-1}u) \in \Pi\text{M}(r, p)$. Thus, $(W_g(x, u) \cdot x, (W_g(x, u))^{-1} \cdot u)$ and $(O_g(x, u, p, r) \cdot x, (O_g(x, u, p, r))^{-1} \cdot u)$ belong to $\Pi\text{M}(r, p)$. Both $(W_g(x, u) \cdot x, (W_g(x, u))^{-1} \cdot u)$ and $(O_g(x, u, p, r) \cdot x, (O_g(x, u, p, r))^{-1} \cdot u)$ belong to Isoq GR, thus $O_g(x, u, p, r) = W_g(x, u) = 1$, and, therefore, $A_g(x, u, p, r) = 1$. Conversely, assume $A_g(x, u, p, r) = 1$, then $O_g(x, u, p, r) = W_g(x, u)$, and hence, $(O_g(x, u, p, r) \cdot x, (O_g(x, u, p, r))^{-1} \cdot u) = (W_g(x, u) \cdot x, (W_g(x, u))^{-1} \cdot u)$. Since $(x, u) \in \text{GR}$, $u \geq 0$, it is clear that $0 < O_g(x, u, p, r) \leqq 1$. Note that since $O_g(x, u, p, r) = W_g(x, u)$, $O_g(x, u, p, r) > 0$, by property $W_g.2$. We need to show that $(O_g(x, u, p, r) \cdot x, (O_g(x, u, p, r))^{-1} \cdot u) \in \Pi\text{M}(r, p)$. First we show that $(O_g(x, u, p, r) \cdot x, (O_g(x, u, p, r))^{-1} \cdot u) = (W_g(x, u) \cdot x, (W_g(x, u))^{-1} \cdot u) \in \text{GR}$. Since $(p, r) \in R^n_{++} \times R^m_+\backslash\{0\}$, $((\text{K}(W_g(x, u) \cdot x) \times \text{M}((W_g(x, u))^{-1} \cdot u)) \cap \{(y, v): rv - py = r(O_g(x, u, p, r))^{-1} \cdot u - pO_g(x, u, p, r) \cdot x\} = (W_g(x, u) \cdot x, (W_g(x, u))^{-1} \cdot u)$. If $(W_g(x, u) \cdot x, (W_g(x, u))^{-1} \cdot u) \notin \text{GR}$, then since $(\text{K}(x) \times \text{M}(u)) \subset H^+_g(x, u, p, r)$ note that $(p, r) \in R^n_{++} \times R^m_+\backslash\{0\}$, and $\text{K}(W_g(x, u) \cdot x) \times M((W_g(x, u))^{-1} \cdot u) \cap \text{GR} = \emptyset$, which is a contradiction. Thus $(W_g(x, u) \cdot x, (W_g(x, u))^{-1} \cdot u) = (O_g(x, u, p, r) \cdot x, (O_g(x, u, p, r))^{-1} \cdot u) \in \text{GR}$. Finally, by theorem (5.4.6), $(O_g(x, u, p, r) \cdot x, (O_g(x, u, p, r))^{-1} \cdot u) \in \Pi\text{M}(r, p)$.

$A_g.3$: Follows from properties $O_g.2$ and $W_g.3$.

$A_g.4$: Follows from property $O_g.5$. ■

Finally, we note that the overall graph measure is multiplicatively decomposable, i.e.

$$O_g(x, u, p, r) = F_g(x, u) \cdot C_g(x, u) \cdot A_g(x, u, p, r), \tag{5.6.4}$$

or, since $C_g(x, u) = W_g(x, u)/F_g(x, u)$,

$$O_g(x, u, p, r) = W_g(x, u) \cdot A_g(x, u, p, r). \tag{5.6.5}$$

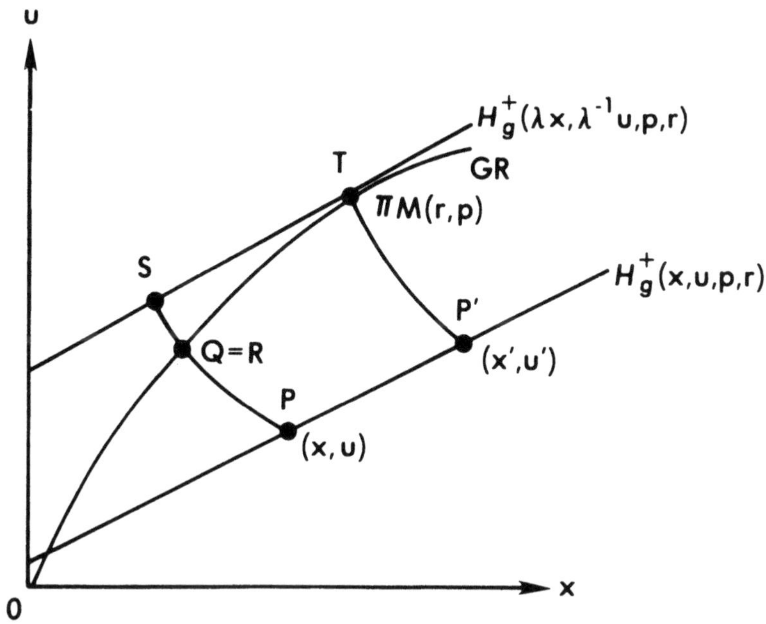

Figure 5-6

5.7 Generalized Hyperbolic Graph Efficiency Measures

The radial input efficiency measures of chapter 3 examined the efficiency of an input vector in the production of a given output vector, while the radial output efficiency measures of chapter 4 examined the efficiency of an output vector produced with a given input vector. The hyperbolic graph efficiency measures of this chapter extend the analyses of chapters 3 and 4 by allowing for the variability of both inputs and outputs in the measurement of efficiency. However, the hyperbolic graph efficiency measures themselves are restrictive, in that they constrain the search for more efficient production plans to a hyperbolic path along which all inputs are reduced, and all outputs are increased, by the same proportion. An obvious generalization of these measures would permit the proportional reduction in all inputs to differ from the proportional increase in all outputs in the search for a more efficient production plan. In this section we introduce just such a generalization by defining and discussing a generalized Farrell graph measure of technical efficiency. We do not pursue the generalization much further, however, leaving the derivation and interpretation of the other four generalized graph measures to the interested reader.

In order to define a generalized Farrell graph measure of technical efficiency for a technology satisfying (GR.1–GR.5), we first define the effective domain of the measure as

$$D(F_g^G) := \{(x, u) : \exists\ \lambda \geqq 0,\ \theta \geqq 0 \text{ such that } (\lambda x, \theta^{-1} u) \in \text{GR}\}. \tag{5.7.1}$$

We can now define the generalized Farrell graph measure as

Definition: The function F_g^G: $R_+^n \times R_+^m \to R_+ \cup \{+\infty\}$ defined by (5.7.2)

$$F_g^G(x, u) := \begin{cases} \min\{(\lambda + \theta)/2 : \lambda \geqq 0,\ \theta \geqq 0 : (\lambda x, \theta^{-1} u) \in \text{GR}\}, \\ \qquad (x, u) \in D(F_g^G), \\ +\infty,\ (x, u) \in \text{Complement } D(F_g^G), \end{cases}$$

is called the Generalized Farrell Graph Measure of Technical Efficiency.

To illustrate this definition, and to compare it with definitions (3.2.2) of $F_i(u, x)$, (4.2.2) of $F_o(x, u)$, and (5.2.2) of $F_g(x, u)$, consider Fig. 5–7. Let $(x, u) \in$ GR at point P. The Farrell input measure $F_i(u, x)$ computes the efficiency of (x, u) by comparing it to (x^i, u) at point Q^i. The Farrell output measure $F_o(x, u)$ computes the efficiency of (x, u) by comparing it to (x, u°) at point Q°. Between these two extremes, the Farrell graph measure $F_g(x, u)$ computes the efficiency of (x, u) by comparing it to (x^g, u^g) at point Q^g. The path from P to Q^g used by $F_g(x, u)$ involves an equiproportionate input reduction and output expansion, and so traces out a rectangular hyperbola. Finally, the generalized Farrell graph measure $F_g^G(x, u)$ computes the efficiency of (x, u) by comparing it to (x^G, u^G) at point Q^G. The path from P to Q^G used by $F_g^G(x, u)$ involves a proportionate input reduction that may differ from the proportionate output increase, and so traces out a (not necessarily rectangular) hyperbola. The point Q^G lies northeast or southwest of the point Q^g along Isoq GR according as $\theta \gtrless \lambda$. Clearly if $\theta = \lambda$ then the two points coincide and $F_g^G(x, u) = F_g(x, u)$. If $\theta \neq \lambda$ then $F_g^G(x, u) < F_g(x, u)$.

Despite the fact that $F_g(x, u)$ and $F_g^G(x, u)$ typically assign different values of technical efficiency to any given (x, u) vector, they have the same reference set, namely Isoq GR, and they have the same properties. The same statement applies, for the same reasons, to $W_g(x, u)$ and a generalized weak

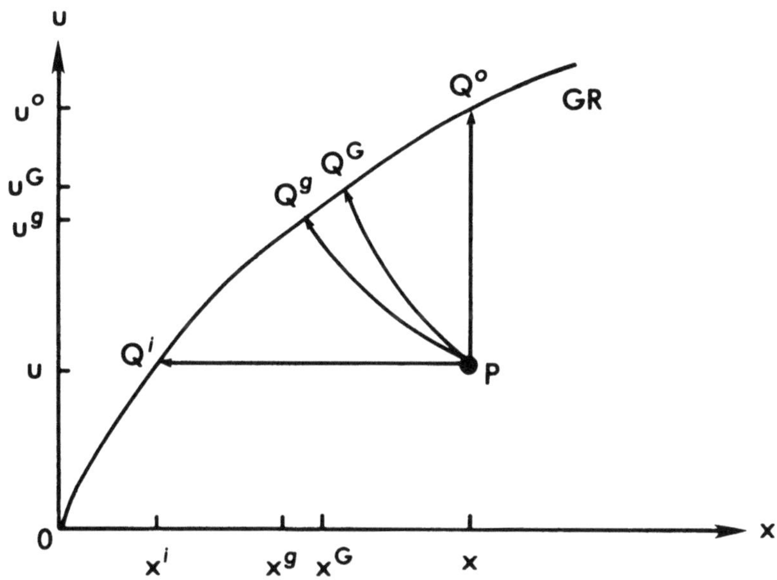

Figure 5-7

graph measure of technical efficiency, except that their common reference set is WEffGR. However $O_g(x, u)$ and a generalized overall graph efficiency measure must assign the same overall efficiency value to any given (x, u) vector, since all points in their common reference set $\Pi M(r, p)$ are equally profitable. Thus the main consequence of the generalization suggested in this section is a reallocation of overall efficiency among its four components.

5.8 Linear Programming Example

In this section, the hypothetical data summarized in Table 5–1 are used to calculate the graph measures discussed in sections 5.2–5.6 of this chapter.

As for the output and input efficiency measures, we begin with the Farrell measure, with the technology characterized by weak disposability. Due to the nature of the graph, we can choose to set up the problem using either the input or output correspondence. We choose the input correspondence, thus the weakly disposable technology can be written as

$$L^W(u) = \{x: \mu \cdot z \cdot M = u, z \cdot N = \delta \cdot x, \mu, \delta \in (0, 1], z \in R^k_+\}, \tag{5.8.1}$$

Table 5-1

	Input	*Outputs*	
Firm	(x)	(u_1)	(u_2)
1	2	1.5	1
2	2	2	2
3	4	3	2
4	6	6	6
5	7	6	6
6	8	7	4
7	9	7	4

where z is the intensity vector, and M is the $k \times m$ normalized output matrix and N is the $k \times n$ input matrix (see chapter 2).

The Farrell graph measure, $F_g(x, u)$, can now be derived relative to the technology described in (5.8.1). Specifically, to calculate $F_g(x, u)$ for a firm or activity (x°, u°), we have the following programming problem

$$\begin{aligned}
&\min \lambda \\
&\text{subject to} \\
&\mu \cdot z \cdot \mathrm{M} = u^\circ/\lambda \\
&z \cdot \mathrm{N} = \lambda \cdot \delta \cdot x^\circ \\
&\mu, \delta \in (0, 1] \\
&z \in R^k_+. \qquad (5.8.2)
\end{aligned}$$

The problem as stated in (5.8.2) can be transformed into the simpler linear programming problem below

$$\begin{aligned}
&\min \Lambda \\
&\text{subject to} \\
&z' \cdot \mathrm{M} = \xi \cdot u^\circ \\
&z' \cdot \mathrm{N} = \Lambda \cdot x^\circ \\
&\xi \geqq 1 \\
&z' \in R^k_+, \qquad (5.8.3)
\end{aligned}$$

where $\Lambda = \lambda^2$, $z' = z \cdot \lambda/\delta$, and $\xi = 1/(\mu \cdot \delta)$.

To derive the graph measure of weak efficiency, we exploit theorem (5.3.9), which states that the Farrell and weak graph measures are equivalent if and only if the technology satisfies strong disposability of inputs (outputs). As in the earlier chapters, we specify the strongly disposable technology as

$$L^S(u) = \{x: z \cdot M \geqq u, z \cdot N \leqq x, z \in R^k_+\}. \qquad (5.8.4)$$

To calculate $W_g(x, u)$ we modify the programming problem (5.8.2) to account for strong disposability as follows

$$\begin{aligned} &\min \lambda \\ &\text{subject to} \\ &z \cdot M \geqq u^\circ/\lambda \\ &z \cdot N \leqq \lambda \cdot x^\circ \\ &z \in R^k_+. \end{aligned} \qquad (5.8.5)$$

This programming problem can also be simplified along the lines used in (5.8.3)

$$\begin{aligned} &\min \Lambda \\ &\text{subject to} \\ &z' \cdot M \geqq u^\circ \\ &z' \cdot N \leqq \Lambda \cdot x^\circ \\ &z' \in R^k_+, \end{aligned} \qquad (5.8.6)$$

where $z' = \lambda \cdot z$ and $\Lambda = \lambda^2$ as before.

In order to calculate the overall graph measure, we make use of theorem (5.4.6) which states that if $O_g(x, u, p, r)$ is a minimum, then it satisfies the following equality: $(O_g(x,u,p,r))^2 \cdot px + O_g(x,u,p,x) \cdot \pi(r,p) = ru$. Thus we can calculate $O_g(x, u, p, r)$ directly once $\pi(r, p)$ (i.e., maximum profits) are derived. $\pi(r,p)$ can be calculated from the following linear programming problem

$$\max(ru - px)$$

subject to

$$z \cdot \mathrm{M} \geqq u^{\circ}$$
$$z \cdot \mathrm{N} \leqq x^{\circ}$$
$$z \in R^{k}_{+}. \tag{5.8.7}$$

To calculate the derived graph measures, we make use of their definitions, i.e., the graph measure of input (output) loss due to lack of disposability is calculated from (5.5.1) as $C_g(x, u) = W_g(x, u)/F_g(x, u)$, and the allocative graph measure is calculated from (5.6.1) as $A_g(x, u, p, r) = O_g(x, u, p, r)/W_g(x, u)$.

We now use the data from Table 5–1, given $r_1 = 2, r_2 = 1$ and $p = 3$, to calculate the five measures of graph efficiency discussed above. These are summarized in Table 5–2.

The maximum profit allowed in this example is 0. It should be noted, however, that the linear specifications of the technology in (5.8.1) and (5.8.4) construct the graph as a cone, i.e., the technology is homogeneous of degree one, thus $\pi(r, p) = 0$. This implies that the overall measure can be calculated as $O_g(x, u, p, r) = \sqrt{ru/px}$.

Table 5-2

Firm	$F_g(x, u)$	$W_g(x, u)$	$O_g(x, u, p, r)$	$C_g(x, u)$	$A_g(x, u, p, r)$
1	.913	.866	.817	.949	.943
2	1.000	1.000	1.000	1.000	1.000
3	.913	.866	.817	.949	.943
4	1.000	1.000	1.000	1.000	1.000
5	.926	.926	.926	1.000	1.000
6	1.000	.935	.866	.935	.926
7	.943	.882	.817	.935	.926

6 A COMPARISON OF INPUT, OUTPUT, AND GRAPH EFFICIENCY MEASURES

6.0 Introduction

In the three previous chapters we established some relationships among various radial input measures of efficiency (chapter 3), among various radial output measures of efficiency (chapter 4), and among various hyperbolic graph measures of efficiency (chapter 5). In this brief chapter we establish some relationships among input, output, and graph measures of various types of efficiency. Our motivation for so doing is that we seek answers to questions such as (1) Under what conditions, if any, do input, output, and graph measures of a certain type of efficiency attach the same efficiency value to a given input-output vector? (2) Under what conditions, if any, can the three measures of a certain type of efficiency be ordered? And, (3) If an input-output vector is labeled efficient by one measure, when, if ever, is it labeled efficient by the other two measures?

The relationship between radial input efficiency measures and the corresponding radial output efficiency measures is investigated in section 6.1. We establish various restrictions on the technology under which input and output measures of technical efficiency are equal, or can be ordered. No such results are available for input and output measures of congestion, allocative efficiency, or overall efficiency.

The relationship between hyperbolic graph efficiency measures on the one hand, and corresponding radial input and output efficiency measures on the other hand, is examined in section 6.2. We are able to come up with rankings of measures of technical and overall efficiency, but we can say little about the relationship among the three measures of congestion or allocative efficiency.

6.1 Comparison of Radial Input and Output Measures

In this section we seek to establish conditions on the production technology under which relationships between measures of input efficiency and output efficiency can be determined. It turns out that we can establish such relationships for the Farrell input and output measures, but not much more is possible.

The following theorem provides a complete characterization of the conditions under which the Farrell input and output measures of technical efficiency are equal. For the single output case this result is stated somewhat loosely by Farrell (1957, p. 259), and more formally by Färe and Lovell (1978, p. 156).

Theorem: $F_i(u,x) = (F_o(x,u))^{-1}$ for all $(x,u) \in R^n_+ \times R^m_+$ if and only if the production technology is homogeneous of degree one, i.e., $\mathrm{L}(\theta u) = \theta \cdot \mathrm{L}(u)$, $\theta > 0$, or equivalently, $\mathrm{P}(\lambda x) = \lambda \cdot \mathrm{P}(x)$, $\lambda > 0$. (6.1.1)

Proof: Assume first that the technology is homogeneous of degree one, and that $(u,x) \in D(F_i)$, then

$$\begin{aligned} F_i(u,x) &= \min\{\lambda: \lambda x \in \mathrm{L}(u)\} \\ &= \min\{\lambda: u \in \mathrm{P}(\lambda x)\} \\ &= \min\{\lambda: u/\lambda \in \mathrm{P}(x)\} \\ &= \max\{\lambda^{-1}: u/\lambda \in \mathrm{P}(x)\} \\ &= (F_o(u,x))^{-1}. \end{aligned}$$

Clearly, since L is homogeneous of degree +1, $D(F_i)$ and $D(F_o)$ contain the same input and output vectors. To prove the converse, we note that by property $F_i.5$ or $F_o.5$, the technology is completely described by F_i or F_o. Thus we need only to show that if $F_i(u,x) = (F_o(x,u))^{-1}$, then the technology is homogeneous of degree +1. Consider θu, then $F_i(\theta u, x) = (F_o(x, \theta u))^{-1} = \theta(F_o(x, u))^{-1} = \theta F_i(u, x)$. Thus F_i is homogeneous of degree +1 in u. Now we have

$$\begin{aligned} L(\theta u) &= \{x: 0 < F_i(\theta u, x) \leqq 1\} \\ &= \{x: 0 < \theta \cdot F_i(u, x) \leqq 1\} \\ &= \{x: 0 < F_i(u, \theta^{-1} x) \leqq 1\} \\ &= \theta \cdot \{y: 0 < F_i(u, y) \leqq 1\} \\ &= \theta \cdot L(u). \quad \blacksquare \end{aligned}$$

To continue the comparison of the two efficiency measures, introduce

Definition: The input correspondence is Sub-Homogeneous (for increases in output) if $L(\theta u) \subseteqq \theta \cdot L(u)$, $\theta \geqq 1$. It is Super-Homogeneous (for increases in output) if $L(\theta u) \supseteqq \theta \cdot L(u)$, $\theta \geqq 1$. (6.1.2)

Sub-homogeneity is commonly used to describe non-increasing returns to scale, while super-homogeneity is used to describe non-decreasing returns to scale. With these notions one can prove

Theorem: If the input correspondence is sub- (super-) homogeneous then $F_i(u, x) \leqq (\geqq) (F_o(x, u))^{-1}$. (6.1.3)

Proof: Assume that L is sub-homogeneous, then

$$\begin{aligned} F_o(x, u) &= \max\{\theta: \theta u \in P(x)\} \\ &= \max\{\theta: x \in L(\theta u)\} \\ &\leqq \max\{\theta: x \in \theta \cdot L(u)\} \\ &= \min\{1/\theta: x/\theta \in L(u)\} \\ &= (F_i(u, x))^{-1}. \end{aligned}$$

The proof for super-homogeneity is similar and therefore is omitted. ■

Theorem (6.1.3) is illustrated in Fig. 6–1 for the sub-homogeneous case. Input-output vector $(x, u) \in GR$ is called technically inefficient by both $F_i(u, x)$ and $F_o(x, u)$. However, under sub-homogeneity, the proportionate decrease in inputs consistent with continued production of outputs u exceeds the proportionate increase in outputs obtainable from continued usage of inputs x. Hence $F_i(u, x) < (F_o(x, u))^{-1}$ as required by the theorem.

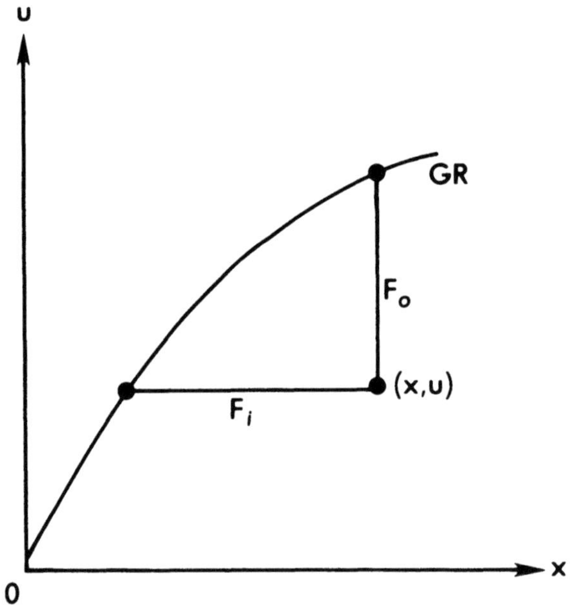

Figure 6-1

Analogous results can be drawn for the linearly homogeneous and super-homogeneous cases.

Theorem (6.1.3) enables us to rank $F_i(u,x)$ and $(F_o(x,u))^{-1}$ provided the input correspondence is sub- or super-homogeneous. But it gives no information concerning the magnitude of the difference between $F_i(u,x)$ and $(F_o(x,u))^{-1}$. Such information is available if we are willing to sharpen our notions of decreasing and increasing returns to scale, as the following theorem shows.

Theorem: If the output correspondence is homogeneous of degree $+\beta$, then $(F_i(u,x))^{\beta} = (F_o(x,u))^{-1}$. (6.1.4)

Proof:
$$\begin{aligned} F_i(u,x) &:= \min\{\lambda: \lambda x \in L(u)\} \\ &= \min\{\lambda: u \in P(\lambda x)\} \\ &= \min\{\lambda: F_o(\lambda x, u) \geqq 1\} \text{ (theorem 4.2.4)} \\ &= \min\{\lambda: \lambda^{\beta} F_o(x,u) \geqq 1\} \text{ (theorem 4.2.5)} \\ &= (F_o(x,u))^{-1/\beta}. \end{aligned}$$

Therefore $(F_i(u, x))^\beta = (F_o(x, u))^{-1}$. ■

Not surprisingly, when the assumptions on technology are strengthened, results are sharpened. If the assumption of sub- or super-homogeneity is strengthened to homogeneity, the inequalities of theorem (6.1.3) become an equality involving the degree of homogeneity in theorem (6.1.4). We also note that theorem (6.1.1) is a special case of theorem (6.1.4).

Theorems (6.1.1), (6.1.3), and (6.1.4) focus on the role of economies of scale in the relationship between the Farrell input and output measures of technical efficiency. The following theorem ignores scale economies, and provides a set of sufficient conditions for the two measures simultaneously to call an input-output vector technically efficient.

Theorem: Let the technology satisfy (L.1–L.5) and conditions I:1 and I:2 of definition (2.2.9). Then $F_o(x, u) = 1$ if and only if $F_i(u, x) = 1$. (6.1.5)

The proof follows directly from lemma (2.2.10). Examples (2.2.13) and (2.2.14) of chapter 2 illustrate technologies satisfying (L.1–L.5) but not conditions I:1 and I:2 of definition (2.2.9), and for which $F_i(u, x) = 1 \not=> F_o(x, u) = 1$ and $F_o(x, u) = 1 \not=> F_i(u, x) = 1$.

We now turn from the Farrell input and output measures to the weak input and output measures. The following theorem provides a set of sufficient conditions for the two weak measures to simultaneously call an input-output vector technically efficient.

Theorem: Let the technology satisfy (L.1–L.5) and conditions W:1 and W:2 of definition (2.2.16). Then $W_o(x, u) = 1$ if and only if $W_i(u, x) = 1$. (6.1.6)

The proof follows directly from lemma (2.2.17). Again, examples (2.2.13) and (2.2.14) of chapter 2 illustrate conditions under which the theorem does not hold.

Unfortunately, not much more can be said about the relationship between the weak input and output measures of technical efficiency. Only under the additional assumption of strong disposability of both inputs and outputs can we obtain results analogous to those of theorems (6.1.1), (6.1.3), and (6.1.4). Under strong disposability of inputs and outputs $F_i(u, x) = W_i(u, x)$ and $F_o(x, u) = W_o(x, u)$, from theorems (3.3.10) and (4.3.11), in which case the results of theorems (6.1.1), (6.1.3), and (6.1.4) hold for $W_i(u, x)$ and $W_o(x, u)$ also.

Furthermore, since input disposability neither implies nor is implied by output disposability, nothing can be said about the relationship between the input and output congestion measures $C_i(u, x)$ and $C_o(x, u)$. Similarly, since input allocative efficiency neither implies nor is implied by output allocative efficiency, nothing can be said about the relationship between the input and output allocative efficiency measures $A_i(u, x, p)$ and $A_o(x, u, r)$. Consequently, nothing can be said about the relationship between the two overall efficiency measures $O_i(u, x, p)$ and $O_o(x, u, r)$.

6.2 Graph Measures Compared to Input and Output Measures

In this section we compare hyperbolic graph measures to the corresponding pairs of radial input and output measures. Consider first the three Farrell measures, the graph measure $F_g(x, u)$, the input measure $F_i(u, x)$, and the output measure $F_o(x, u)$. The following relationship holds

Theorem: Let technology satisfy (GR.1–GR.5). Then for $(x, u) \in \text{GR}$, $F_g(x, u) \geqq \max\{F_i(u, x), (F_o(x, u))^{-1}\}$. (6.2.1)

Proof: Since $(x, u) \in \text{GR}$, property $F_g.6$ implies that $F_g(x, u) \leqq 1$. Moreover, $(F_g(x, u) \cdot x, (F_g(x, u))^{-1} \cdot u) \in \text{GR}$, by the definition of F_g. Thus, $F_g(x, u) \cdot x \in \text{L}((F_g(x, u))^{-1} \cdot u)$ or equivalently, $(F_g(x, u))^{-1} \cdot u \in \text{P}(F_g(x, u) \cdot x)$. From the first of these expressions and from weak disposability of outputs, $F_g(x, u) \cdot x \in \text{L}(u)$. Thus, from the definition of F_i, $F_g(x, u) \geqq F_i(u, x)$. Similar arguments using weak disposability of inputs apply to show that $F_g(x, u) \geqq (F_o(x, u))^{-1}$. Thus $F_g(x, u) \geqq \max\{F_i(u, x), (F_o(x, u))^{-1}\}$. ■

Theorem (6.2.1) is illustrated in Fig. 6–2. Input-output vector $(x, u) \in \text{GR}$ is technically inefficient for all three measures. But the technical efficiency of (x, u) is at least as great according to $F_g(u, x)$ as it is according to either $F_i(u, x)$ or $F_o(x, u)$. This is because, regardless of the nature of economies of scale, the proportionate adjustment required to reach Isoq GR is not larger when both inputs and outputs are variable then when only inputs or only outputs are variable.

To see that the equality in (6.2.1) does not necessarily hold, consider the following technology

$$\text{GR}: = \{(x, u): u \leqq x, x \in R_+\}. \tag{6.2.2}$$

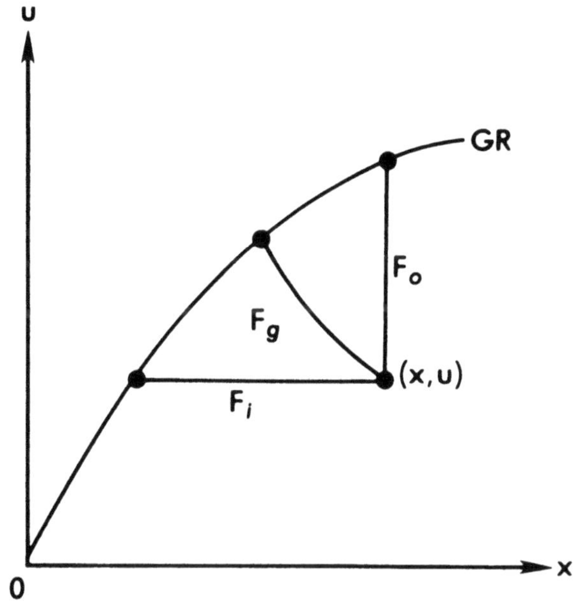

Figure 6-2

This technology satisfies (GR.1–GR.5). Let $(x, u) = (2, 1) \in$ GR. Then $1 \in$ P(2) and $2 \in$ L(1). The measures are $F_i(1, 2) = ½$, $F_o(2, 1) = 2$ and $F_g(1, 2) = \sqrt{½}$. This example shows that the strict inequality may hold.

We next establish sufficient conditions for the Farrell graph measure to call an input-output vector technically efficient.

Theorem: If either $F_i(u, x) = 1$ or $F_o(x, u) = 1$, then $F_g(x, u) = 1$. (6.2.3)

Proof: Assume first that $F_i(u, x) = 1$. Then $x \in L(u)$ and thus $(x, u) \in$ GR. Therefore, by property F_g.6, $F_g(x, u) \leqq 1$. Since $x \in L(u)$, $u \in P(x)$ and thus $F_o(x, u) \geqq 1$ (see property F_o.5). Thus by theorem (6.2.1), $F_g(x, u) = 1$. Similar arguments apply to show that if $F_o(x, u) = 1$, then $F_g(x, u) = 1$. ■

To show that the converse of theorem (6.2.3) is not in general true, consider the following technology, satisfying properties (GR.1–GR.5)

$$\text{GR:} = \{(x, u): u \leqq x, x \in [0, 1]; u \leqq 1, x \in [1, 2); u \leqq x, x \geqq 2\}. \tag{6.2.4}$$

The input-output vector $(2, 1) \in \text{GR}$. Also, $(2, 1) \in \text{Isoq GR}$, thus $F_g(2, 1) = 1$. Also, $2 \in L(1)$ but $2 \notin \text{Isoq } L(1)$, thus $F_i(1, 2) < 1$ and $1 \in P(2)$ but $1 \notin \text{Isoq } P(2)$, hence $F_g(2, 1) > 1$. This shows that the converse of theorem (6.2.3) is, in general, not true. However if $x \in \text{Isoq } L(u) \Leftrightarrow u \in \text{Isoq } P(x)$, i.e., if properties I:1 and I:2 of definition (2.2.9) hold, then by theorem (6.2.1) and lemma (2.2.10), theorem (6.2.3) can be strengthened to

Theorem: Let the technology satisfy properties (GR.1–GR.5), and let properties I:1 and I:2 of definition (2.2.9) hold. Then $F_g(x, u) = 1$ if and only if either $F_i(u, x) = 1$ or $F_o(x, u) = 1$. (6.2.5)

Turning now to the weak efficiency measures, the following result can be established

Theorem: Let the technology satisfy properties (GR.1–GR.5). Then for $(x, u) \in \text{GR}$, $W_g(x, u) \geqq \max\{W_i(u, x), (W_o(x, u))^{-1}\}$. (6.2.6)

The proof of this theorem parallels the proof of theorem (6.2.1), and is omitted.

The graph in example (6.2.2), in addition to satisfying (GR.1–GR.5), also satisfies GR.6. Therefore, by theorem (5.3.9), $W_g(x, u) = F_g(x, u)$. Also, $W_i(u, x) = F_i(u, x)$ and $W_o(x, u) = F_o(x, u)$ by theorems (3.3.10) and (4.3.11) respectively, since GR.6 implies L.3.S and P.5.S. Hence (6.2.2) shows that strict inequality can hold in theorem (6.2.6).

For the weak efficiency measures, it is also true (based on arguments similar to those used to prove theorem (6.2.3) that

Theorem: If either $W_i(u, x) = 1$ of $W_o(x, u) = 1$, then $W_g(x, u) = 1$. (6.2.7)

The graph given by (6.2.4) shows that the converse of theorem (6.2.7) is not true. However if $x \in \text{WEff } L(u)$ if and only if $u \in \text{WEff } P(x)$, then we have

Theorem: Let the technology satisfy properties (GR.1–GR.5) and conditions W:1 and W:2 of definition (2.2.16).

Then $W_g(x, u) = 1$ if and only if either $W_i(u, x) = 1$ or $W_o(x, u) = 1$. (6.2.8)

The proof follows directly from theorems (6.2.6) and (6.2.7), together with lemma (2.2.17).

For reasons similar to those experienced in section 6.1, we cannot compare graph measures of congestion or allocative efficiency to input and output measures of congestion or allocative efficiency. However, we can state the following relationship among the three measures of overall efficiency.

Theorem: Let $(p, r) \in R^n_{++} \times R^m_{++}$, and $\pi(r, p) = \mathrm{R}(x, r) - \mathrm{Q}(u, p)$ together with $O_g(x, u, p, r)$ being a minimum. Then $O_g(x, u, p, r) = 1$ if and only if $O_i(u, x, p) = O_o(x, u, r) = 1$. (6.2.9)

Proof: From the assumptions of the theorem, the following holds: (1) $px = \mathrm{Q}(u, p)/O_i(u, x, p)$ by theorem (3.4.5), (2) $ru = \mathrm{R}(x, r)/O_o(x, u, r)$ by theorem (4.4.5), (3) $(O_g(x, u, p, r))^2 \cdot px + O_g(x, u, p, r) \cdot \pi(r, p) = ru$ by theorem (5.4.6). Hence, from (1)–(3) and the requirements on $\pi(r, p)$, we have (omitting the arguments of the functions)

$$O_g \cdot O_o \cdot \mathrm{Q} \cdot (O_g - O_i) + \mathrm{R} \cdot O_i \cdot (O_g \cdot O_o - 1) = 0. \tag{6.2.10}$$

Now if $O_g = 1$, then from (6.2.10) we have

$$O_o \cdot \mathrm{Q} \cdot (1 - O_i) + \mathrm{R} \cdot O_i(O_o - 1) = 0. \tag{6.2.11}$$

Since $O_g = 1$, $(x, u) \in \mathrm{GR}$, and since $(p, r) \in R^n_{++} \times R^m_{++}$, $0 < O_i \leqq 1$, $O_o \geqq 1$. Therefore since Q and $\mathrm{R} > 0$, it follows from (6.2.11) that $O_i = O_o = 1$. To prove the converse, assume that $O_i = O_o = 1$. Since Q and $\mathrm{R} > 0$, it then follows from (6.2.10) that

$$O_g \cdot \mathrm{Q} \cdot (O_g - 1) + \mathrm{R} \cdot (O_g - 1) = 0, \tag{6.2.12}$$

therefore $O_g = 1$. ∎

7 NONRADIAL EFFICIENCY MEASURES

7.0 Introduction

In chapters 3 and 4 we introduced radial input and output efficiency measures. The hyperbolic graph efficiency measure introduced in chapter 5, though not a radial measure in the strict sense, nonetheless possesses many of the characteristics of the radial input and output efficiency measures. Among the virtues of this family of efficiency measures are their consistency with the original formulations of Farrell (1957), their ease of computation, their straightforward cost or revenue interpretation, and their consequent decomposability. That is, measures of overall (input, output, and graph) efficiency each have a multiplicative decomposition into technical, congestion, and allocative components.

In addition to these virtues, however, this family of efficiency measures shares a common defect. Each is constructed around a technical component that involves an equiproportionate reduction in all inputs, or an equiproportionate expansion of all outputs, or both. Unfortunately there is no guarantee that such a process must intersect the appropriate efficient subset of the technology. Each of these measures has the appropriate isoquant as its reference set, and although isoquants include efficient subsets, the converse is not necessarily true. This can lead to an overstatement of the true technical efficiency of a vector, perhaps to the extent that a vector is labeled technically efficient when it is not, and so to an improper decomposition of overall efficiency.

Moreover, this is not merely a pathological possibility. It can occur in a wide variety of popular specifications of production technology, including Leontief, variable elasticity of substitution, and apparently all flexible functional forms (see Kopp (1981b) and Färe and Lovell (1981)).

Consequently, in this chapter we introduce a family of nonradial input, output, and graph efficiency measures. Each has a technical component that, by virtue of its nonradial nature, has the flexibility to select a vector from the appropriate efficient subset against which to compute the technical efficiency of an observed vector. Hence these nonradial measures call a vector technically efficient if and only if it belongs to an efficient subset. Thus their reference sets are narrower, and more appropriate for the purpose of efficiency measurement, than are the reference sets of the analogous radial measures. Moreover, these nonradial measures contain their radial counterparts as testable special cases. These nonradial measures are not without their drawbacks. They are somewhat more difficult to calculate than are the corresponding radial measures, they have no straightforward cost or revenue interpretation, and they do not generate a natural decomposition of overall efficiency. The last two problems can be resolved by means of a slight modification of the technical component, however.

In sections 7.1–7.3 we introduce nonradial measures of input, output, and graph technical efficiency respectively. We also obtain their properties, and relate each to the corresponding radial measures of technical efficiency. As already noted, an important property of these nonradial measures of technical efficiency is that they relate an observed vector directly to an element of the appropriate efficient subset. This enables us to dispense with measures of weak technical efficiency and congestion, leaving us with only three efficiency measures (technical, allocative, and overall) instead of five.

Finally, we show how each nonradial measure of technical efficiency can be modified so as to permit a decomposition of the appropriate overall measure of efficiency into technical and allocative components. In section 7.4 we compare the nonradial measures of input, output, and graph technical efficiency. In section 7.5 we continue our practice of working through a linear programming example to illustrate the computation of the various nonradial efficiency measures.

7.1 The Russell Input Measure of Technical Efficiency

The Russell input measure of technical efficiency, introduced by Färe and Lovell (1978) for the single output case and extended by Färe, Lovell and Zieschang (1983) to the multiple output case, terms an input vector technically efficient if and only if it belongs to an efficient subset. In order to define the Russell input measure of technical efficiency in the context of an input correspondence satisfying (L.1–L.5) we need the following notation

$$(x_1, x_2, \ldots, x_k; \ldots). \tag{7.1.1}$$

This denotes the input vector $x \in R^n_+$ with $x_i > 0$ for $i = 1, \ldots, k$, $k \leqq n$, and $x_i = 0$ for $i = k + 1, \ldots, n$. With this notation we can define the effective domain of the Russell input measure as

$$D(R_i) := \{u, x): \exists\ \lambda_i \in [0, 1], i = 1, \ldots, k, \text{ such that } (\lambda_1 x_1, \lambda_2 x_2, \ldots, \lambda_k x_k; \ldots) \in L(u)\}. \tag{7.1.2}$$

The Russell input measure is now defined as

Definition: The function $R_i: R^m_+ \times R^n_+ \to R_+ \cup \{+\infty\}$ defined by (7.1.3)

$$R_i(u, x) := \begin{cases} \min\{\sum_{i=1}^{k} \lambda_i/k : (\lambda_1 x_1, \lambda_2 x_2, \ldots, \lambda_k x_k; \ldots) \in L(u), \lambda_i \in [0, 1]\}, & (u, x) \in D(R_i), \\ +\infty, & (u, x) \in \text{Complement } D(R_i), \end{cases}$$

is called the Russell Input Measure of Technical Efficiency.

To illustrate this definition, consider Fig. 7–1.

Let $x \in L(u)$, at point P. Then the Russell input measure of technical efficiency minimizes $(\lambda_1 + \lambda_2)/2$ under the condition that $\lambda_i \in [0, 1]$, $i = 1, 2$, i.e., that $(\lambda_1 x_1, \lambda_2 x_2)$ belongs to the region to the southwest of P, and that $(\lambda_1 x_1, \lambda_2 x_2)$ remain in $L(u)$. The resulting technically efficient input vector $(\lambda_1 x_1, \lambda_2 x_2)$ occurs at point Q, the efficient subset of $L(u)$. If the efficient subset of $L(u)$ contains more than one vector, then $(\lambda_1 x_1, \lambda_2 x_2) \in \text{Eff } L(u)$.

Suppose, to the contrary, that $(\lambda_1 x_1, \lambda_2 x_2)$ occurs at point R outside Eff $L(u)$. But then a further reduction in λ_1, and hence in $(\lambda_1 + \lambda_2)/2$, pushes $(\lambda_1 x_1, \lambda_2 x_2)$ to point Q, and so the values of λ_1 and λ_2 leading to point R could not have minimized $(\lambda_1 + \lambda_2)/2$. This minimization process guarantees

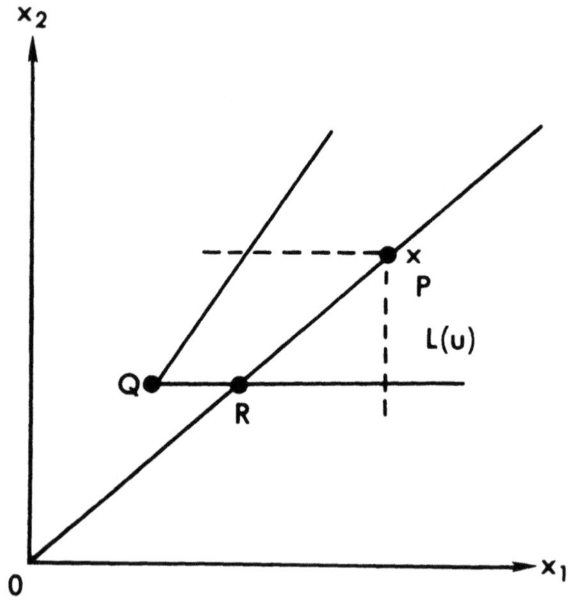

Figure 7-1

that the reference set of the Russell input measure is Eff L(u). In contrast, the Farrell input measure compares point P to point R, since its more restrictive minimization process generates Isoq L(u) as a reference set.

From the definition of the Russell input measure of technical efficiency, it is clear that the minimum exists, and so the measure is well-defined. The properties that the Russell input measures satisfies are summarized in the following theorem

Theorem: If L satisfies (L.1–L.5), then (7.1.4)

$R_i.1$ $R_i(0, x) = 0, x \in R^n_+,$

$R_i.2$ $0 < R_i(u, x) \leqq 1, u \geq 0, (u, x) \in D(R_i),$

$R_i.3$ $R_i(u, \lambda x) \leqq \lambda^{-1} R_i(u, x), \lambda \geqq 1, (u, x) \in D(R_i),$

$R_i.4$ $R_i(\theta u, x) \geqq R_i(u, x), \theta \geqq 1,$

$R_i.5$ $\mathrm{L}(u) \subsetneqq \{x\colon 0 < R_i(u, x) \leqq 1\}, u \geq 0,$

$R_i.6$ $\mathrm{Eff\ L}(u) = \{x\colon R_i(u, x) = 1\}, u \geq 0.$

Proof: Property $R_i.1$ follows from the assumption that $L(0) = R^n_+$.

$R_i.2$: Since $u \geq 0$, $x \geq 0$ for $x \in L(u)$ (see L.1). Thus, since $(u, x) \in D(R_i)$, property $R_i.2$ follows from the definition of the Russell input measure.

$$R_i.3: \ R_i(u, \lambda x) = \min\left\{\sum_{i=1}^{k} \delta_i/k : (\lambda\delta_1 x_1, \lambda\delta_2 x_2, \ldots, \lambda\delta_k x_k; \ldots) \in L(u),\ \delta_i \in [0, 1]\right\},$$

$$= \frac{1}{\lambda}\min\left\{\sum_{i=1}^{k} \lambda\delta_i/k : (\lambda\delta_1 x_1, \lambda\delta_2 x_2, \ldots, \lambda\delta_k x_k; \ldots) \in L(u),\ \lambda\delta_i \in [0, \lambda]\right\},$$

$$\leqq \frac{1}{\lambda}\min\left\{\sum_{i=1}^{k} \mu_i/k : (\mu_1 x_1, \mu_2 x_2, \ldots, \mu_k x_k; \ldots) \in L(u),\ \mu_i \in [0, 1]\right\},$$

$$= \lambda^{-1} R_i(u, x).$$

We note that inequality occurs since $\lambda \geqq 1$.

$R_i.4$: This property follows from the fact that outputs are weakly disposable.

$R_i.5$: Let $x \in L(u)$, $u \geq 0$, then $x \geq 0$ (see L.1), and $R_i(u, x) > 0$. Moreover, from the definition of the Russell input measure, $1 \geqq R_i(u, x)$.

$R_i.6$: Let $x \in \text{Eff } L(u)$, $u \geq 0$, then by L.1, $x \geq 0$. Since x is efficient, there does not exist a $y \in L(u)$ such that $y \leq x$. Thus, $R_i(u, x) = 1$. Next assume that $x \in L(u)$, but $x \notin \text{Eff } L(u)$. Then there exists a $y \in L(u)$ such that $y \leq x$. Thus, $R_i(u, x) < 1$. Finally, assume $x \notin L(u)$. If $\{y: y \leqq x\} \cap L(u)$ is empty, then $(u, x) \in \text{Complement } D(R_i)$, and $R_i(u, x) = +\infty$. Finally, let $\{y: y \leqq x\} \cap L(u) \neq \emptyset$. But then since $x \notin L(u)$, there exists a $y \in L(u)$ such that $y \leq x$. Therefore, $R_i(u, x) < 1$. ■

Properties $R_i.1$ and $R_i.4$ are the same as properties $F_i.1$ and $F_i.4$ of the Farrell input measure of technical efficiency, and share the same interpretation. Property $R_i.2$ differs from $F_i.2$ in that $R_i.2$ shows $R_i(u, x)$ to be bounded above by a value of unity since $\lambda_i \in [0, 1]$, $i = 1, \ldots, k$. Property $R_i.3$ states that the Russell input measure is not homogeneous of degree minus one in inputs. Property $R_i.6$ states that an input vector is technically efficient if and only if the input vector belongs to an efficient subset. Property $R_i.5$ shows that the Russell input measure does not provide a complete characterization of the production technology as given by L(u). However property R_i.5 can be strengthened to provide such a complete characterization if inputs are assumed to be strongly disposable, as the following theorem demonstrates

Theorem: Let L satisfy (L.1–L.5) and L.3.S, then for $u \geq 0$,
$L(u) = \{x: 0 < R_i(u,x) \leqq 1\}$. (7.1.5)

Proof: Since by property R_i.5, $L(u) \subsetneqq \{x: 0 < R_i(u, x) \leqq 1\}$, choose $x \notin L(u)$, $u \geq 0$. Since inputs are strongly disposable, L.3.S holds, and there is no $(\lambda_1, \lambda_2, \ldots, \lambda_k) \leqq 1$, such that $(\lambda_1 x_1, \lambda_2 x_2, \ldots, \lambda_k x_k; \ldots) \in L(u)$. Thus $R_i(u, x) = +\infty$. ■

In general, $F_i(u,x)$ and $R_i(u,x)$ do not assign the same efficiency value to an input vector $x \in L(u)$, $u \geq 0$. This is true even if both $F_i(u,x)$ and $R_i(u, x)$ compare $x \in L(u)$ to an element of Eff L(u), since even then they typically compare $x \in L(u)$ to different elements of Eff L(u). Only when the observed input vector $x \in$ Eff L(u) can one be sure that $F_i(u,x) = R_i(u,x)$, and then of course $F_i(u,x) = R_i(u,x) = 1$. However, it is possible to order the two input measures, as the following theorem demonstrates

Theorem: For $x \in L(u)$, $u \geq 0$, $F_i(u,x) \geqq R_i(u,x)$. (7.1.6)

Proof: Let $(\lambda_1^\circ, \lambda_2^\circ, \ldots, \lambda_k^\circ)$ yield the minimum for $R_i(u, x)$ and $\bar{\lambda}$ yield the minimum for $F_i(u, x)$. Assume $(\Sigma_{i=1}^k \lambda_i^\circ/k) > \bar{\lambda} = (\Sigma_{i=1}^k \bar{\lambda}/k)$. Then choose $\lambda_i^\circ = \bar{\lambda}$, $i = 1, 2, \ldots, k$; (this is possible since $\bar{\lambda} x \in L(u)$, $x \in L(u)$ by assumption) so that $(\Sigma_{i=1}^k \lambda_i^\circ/k)$ is not the minimum for $R_i(u, x)$. This contradicts the definition of $R_i(u, x)$ and shows that $(\Sigma_{i=1}^k \lambda_i^\circ/k) \leqq \bar{\lambda}$. ■

Thus for a technology satisfying (L.1–L.5) an input vector $x \in L(u)$, $u \geq 0$, is at least as efficient by $F_i(u, x)$ as by $R_i(u, x)$. This is so because the reference set for $R_i(u,x)$ is contained in the reference set for $F_i(u,x)$, i.e., Eff $L(u) \subsetneqq$ Isoq L(u), $u \geq 0$.

The next task is to relate $R_i(u,x)$ to $W_i(u,x)$ for $x \in L(u)$, $u \geq 0$. We first demonstrate that $W_i(u,x) \geqq R_i(u,x)$ for $x \in L(u)$, $u \geq 0$, which by (3.3.9) implies that $F_i(u, x) \geqq W_i(u, x) \geqq R_i(u, x)$. This relationship corresponds to the fact that Isoq L(u) $\supseteqq$ WEff L(u) $\supseteqq$ Eff L(u). We first need the following lemmata

Lemma: Let L satisfy (L.1–L.5), then Eff L(u) = Eff $L^{SI}(u)$,
where $L^{SI}(u) := \{x: x = y + z, y \in L(u), z \in R_+^n\}$. (7.1.7)

Lemma: If $x \in L(u)$, $u \geq 0$, and $x \notin \text{Eff } L(u)$, then $R_i(u, x)$ compares x to some $x^\circ \in \text{Eff } L(u)$. (7.1.8)

The proof of lemma (7.1.7) is a direct generalization of Färe (1975; Proposition 2, p. 319). To prove lemma (7.1.8), assume that $(\lambda_1^\circ, \lambda_2^\circ, \ldots, \lambda_k^\circ)$ is the vector of scalars that determines $R_i(u, x)$. We need to show that $(\lambda_1^\circ x_1, \lambda_2^\circ x_2, \ldots \lambda_k^\circ x_k; \ldots) \in \text{Eff } L(u)$, $u \geq 0$, so that $x \in L(u)$ is compared with an efficient input vector. Assume that $(\lambda_1^\circ x_1, \lambda_2^\circ x_2, \ldots, \lambda_k^\circ x_k; \ldots) \notin \text{Eff } L(u)$. Then there is a $y \in L(u)$, $y \leq (\lambda_1^\circ x_1, \lambda_2^\circ x_2, \ldots, \lambda_k^\circ x_k; \ldots)$ implying that $(\lambda_1^\circ, \lambda_2^\circ, \ldots, \lambda_k^\circ)$ is not the vector that determines $R_i(u, x)$. This contradiction shows that lemma (7.1.8) holds.

Using these results, we can now state

Theorem: For $x \in L(u)$, $u \geq 0$, $W_i(u, x) \geqq R_i(u, x)$. (7.1.9)

Proof: From lemmata (7.1.7) and (7.1.8) we have that $R_i(u, x)$ for $x \in L(u)$, $u \geq 0$, equals $R_i(u, x)$ for $x \in L^{SI}(u)$, $u \geq 0$. Next, since $L^{SI}(u)$ satisfies strong disposability of inputs, $F_i(u, x) = W_i(u, x)$ for $x \in L^{SI}(u)$. Therefore by theorem (7.1.6), $W_i(u, x) \geqq R_i(u, x)$. ■

This result, in conjunction with (3.3.9), suffices to establish the ordering $F_i(u, x) \geqq W_i(u, x) \geqq R_i(u, x)$. Furthermore, as noted in the proof of theorem (7.1.9), since $R_i(u, x)$ computes the efficiency of $x \in L(u)$ relative to some $x^\circ \in \text{Eff } L(u)$, it yields the same efficiency value whether measured relative to a technology satisfying weak or strong disposability of inputs. This explains why there is no need for separate measures of weak technical efficiency and congestion when the nonradial Russell measure of technical efficiency is used. This result will also prove particularly useful in the computation of $R_i(u, x)$ by programming techniques in section 7.5.

We now consider a decomposition of overall input efficiency into technical and allocative components. The overall input efficiency measure was introduced in chapter 3, section 4, and remains applicable here. Thus, using definition (3.4.4) and theorem (3.4.5), $O_i(u, x, p) = Q(u, p)/px$ measures the ratio of the minimum cost of producing output vector u at input prices p to the actual cost of producing output vector u with input vector x at input prices p. However since the Russell input measure of technical efficiency is not a radial measure, it does not possess a natural cost interpretation as the radial Farrell input measure does. Consequently the Russell input measure of technical efficiency must be modified if a decomposition of $O_i(u, x, p)$ into technical and allocative components is to be achieved. This we do in the following

Definition: For $x \in L(u)$, $u \geq 0$, $p \in R^n_{++}$, let $x^\circ \in$ Eff $L(u)$ be the input vector that is obtained as the solution to the Russell input measure of technical efficiency, i.e., $x^\circ = (\lambda_1^\circ x_1, \ldots \lambda_k^\circ x_k; \ldots)$ where $(\Sigma_{i=1}^k \lambda_i^\circ/k) = R_i(u, x)$. Then $R_i^c(u, x, p): = px^\circ/px$ is called the Russell Input Cost Measure of Technical Efficiency. (7.1.10)

It follows directly from definition (7.1.10) that allocative efficiency may be obtained from $O_i(u, x, p)$ and $R_i^c(u, x, p)$ by means of the ratio

$$A_i^c(u, x, p): = O_i(u, x, p)/R_i^c(u, x, p) = Q(u, p)/px^\circ. \tag{7.1.11}$$

It should be emphasized that the overall input efficiency measure $O_i(u, x, p) = Q(u, p)/px$ is defined independently of the particular input measure of technical efficiency being used. However since $F_i(u, x)$ and $R_i(u, x)$, typically yield different values of technical input efficiency, they typically generate different decompositions of $O_i(u, x, p)$.

7.2 The Russell Output Measure of Technical Efficiency

In order to define a Russell output measure of technical efficiency on the output correspondence satisfying (P.1–P.5), we need the following notation

$$(u_1, u_2, \ldots, u_l; \ldots). \tag{7.2.1}$$

This denotes the output vector $u \in R^m_+$ with $u_i > 0$ for $u = 1, 2, \ldots, l; l \leqq m$, and $u_i = 0$ for $i = l + 1, l + 2, \ldots, m$. With this notation we can define the effective domain of the Russell output measure R_o as

$D(R_o): = \{(x, u): \exists\, \theta_i \geqq 1,\ i = 1, 2, \ldots, l$, such that $(\theta_1 u_1, \theta_2 u_2, \ldots, \theta_l u_l; \ldots) \in P(x)\}$. (7.2.2)

The Russell output measure may now be defined.

Definition: The function R_o: $R^n_+ \times R^m_+ \rightarrow R_+ \cup \{+\infty\}$ defined by

$$R_o(x, u) := \begin{cases} \max\left\{ \sum_{i=1}^{l} \theta_i/l;\ (\theta_1 u_1, \theta_2 u_2, \ldots, \theta_l u_l; \ldots) \in \right. \\ \left. P(x),\ \theta_i \geqq 1 \right\},\ (x, u) \in D(R_o), \\ +\infty,\ (x, u) \in \text{Complement } D(R_o), \end{cases} \tag{7.2.3}$$

is called the Russell Output Measure of Technical Efficiency.

To illustrate this definition, consider Fig. 7–2.

Let $u \in P(x)$ at point P. Then the Russell output measure of technical efficiency maximizes $(\theta_1 + \theta_2)/2$ under the conditions that $\theta_i \geqq 1, i = 1, 2$, i.e., that $(\theta_1 u_1, \theta_2 u_2)$ belongs to the region to the northeast of P, and that $(\theta_1 u_1, \theta_2 u_2)$ remains in P(x). The resulting technically efficient output vector occurs at point B, the efficient subset of P(x). If the efficient subset of P(x) contains more than one vector, then $(\theta_1 u_1, \theta_2 u_2) \in$ Eff P(x).

Suppose, to the contrary, that $(\theta_1 u_1, \theta_2 u_2)$ occurs at point C outside Eff P(x). But a further increase in θ_2, and hence $(\theta_1 + \theta_2)/2$, is possible such that $(\theta_1 u_1, \theta_2 u_2)$ is pushed to point B, and so the values of θ_1 and θ_2 leading to

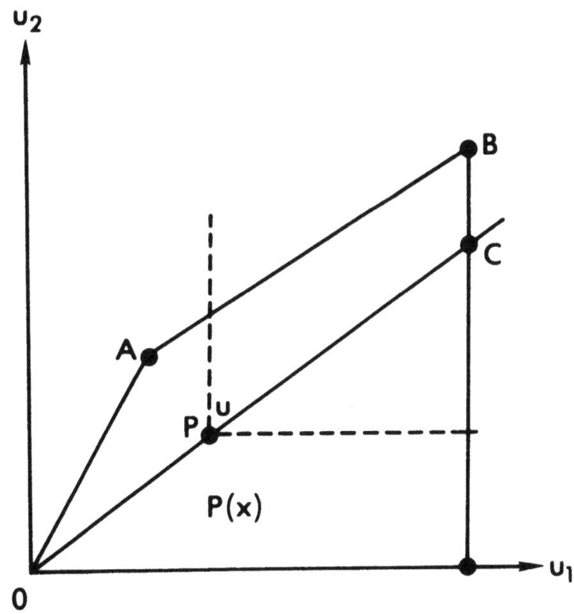

Figure 7-2

point B could not have maximized $(\theta_1 + \theta_2)/2$. This maximization process guarantees that the reference set of the Russell output measure is Eff P(x). In contrast, the Farrell output measure compares point P to point C, since its more restrictive maximization process generates Isoq P(x) as its reference set.

From the definition of the Russell output measure of technical efficiency, it is clear that the maximum exists, and thus the measure is well-defined. The properties that the Russell output measure satisfies are summarized below

Theorem: If P satisfies (P.1–P.5), then (7.2.4)

$R_o.1$ $R_o(0, u) = +\infty$,

$R_o.2$ $R_o(x, u) \geqq 1$, $(x, u) \in D(R_o)$, $P(x) \neq \{0\}$,

$R_o.3$ $R_o(x, \theta u) \geqq \theta^{-1} R_o(x, u)$, $\theta \in (0, 1]$, $(x, u) \in D(R_o)$,

$R_o.4$ $R_o(\lambda x, u) \geqq R_o(x, u)$, $\lambda \geqq 1$,

$R_o.5$ $P(x) \subsetneqq \{u: R_o(x, u) \geqq 1\}$, $P(x) \neq \{0\}$,

$R_o.6$ Eff $P(x) = \{u: R_o(x, u) = 1\}$, $P(x) \neq \{0\}$.

Proof: Property $R_o.1$ follows from P.1.

$R_o.2$: Since $P(x) \neq \{0\}$, this property follows from the definition of the Russell output measure.

$$\begin{aligned}
R_o.3: R_o(x, \theta u) &= \max\{\sum_{i=1}^{l} \delta_i/l: (\theta\delta_1 u_1, \theta\delta_2 u_2, \ldots, \theta\delta_l u_l; \ldots) \in \\
&\quad P(x), \delta_i \geqq 1\} \\
&= \frac{1}{\theta}\max\{\sum_{i=1}^{l} \theta\delta_i/l: (\theta\delta_1 u_1, \theta\delta_2 u_2, \ldots, \theta\delta_l u_l; \ldots) \in \\
&\quad P(x), \theta\delta_i \geqq \theta\} \\
&\geqq \frac{1}{\theta}\max\{\sum_{i=1}^{l} \mu_i/l: (\mu_1 u_1, \mu_2 u_2, \ldots, \mu_l u_l; \ldots) \in \\
&\quad P(x), \mu_i \geqq 1\} \\
&= \theta^{-1} R_o(x, u).
\end{aligned}$$

We note that the inequality occurs since $\theta \in (0, 1]$.

$R_o.4$: This property follows from weak disposability of inputs.

$R_o.5$: Let $u \in P(x) \neq \{0\}$. Then from the definition of the Russell input measure, $R_o(x, u) \geqq 1$.

R_o.6: Let $u \in$ Eff P(x), P(x) $\neq \{0\}$. Since u is efficient, there does not exist a $v \in$ P(x), $v \geq u$. Thus $R_o(x, u) = 1$. Next, assume $u \in$ P(x), $u \notin$ Eff P(x). Then there exists a $v \in$ P(x), with $v \geq u$, and thus $R_o(x, u) > 1$. Finally, assume that $u \notin$ P(x), if $\{v: v \geqq u\} \cap$ P(x) is empty, then $R_o(x, u) = +\infty$, thus let $\{v: v \geqq u\} \cap$ P(x) be nonempty. But since $u \notin$ P(x), there exists a $v \in$ P(x), $v \geq u$. Thus $R_o(x, u) > 1$. ■

Properties R_o.1 and R_o.4 are the same as properties F_o.1 and F_o.4 of the Farrell output measure of technical efficiency. Property R_o.2 differs from property F_o.2 in that $R_o(x, u)$ is bounded below by unity since $\theta_i \geqq 1$, $i = 1, \ldots, l$. Property R_o.3 states that the Russell output measure is not homogeneous of degree minus one in outputs. Property R_o.6 states that the Russell output measure calls an output vector technically efficient if and only if it belongs to an efficient subset. Property R_o.5 shows that the Russell output measure does not fully characterize the production technology as given by P(x). However property R_o.5 can be strengthened so as to provide such a complete characterization if outputs are assumed to be strongly disposable, as the following theorem demonstrates.

Theorem: Let P satisfy (P.1–P.5) and P.5.S, then for P(x) $\neq \{0\}$, P(x) $= \{u: R_o(x, u) \geqq 1\}$. (7.2.5)

Proof: By property R_o.5, P(x) $\subseteqq \{u: R_o(x, u) \geqq 1\}$. Assume $u \notin$ P(x). Since inputs are strongly disposable, P.5.S holds, and there is no $(\theta_1, \theta_2, \ldots, \theta_l) \geqq 1$ such that $(\theta_1 u_1, \theta_2 u_2, \ldots, \theta_l u_l; \ldots) \in$ P(x). Thus $R_o(x, u) = +\infty$. ■

In general, the Farrell and the Russell output measures do not assign the same technical efficiency value to an output vector $u \in$ P(x), although if $u \in$ Eff P(x) it is true that $F_o(u, x) = R_o(x, u) = 1$. However it is possible to order the two output measures, as the following theorem demonstrates

Theorem: For $u \geq 0$, $u \in$ P(x), $F_o(x, u) \leqq R_o(x, u)$. (7.2.6)

Proof: Let $(\theta_1^\circ, \theta_2^\circ, \ldots, \theta_l^\circ)$ yield the maximum for $R_o(x, u)$ and $\bar{\theta}$ yield the maximum for $F_o(x, u)$. Assume that $(\sum_{i=1}^{l} \theta_i^\circ/l) < \bar{\theta}$. Then choose $\theta_i^\circ = \bar{\theta}$, $i = 1, 2, \ldots, l$ (this is possible since $\bar{\theta}u \in$ P(x)) so that $(\sum_{i=1}^{l} \theta_i^\circ/l)$ is not the maximum for $R_o(x, u)$. This contradiction shows that $F_o(x, u) \leqq R_o(x, u)$. ■

The next task is to relate $R_o(x, u)$ to $W_o(x, u)$. For this purpose the following two lemmata are needed

Lemma: Let L satisfy (L.1–L.5), then Eff P(x) = Eff $P^{SO}(x)$, where $P^{SO}(x) := (\text{Eff } P(x) + R^m_-) \cap R^m_+$. (7.2.7)

Proof: It has been shown elsewhere (Färe and Shephard, 1977), that $P^{SO}(x)$ satisfies strong disposability of outputs. From the definition of $P^{SO}(x)$, it is clear that Eff P(x) $\subseteqq$ Eff $P^{SO}(x)$. Thus assume that $u \notin$ Eff P(x). That implies, however, that $u \notin P^{SO}(x)$. Therefore, Eff P(x) = Eff $P^{SO}(x)$. ■

Lemma: If $u \in P(x), u \geq 0$, and $u \notin$ Eff P(x), then $R_o(x, u)$ compares u to some $u° \in$ Eff P(x). (7.2.8)

The proof is omitted since it closely follows the proof of lemma (7.1.8).

As a consequence of these two lemmata, we note that in calculating the Russell output measure of technical efficiency we can use either the strongly disposable or the weakly disposable representation of technology. This is because $R_o(x, u)$ calculates the efficiency of $u \in P(x)$ to some $u° \in$ Eff P(x). Since $R_o(u, x)$ bypasses Isoq P(x) and WEff P(x) and goes directly to Eff P(x) for its reference sets there is no need to develop measures of weak technical efficiency or congestion. We now use the two lemmata to prove

Theorem: For $u \in P(x), u \neq 0, R_o(x, u) \geqq W_o(x, u)$. (7.2.9)

Proof: From lemmata (7.2.7) and (7.2.8) we have that $R_o(u, x), u \in P(x), u \neq 0$, is the same as $R_o(u, x)$ for $u \in P^{SO}(x), u \neq 0$. Next, since $P^{SO}(x)$ satisfies strong disposability of outputs, $F_o(u, x) = R_o(u, x)$ (theorem (4.3.11)). Therefore by theorem (7.2.6), $R_o(x, u) \geqq W_o(x, u)$. ■

This theorem, together with the observation that $W_o(x, u) \geqq F_o(x, u)$ (see (4.3.9)), implies that for $u \in P(x), u \neq 0, R_o(x, u) \geqq W_o(x, u) \geqq F_o(x, u)$. This relation is the reverse of the relation among the three subsets Eff P(x), WEff P(x), and Isoq P(x), since Eff P(x) $\subseteqq$ WEff P(x) $\subseteqq$ Isoq P(x).

Since the Russell output measure of technical efficiency is not a radial measure, we cannot obtain a natural decomposition of overall output efficiency into a price-independent Russell output measure of technical efficiency and a price-dependent allocative measure. Consequently $R_o(x, u)$ must be modified if such a decomposition is to be achieved.

Definition: For $u \in P(x), u \neq 0, r \in R^m_+, r \neq 0$, let $u° = (\theta_1^\circ u_1, \ldots, \theta_i^\circ u_i; \ldots) \in$ Eff P(x) be the output vector that yields the Russell output measure of technical efficiency, i.e.,

$(\sum_{i=1}^{l} \theta_i^o/l) = R_o(x, u)$. Then $R_o^r(x, u, r) := ru^o/ru$ is called the Russell Output Revenue Measure of Technical Efficiency. (7.2.10)

From chapter 4, section 4, the overall output efficiency measure is $O_o(x, u, r) = R(x, r)/ru$, $ru > 0$. It follows immediately that an allocative output efficiency measure can be obtained from $O_o(x, u, r)$ and $R_o^r(x, u, r)$ by means of the ratio

$$A_o^r(x, u, r) := O_o(x, u, r)/R_o^r(x, u, r) = R(x, r)/ru^o. \quad (7.2.11)$$

Note that the use of $R_o^r(x, u, r)$ instead of $F_o(x, u)$ leads to a different decomposition of the same overall output efficiency measure $O_o(x, u, r)$ into technical and allocative components.

7.3 The Russell Graph Measure of Technical Efficiency

In order to define a Russell graph measure of technical efficiency for a technology whose graph satisfies (GR.1–GR.5), we need the following notation

$$(x_1, x_2, \ldots, x_k; \ldots, u_1, u_2, \ldots, u_l; \ldots) \quad (7.3.1)$$

This denotes an input-output vector $(x, u) \in R_+^{n+m}$ with $x_i > 0, i = 1, \ldots, k$; $x_i = 0, i = k+1, \ldots, n$; and $u_i > 0, i = 1, \ldots, l$; $u_i = 0, i = l+1, \ldots, m$. With this notation we can introduce the effective domain of the Russell graph measure R_g as

$$D(R_g) := \{(x, u): \exists\, \lambda_i \in [0, 1], i = 1, 2, \ldots, k, \text{ and } \mu_j \in (0, 1], j = 1, 2, \ldots, l, \text{ such that } (\lambda_1 x_1, \lambda_2 x_2, \ldots, \lambda_\kappa x_k; \ldots, \mu_1^{-1} u_1, \mu_2^{-1} u_2, \ldots, \mu_l^{-1} u_l; \ldots) \in GR\}. \quad (7.3.2)$$

The Russell graph measure can now be defined.

Definition: The function $R_g: R_+^n \times R_+^m \rightarrow R_+ \cup \{+\infty\}$ defined by (7.3.3)

$$R_g(x, u) := \begin{cases} \min\left\{ \left(\dfrac{\sum_{i=1}^{k} \lambda_i + \sum_{j=1}^{l} \mu_j}{k + l} \right) : (\lambda_1 x_1, \lambda_2 x_2, \ldots, \right. \\ \quad \lambda_k x_k; \ldots, \mu_1^{-1} u_1, \mu_2^{-1} u_2, \ldots, \mu_l^{-1} u_l; \ldots) \in \mathrm{GR}, \\ \quad \left. \lambda_i, \mu_j \in (0, 1] \right\}, (x, u) \in D(R_g), \\ +\infty, (x, u) \in \text{Complement } D(R_g), \end{cases}$$

is called the Russell Graph Measure of Technical Efficiency.

The Russell graph measure is illustrated in Fig. 7–3. For (x, u) in the graph at point P, $R_g(x, u)$ minimizes $(\lambda + \mu)/2$ under the conditions that $(\lambda, \mu) \in (0, 1]$ and that $(\lambda x, \mu^{-1} u)$ belongs to the graph, i.e., that the minimizing input-output vector must belong to the intersection of the region to the northwest of point P and the graph. The path traced out by $R_g(x, u)$ is a hyperbola but not necessarily a rectangular hyperbola. If the minimizing values of λ and μ are equal, then the path is a rectangular hyperbola, and consequently $R_g(x, u) = F_g(x, u)$. Even if the minimizing values of λ and μ

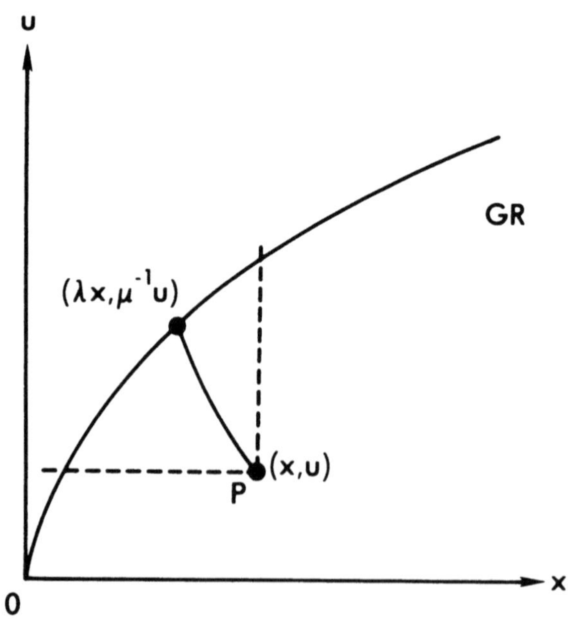

Figure 7-3

are not equal, in the single-output, single-input case $R_g(x, u)$ and $F_g^G(x, u)$ are equal. It is in the multiple-output, multiple-input case that $R_g(x, u)$ is a generalization of $F_g^G(x, u)$, which in turn is a generalization of $F_g(x, u)$.

From the definition of the Russell graph measure and from properties (GR.1–GR.5), it is clear that the Russell graph measure is well-defined. In addition, this graph measure satisfies the properties summarized in the following theorem

Theorem: If GR satisfies (GR.1–GR.5), then

$$
\begin{aligned}
&R_g.1\ R_g(0, 0) = 0,\\
&R_g.2\ 0 < R_g(x, u) \leqq 1,\ u \geq 0,\ (x, u) \in D(R_g),\\
&R_g.3\ R_g(\theta x, \theta^{-1} u) \leqq \theta^{-1} R_g(x, u),\ \theta \geqq 1,\ (x, u) \in D(R_g),\\
&R_g.4\ R_g(\lambda x, u) \leqq R_g(x, u),\ \lambda \geqq 1,\\
&R_g.5\ R_g(x, \theta u) \leqq R_g(x, u),\ \theta \in [0, 1],\\
&R_g.6\ \text{GR} \subseteqq \{(x, u)\colon 0 < R_g(x, u) \leqq 1\},\ u \geq 0,\\
&R_g.7\ \text{Eff GR} = \{(x, u)\colon R_g(x, u) = 1\},\ u \geq 0.
\end{aligned} \tag{7.3.4}
$$

Proof: Property $R_g.1$ follows from $0 \in \text{GR}$ and the definition of R_g.

$R_g.2$: This property follows from the definition of R_g.

$$
\begin{aligned}
R_g.3\colon R_g(\theta x, \theta^{-1} u) = \min\{ &\left(\frac{\sum_{i=1}^{k} \lambda_i + \sum_{j=1}^{l} \mu_j}{k + l} \right) \colon (\theta\lambda_1 x_1, \theta\lambda_2 x_2, \ldots,\\
&\theta\lambda_k x_k; \ldots, (\theta\mu_1)^{-1} u_1, (\theta\mu_2)^{-1} u_2, \ldots,\\
&\quad (\theta\mu_l)^{-1} u_l; \ldots)\\
&\in \text{GR},\ \lambda_i,\ \mu_j \in (0, 1]\}.\\
= \frac{1}{\theta}\min\{ &\left(\frac{\sum_{i=1}^{k} \theta\lambda_i + \sum_{j=1}^{l} \theta\mu_j}{k + l} \right) \colon (\theta\lambda_1 x_1, \theta\lambda_2 x_2, \ldots,\\
&\theta\lambda_k x_k; \ldots, (\theta\mu_1)^{-1} u_1, (\theta\mu_2)^{-1} u_2, \ldots,\\
&(\theta\mu_l)^{-1} u_l; \ldots) \in \text{GR},\ \theta\lambda_i,\ \theta\mu_j \in (0, \theta]\}\\
\leqq \theta^{-1} &R_g(x, u).
\end{aligned}
$$

We note that the inequality occurs since $\theta \geqq 1$.

R_g.4: This property follows from the definition of the Russell graph measure R_g and property GR.3.

R_g.5: Follows from property GR.5 and the definition of $R_g(x, u)$.

R_g.6: Let $(x, u) \in \text{GR}$, $u \geq 0$. Then $x \geq 0$ and $R_g(x, u) > 0$. Moreover, from the definition of $R_g(x, u)$ and $(x, u) \in \text{GR}$, $R_g(x, u) \geq 1$.

R_g.7: Let $(x, u) \in \text{Eff GR}$, $u \geq 0$. $u \geq 0$ implies that $x \geq 0$, (see GR.1). Now since $(x, u) \in \text{Eff GR}$, there does not exist a vector $(y, v) \in \text{GR}$ such that $(y, -v) \leq (x, -u)$. Thus, $R_g(x, u) = 1$. Next assume $(x, u) \in \text{GR}$, such that $(y, -v) \leq (x, -u)$. Therefore, $R_g(x, u) < 1$. Finally, assume that $(x, u) \notin \text{GR}$. If $\{(y, v):(y, -v) \leqq (x, -u)\} \cap \text{GR}$ is empty, then $R_g(x, u) = +\infty$, by definition. If this intersection is nonempty, then there exists a $(y, v) \in \text{GR}$, $(y, -v) \leq (x, -u)$. Thus $R_g(x, u) < 1$. ■

Properties R_g.1, R_g.4, and R_g.5 are the same as properties F_g.1, F_g.4, and F_g.5 of the Farrell graph measure of technical efficiency. Property R_g.2 states that $R_g(x, u)$ is positive and bounded above by unity since $(\lambda_i, \mu_j \in (0, 1]$. Property R_g.3 shows that $R_g(x, u)$ is not homogeneous of degree minus one in (x, u) since it is a nonradial measure. Property R_g.7 states that $R_g(x, u)$ terms an input-output vector technically efficient if and only if it belongs to the efficient subset of the graph. Property R_g.6 states that the graph is contained among the input-output vectors that yield $R_g(x, u) \in (0, 1]$. This property can be strengthened by assuming strong disposability of both inputs and outputs, i.e., that GR.6 holds in addition to (GR.1–GR.5), as we now demonstrate.

Theorem: Let GR satisfy (GR.1–GR.6), then for $u \geq 0$,
$$\text{GR} = \{(x, u): 0 < R_g(x, u) \leqq 1\}. \tag{7.3.5}$$

Proof: By property R_g.6, $\text{GR} \subseteq \{(x, u): 0 < R_g(x, u) \leqq 1\}$. Thus assume that $(x, u) \notin \text{GR}$. Then since GR.6 holds, there is no $(\lambda_1, \lambda_2, \ldots, \lambda_k; \ldots, \theta_1, \theta_2, \ldots, \theta_l; \ldots) \leqq 1$, such that $(\lambda_1 x_1, \lambda_2 x_2, \ldots, \lambda_k x_k; \ldots, \theta_1^{-1} u_1, \theta_2^{-1} u_2, \ldots, \theta_l^{-1} u_l; \ldots) \in \text{GR}$. Thus $R_g(x, u) = +\infty$. ■

If an input-output vector belongs to the efficient subset of the graph, then the Farrell and Russell graph measures yield the same value, namely unity. In general, however, they assign different efficiency values to an input-output vector. In fact

Theorem: For $(x, u) \in \text{GR}$, $u \geq 0$, $F_g(x, u) \geqq R_g(x, u)$. (7.3.6)

Proof: Let $(\lambda_1^\circ, \lambda_2^\circ, \ldots, \lambda_k^\circ; \ldots, \mu_1^\circ, \mu_2^\circ, \ldots, \mu_l^\circ; \ldots)$ yield the minimum for $R_g(x, u)$ and $\bar{\lambda}$ yield the minimum for $F_g(x, u)$. Assume $(\sum_{i=1}^{k} \lambda_i^\circ + \sum_{j=1}^{l} \mu_j^\circ)/(k + l) > \bar{\lambda}$. Then choose $\lambda_i^\circ = \mu_j^\circ = \bar{\lambda}$. This is possible since $(\bar{\lambda}x, \bar{\lambda}^{-1}u) \in GR$. Hence $(\lambda_1^\circ, \lambda_2^\circ, \ldots, \lambda_k^\circ; \ldots, \mu_1^\circ, \mu_2^\circ, \ldots, \mu_l^\circ; \ldots)$ does not yield the minimum for $R_g(x, u)$. This contradiction proves the theorem. ■

In order to investigate the relationship between the weak graph measure and the Russell graph measure, the following lemmata are useful

Lemma: For $u \geq 0$, if $(x, u) \in \text{Eff GR}$, then $x \in \text{Eff L}(u)$ and $u \in \text{Eff P}(x)$. (7.3.7)

Proof: The proof is given in contrapositive form. Thus there are three cases to consider: (i) $x \in \text{Eff L}(u)$ but $u \notin \text{Eff P}(x)$, (ii) $u \in \text{Eff P}(x)$ but $x \notin \text{Eff L}(u)$ and (iii) $x \notin \text{Eff L}(u)$ and $u \notin \text{Eff P}(x)$. (i) Assume $x \in \text{Eff L}(u)$ but $u \notin \text{Eff P}(x)$. Since $x \in \text{Eff L}(u)$, then it follows that $x \in L(u)$ and $u \in P(x)$. Therefore, since $u \notin \text{Eff P}(x)$, there exists a $v \in P(x)$, such that $v \geq u$. Thus $(x, v) \in GR$ and since $(x, u) \in GR$ and $(x, -v) \leq (x, -u)$, $(x, u) \notin \text{Eff GR}$. (ii) Assume $u \in \text{Eff P}(x)$ but $x \notin \text{Eff L}(u)$. Since $u \in \text{Eff P}(x)$, $x \in L(u)$, and since $u \geq 0$, $x \geq 0$. Therefore, since $x \notin \text{Eff L}(u)$, there exists a $y \in L(u)$, $y \leq x$. Thus $(y, u) \in GR$ and since $(y, -u) \leq (x, -u)$, $(x, u) \notin \text{Eff GR}$. (iii) Assume that $x \notin \text{Eff L}(u)$ or $u \notin \text{Eff P}(x)$. If $x \notin L(u)$, then $(x, u) \notin GR$, thus $(x, u) \notin \text{Eff GR}$. Instead, assume that $x \in L(u)$ and $u \in P(x)$. Since $u \notin \text{Eff P}(x)$, there exists a $v \in P(x)$, such that $v \geq u$. Thus, $(x, v) \in GR$, and, since $(x, u) \in GR$ and $(x, -v) \leq (x, -u)$, then $(x, u) \notin \text{Eff GR}$. ■

Lemma: Assume that either inputs or outputs are strongly disposable (i.e., L.3.S or L.5.S hold). For $u \geq 0$, if $x \in \text{Eff L}(u)$ and $u \in \text{Eff P}(x)$, then $(x, u) \in \text{Eff GR}$. (7.3.8)

Proof: The proof is given in contrapositive form. Thus assume $(x, u) \notin \text{Eff GR}$. If $(x, u) \notin GR$, the theorem holds. Thus let $(x, u) \in GR$. Since (x, u) is not efficient and $u \geq 0$, there exists an input-output vector $(y, v) \in GR$ such that $(y, -v) \leq (x, -u)$. This inequality yields three cases: (i) $y \leq x$ and $u = v$, (ii) $u \leq v$ and $x = y$, and (iii) $y \leq x$ and $u \leq v$. In case (i) since $y \leq x$ and $x, y \in L(u) = L(v)$, $x \notin \text{Eff L}(u)$, for case (ii), since $u \leq v$ and $u, v \in P(x) = P(y)$, $u \notin \text{Eff P}(x)$. In the last case, we first let outputs be strongly disposable, then $L(v) \subsetneqq L(u)$ since $v \geq u$. Thus $y \in L(u)$ and $x \in L(u)$ but y

$\leq x$, therefore $x \notin$ Eff L(u). Finally, in case (iii), let inputs be strongly disposable, then P(x) $\supseteqq$ P(y) since $x \geq y$. Thus, $v \in$ P(y) $\supseteqq$ P(x), and, since $v \geq u$, $u \notin$ Eff P(x). ■

For both the Russell input and output measures it was proved that for a feasible nonefficient vector, to measure the degree of inefficiency, that vector was compared to an efficient vector. A similar result holds for the graph measure (the proof follows the earlier ones and is omitted).

Lemma: If $(x, u) \in$ GR, $u \geq 0$, and $(x, u) \notin$ Eff GR, then $R_g(x, u)$ compares (x, u) to some $(x^\circ, u^\circ) \in$ Eff GR. (7.3.9)

The following relationship holds between the weak efficient graph measure and the Russell graph measure

Theorem: Let inputs or outputs be strongly disposable, (i.e., L.3.S or L.5.S hold). For $(x, u) \in$ GR, $u \geq 0$, $W_g(x, u) \geqq R_g(x, u)$. (7.3.10)

Proof: From lemmata (7.1.7), (7.2.7), and (7.3.8), we have that if inputs and outputs are strongly disposable, then $R_g(x, u)$ equals $W_g(x, u)$, where $R_g(x, u)$ is a Russell measure given that inputs or outputs are strongly disposable. Thus by theorems (5.3.9) and (7.3.6), $W_g(x, u) \geqq R_g(x, u)$ if inputs or outputs are strongly disposable. ■

Since the Russell graph measure of technical efficiency is not a radial measure, it cannot be used to obtain a decomposition of overall graph efficiency into a price-independent Russell graph measure of technical efficiency and a price-dependent allocative measure. Hence we suggest the following modification of the Russell graph measure

Definition: Let $(x, u) \in$ GR, $u \geq 0$, $(p, r) \in R^{n+m}_{++}$ and let (x°, u°) be the technically efficient input-output vector that the Russell graph measure compares (x, u) with, i.e., $(\sum_{i=1}^{k} \lambda_i^\circ + \sum_{j=1}^{l} \mu_j^\circ)/(k + l) = R_g(x, u)$. Then $R_g^\pi(x, u, p, r) := (ru^\circ - px^\circ)/(ru - px)$ is called the Russell Graph Profit Measure of Technical Efficiency. (7.3.11)

Now let $O_g(x, u, p, r)$ as defined in chapter 5, section 4 be the overall graph measure of efficiency. An allocative graph efficiency measure can now be defined as the ratio

$$A_g(x, u, p, r) := O_g(x, u, p, r)/R_g^{\pi}(x, u, p, r). \qquad (7.3.12)$$

7.4 Comparison of Russell Measures

We can only compare the three Russell measures when efficiency is implied. Specifically, we have

Theorem: For $u \geq 0$, $(x, u) \in \text{GR}$, if $R_g(x, u) = 1$ then $R_i(u, x) = R_o(x, u) = 1$. (7.4.1)

Theorem: Let inputs or outputs be strongly disposable (i.e., L.3.S or L.5.S hold). For $u \geq 0$, $(x, u) \in \text{GR}$, if $R_i(u, x) = R_o(x, u) = 1$ then $R_g(x, u) = 1$. (7.4.2)

The proofs of these theorems follow from lemmata (7.3.7) and (7.3.8), respectively.

7.5 Computing the Russell Measures

In this section we construct linear programming examples of the Russell input, Russell output, and Russell graph measures discussed in the previous sections of this chapter. In calculating these measures, we use the same data used in previous chapters for the input, output, and graph measures.

For all of the Russell measures, it should be noted that specification of the linear programming problem is complicated by the nature of the objective function. The complication arises because the measure is not a simple radial expansion or contraction of the observed point, but rather a more complicated vector operation.

In constructing the Russell input measure, we note that from lemmata (7.1.7) and (7.1.8) it follows that the value of $R_i(u, x)$ does not change whether measured relative to the weakly or strongly disposable technology. Thus, we measure $R_i(u, x)$ relative to the following linear technology satisfying strong disposability of inputs and outputs

$$\text{L}^{\text{S}}(u) := \{x : z \cdot \text{M} \geqq u, z \cdot \text{N} \leqq x, z \in R_{+}^{k}\}, \qquad (7.5.1)$$

where the matrices N and M are as in chapter 2, and z is the intensity vector. Following definition (7.1.3) of the Russell input measure, we can specify the following programming problem

$$\text{minimize} \sum_{i=1}^{k} \lambda_i/k$$
$$\text{subject to}$$
$$z \cdot \mathrm{N} \leqq \lambda \odot x^{\circ}$$
$$z \cdot \mathrm{M} \geqq u^{\circ}$$
$$\lambda_i \in [0, 1], i = 1, 2, \ldots, k; z \in R_+^k, \tag{7.5.2}$$

where $\odot$ denotes component-wise multiplication of the λ and x vectors (see the mathematical appendix).

The data (reproduced from chapter 3) and the corresponding values of the Russell input measure calculated using (7.5.2) are summarized in Table 7-1.

As for the case of the Russell input measure, we can calculate the Russell output measure relative to a technology satisfying either weak or strong disposability of outputs, i.e., $R_o(x, u)$ is invariant with the type of disposability of outputs (see lemmata (7.2.7) and (7.2.8)). Thus we can apply the definition of the Russell output measure of efficiency to the strongly disposable technology and specify the following linear programming problem

$$\text{maximize} \sum_{i=1}^{l} \theta_i/l$$

Table 7-1

	Output	Inputs		
Firm	(u)	(x_1)	(x_2)	$R_i(u, x)$
1	2	2	1	1.00
2	2	2	2	.75
3	2	1	2	1.00
4	2	3	1	.83
5	2	4	1	.75
6	2	1.25	3	.73
7	2	1.25	4	.65

subject to

$$z \cdot \mathrm{N} \leqq x^\circ$$
$$z \cdot \mathrm{M} \geqq \theta \odot u^\circ$$
$$z \in R^k_+$$
$$\theta_i \geqq 0,\ i = 1, \ldots, l, \qquad (7.5.4)$$

where the maximum is the Russell output measure.

The data (reproduced from chapter 4) and the corresponding values of the Russell output measure calculated using (7.5.3) are summarized in Table 7–2.

Based on definition (7.3.3) of the Russell graph measure and employing the strongly disposable technology used in chapter 5,[1] we can calculate the Russell graph measure from the following nonlinear programming problem

$$\text{minimize } \Big(\sum_{i=1}^{k} \lambda_i + \sum_{j=1}^{l} \mu_j\Big)/(k + l)$$

subject to

$$z \cdot \mathrm{N} \leqq \lambda \odot x^\circ$$
$$z \cdot \mathrm{M} \geqq \mu^{-1} \odot u^\circ$$
$$\lambda_i \in [0, 1],\ i = 1, \ldots, k,$$
$$\mu_j \in (0, 1],\ j = 1, \ldots, l,$$
$$z \in R^k_+. \qquad (7.5.4)$$

Table 7-2

	Outputs		*Input*	
Firm	(u_1)	(u_2)	(x)	$R_o(x, u)$
1	5	2	5	2.00
2	5	3	5	1.50
3	6	4	5	1.00
4	4	5	5	1.23
5	5	6	5	1.00
6	4	6	5	1.13
7	2	6	5	1.75

Table 7-3

	Input	*Outputs*		
Firm	(x)	(u_1)	(u_2)	$R_g(x, u)$
1	2	1.5	1	.92
2	2	2	2	1.00
3	4	3	2	.92
4	6	6	6	1.00
5	7	6	6	.95
6	8	7	4	.96
7	9	7	4	.93

Although problem (7.5.4) is nonlinear, we can transform it into a simpler problem, i.e., a programming problem with a nonlinear objective function and linear constraints instead of the nonlinear constraints of problem (7.5.4). Thus, we can respecify the problem as

$$\text{minimize } \left(\sum_{i=1}^{k} \lambda_i + \sum_{j=1}^{l} 1/\delta_j\right)/(k+l)$$

subject to

$$z \cdot \mathrm{N} \leqq \lambda \odot x^\circ$$

$$z \cdot \mathrm{M} \geqq \delta \odot u^\circ$$

$$\lambda_i \in [0, 1], i = 1, \ldots, k$$

$$\delta_j \geqq 1, j = 1, \ldots, l,$$

$$z \in R_+^k, \tag{7.5.5}$$

where $\delta_j = 1/\mu_j$.

The data from chapter 5 are reproduced below in Table 7–3 with the corresponding values of $R_g(x, u)$.

Notes

1. From theorem (7.3.8), we know that if inputs or outputs are strongly disposable, we can use strong disposability on both the input and output side without changing $R_g(x, u)$. Since we have only one input in the example, we have chosen strong disposability of inputs.

8 MEASURES OF SCALE EFFICIENCY

8.0 Introduction

From a private perspective, a firm facing a given technology and fixed output and input prices can do no better than to select an input-output vector that yields maximum profit. Indeed in section 5.4, an input-output vector $(x, u) \in \Pi M(r, p)$ is termed overall graph efficient, i.e., the input-output vector is uncongested, technically efficient and allocatively efficient. However the structure of technology and the distribution of output and input prices may combine to yield the result that an overall graph efficient firm earns negative, zero, or positive profit.

In light of the Pareto-optimal characteristics of long run price-taking competitive equilibrium, we are naturally interested in a comparison of an observed input-output vector with an overall efficient zero profit input-output vector. The difference between the two is termed scale inefficiency.

For this purpose, in section 8.1 we introduce the constant returns to scale extended technology, the smallest constant returns to scale technology containing the existing technology. In section 8.2 we introduce the weak input cone measure of technical efficiency, from which we obtain a derived measure of input scale efficiency. We discuss the properties of both measures, and obtain a decomposition of the latter. In section 8.3 we introduce the weak output cone measure of technical efficiency, and obtain a derived measure of output scale efficiency, which also has a decomposition property. In section 8.4 we introduce the weak graph cone measure of technical efficiency and a derived measure of graph scale efficiency along with its decomposition properties.

In section 8.5 we provide a linear programming example of the computation of the graph measure of scale efficiency. In section 8.6 we discuss the sources of each measure of scale efficiency, the actual computation of which is illustrated with another linear programming example in section 8.7.

8.1 The Constant Returns to Scale Extended Technology

In order to introduce the three measures of scale efficiency for a technology satisfying (GR.1–GR.5) we need to introduce a constant returns to scale extended technology as a reference framework. Therefore, define

$$\overline{\mathrm{K(GR)}} := \overline{\{(x,u): (x,u) = (\lambda y, \lambda v), (y,v) \in \mathrm{GR}, \lambda \geqq 0\}}. \tag{8.1.1}$$

$\overline{\mathrm{K(GR)}}$ is the smallest closed cone containing the graph GR. In general when GR satisfies (GR.1–GR.5), $\overline{\mathrm{K(GR)}}$ does not satisfy (GR.1–GR.5) and is thus not a technology. To see this, let

$$\mathrm{GR} = \{(x, u): u \leqq x^2, x \geqq 0\}. \tag{8.1.2}$$

This graph satisfies (GR.1–GR.5), but $\overline{\mathrm{K(GR)}} = R^2_+$, thus $\overline{\mathrm{K(GR)}}$ fails to satisfy GR.2. However, we will restrict ourselves to technologies which yield $\overline{\mathrm{K(GR)}}$ that satisfies GR.2. For all practical purposes, this is a reasonable assumption. Moreover, it is clear that $\overline{\mathrm{K(GR)}}$ satisfies (GR.1, GR.3–GR.5), and so by our restriction, $\overline{\mathrm{K(GR)}}$ becomes a technology as we have defined it in chapter 2. For brevity we will refer to the constant returns to scale extended technology $\overline{\mathrm{K(GR)}}$ as the cone technology.

To illustrate the cone technology $\overline{\mathrm{K(GR)}}$, consider Fig. 8–1.

In this figure, the graph GR is bounded by the surface OB and the x–axis. The cone technology $\overline{\mathrm{K(GR)}}$ generated by this graph is bounded by the ray OA and the x–axis. The input and output correspondences derived from $\overline{\mathrm{K(GR)}}$ are given by

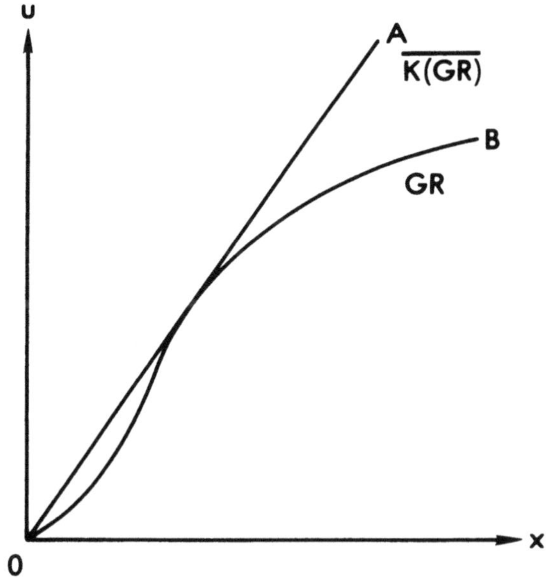

Figure 8-1

$$L^K(u) := \{x: (x, u) \in \overline{K(GR)}\}, \tag{8.1.3}$$

and

$$P^K(x) := \{u: (x, u) \in \overline{K(GR)}\}, \tag{8.1.4}$$

respectively. We now show that the input and output correspondences derived from K(GR) are homogeneous of degree +1.

Theorem: Let $\overline{K(GR)}$ satisfy (GR.1–GR.5). The input correspondence $L^K(u)$ and the output correspondence $P^K(x)$ are homogeneous of degree +1. (8.1.5)

Proof: From theorem (2.4.9) it follows that it is sufficient to show that L^K is homogeneous of degree +1. Therefore consider

$$\begin{aligned} L^K(\theta u) :&= \{x: (x, \theta u) \in \overline{K(GR)}\}, \theta > 0, \\ &= \{x: \theta(x/\theta, u) \in \overline{K(GR)}\} \end{aligned}$$

$$= \theta \cdot \{x/\theta: (x/\theta, u) \in \tfrac{1}{\theta}\, \overline{K(GR)}\}$$
$$= \theta \cdot \{y: (y, u) \in \overline{K(GR)}\}$$
$$= \theta \cdot L^K(u). \blacksquare$$

Regarding the converse of theorem (8.1.5) we have

Theorem: Let L satisfy (L.1–L.5). If $L(\theta u) = \theta \cdot L(u)$, $\theta > 0$, then $L(u) = L^K(u)$. (8.1.6)

Proof: Assume $x \in L(u)$, then $(x, u) \in GR$, and thus $(x, u) \in \overline{K(GR)}$. Therefore, $x \in L^K(u)$. To prove the converse, assume $x \notin L(u)$. Then $(x, u) \notin GR$. If $(x, u) \notin \overline{K(GR)}$, then $x \notin L^K(u)$. Thus assume that $(x, u) \in \overline{K(GR)}$. We have two cases (1) $(x, u) \in K(GR)$ and (2) $(x, u) \in \overline{K(GR)} \setminus K(GR)$. In the first case there exists $\lambda \geqq 0$ and $(y, v) \in GR$ such that $(x, u) = (\lambda y, \lambda x)$. But since $L(\theta u) = \theta \cdot L(u)$, $(x, u) \in GR$, a contradiction. Thus only (2) can be possible. If $(x, u) \in \overline{K(GR)} \setminus K(GR)$, then there exists a sequence $(x^l, u^l) \subseteqq K(GR)$ such that $(x^l, u^l) \to (x, u)$. Thus since $L(\theta u) = \theta \cdot L(u)$, there exists a sequence λ^l and a sequence $(y^l, v^l) \subseteqq GR$, such that $(x^l, u^l) = (\lambda^l y^l, \lambda^l v^l)$ for all l and $(\lambda^l y^l, \lambda^l v^l) \to (x, u)$. Therefore, since the graph is closed, $(y^l, v^l) \to (y, v) \in GR$, and since the input correspondence is homogeneous of degree $+1$, $(x, u) \in GR$. This contradiction completes the proof. $\blacksquare$

Since input and output correspondence are inverses (see 2.1.1) and (2.1.2)) the following corollary holds.

Corollary: Let P satisfy (P.1–P.5). If $P(\lambda x) = \lambda \cdot P(x)$, $\lambda > 0$, then $P(x) = P^K(x)$. (8.1.7)

8.2 The Input Scale Efficiency Measure

In order to introduce a measure of input scale efficiency, we first need to define a weak input measure of technical efficiency for the cone technology $L^K(u)$. Therefore, introduce the effective domain of $K_i(u, x)$, the weak input measure of technical efficiency for the cone technology

$$D(K_i) := \{(u, x): \exists\, \lambda \geqq 0 \text{ such that } (\lambda\, K(x) \cap L^K(u)) \neq \emptyset\} \quad (8.2.1)$$

where $K(x) := \{y: 0 \leqq y \leqq x\}$. Now define

Definition: The function $K_i: R^m_+ \times R^n_+ \rightarrow R_+ \cup \{+\infty\}$ defined by (8.2.2)

$$K_i(u, x) := \begin{cases} \min\{\lambda \geqq 0: (\lambda K(x) \cap L^K(u)) \neq \emptyset\}, (u, x) \in D(K_i), \\ +\infty, (u, x) \in \text{Complement } D(K_i), \end{cases}$$

is called the Weak Input Cone Measure of Technical Efficiency.

To illustrate the weak input cone measure of technical efficiency, consider Fig. 8–2, where $L(u) \subset L^K(u)$.

For $x \in L(u)$ at point P, the weak input cone efficiency measure $K_i(u,x) = \lambda$, where $T = \lambda K(x) \cap L^K(u)$. Verbally, $K_i(u, x)$ pushes the translated nonpositive orthant $K(x)$ as far down as possible along the ray OP through x under the condition that $\lambda K(x)$ has a nonempty intersection with $L^K(u)$. Hence $\lambda = OR/OP$.

From the analysis of the weak input measure of technical efficiency in section 3.3, it is clear that $K_i(u, x)$ is well defined and that it has the following properties

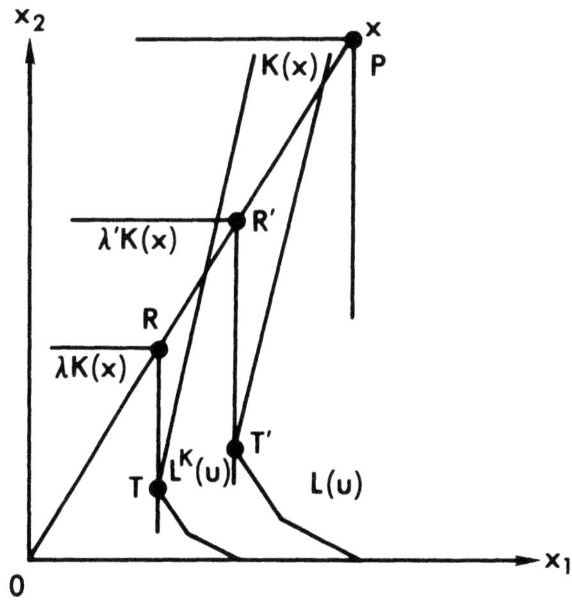

Figure 8-2

Theorem: If $\overline{\mathrm{K(GR)}}$ satisfies (GR.1–GR.5), then (8.2.3)

$K_i.1$ $K_i(0, x) = 0, x \in R^n_+$,

$K_i.2$ $0 < K_i(u, x) < +\infty, (u, x) \in D(K_i)$,

$K_i.3$ $K_i(u, \lambda x) = \lambda^{-1} K_i(u, x), \lambda > 0, (u, x) \in D(K_i)$,

$K_i.4$ $K_i(\theta u, x) \geqq K_i(u, x), \theta \geqq 1$,

$K_i.5$ $\mathrm{L^K}(u) \subseteqq \{x: 0 < K_i(u, x) \leqq 1\}, u \geq 0$,

$K_i.6$ WEff $\mathrm{L^K}(u) = \{x: x \in \mathrm{L^K}(u), K_i(u, x) = 1\}, u \geq 0$.

In addition to these properties we have

Theorem: If $\overline{\mathrm{K(GR)}}$ satisfies (GR.1–GR.5), then $K_i(\theta u, x) = \theta K_i(u, x), (u, x) \in D(K_i), \theta > 0$. (8.2.4)

Proof: From theorem (8.1.5) we know that $\mathrm{L^K}(\theta u) = \theta \cdot \mathrm{L^K}(u)$. Using this and definition (8.2.2) we obtain

$$\begin{aligned} K_i(\theta u, x) &= \min\{\lambda \geqq 0: (\lambda \mathrm{K}(x) \cap \mathrm{L^K}(\theta u)) \neq \emptyset\} \\ &= \min\{\lambda \geqq 0: \lambda \mathrm{K}(x) \cap \theta \cdot \mathrm{L^K}(u) \neq \emptyset\} \\ &= \theta \cdot \min\{\lambda/\theta: \lambda/\theta\, \mathrm{K}(x) \cap \mathrm{L^K}(u) \neq \emptyset\} \\ &= \theta K_i(u, x). \ \blacksquare \end{aligned}$$

It also follows that if inputs are strongly disposable, one can prove

Theorem: If $\overline{\mathrm{K(GR)}}$ satisfies (GR.1–GR.5), then $\mathrm{L^K}(u) = \{x: 0 < K_i(u,x) \leqq 1\}, u \geq 0$, if and only if inputs are strongly disposable. (8.2.5)

The proof follows the proof of theorem (3.3.6) and is thus omitted.

The following relation between $K_i(u, x)$ and $W_i(u, x)$ is valid.

Theorem: If $\overline{\mathrm{K(GR)}}$ satisfies (GR.1–GR.5), then $K_i(u,x) = W_i(u, x)$ for all $(u, x) \in R^m_+ \times R^n_+$ if $\mathrm{L}(\theta u) = \theta \cdot \mathrm{L}(u)$. (8.2.6)

Proof: If the input correspondence is homogeneous of degree +1, then by theorem (8.1.6), $\mathrm{L}(u) = \mathrm{L^K}(u)$. Thus from the definitions of K_i and W_i, the result follows. ■

Regarding the converse of theorem (8.2.6) we have

Theorem: If $\overline{K(GR)}$ satisfies (GR.1–GR.5) and if inputs are strongly disposable (i.e., L.3.S holds), then $K_i(u,x) = W_i(u, x)$ for all $(u,x) \in R_+^m \times R_+^n$ implies that $L(\theta u) = \theta \cdot L(u)$. (8.2.7)

Proof: Since $K_i(u,x) = W_i(u,x)$ for all $(u,x) \in R_+^m \times R_+^n$, it follows from theorem (8.2.4) that $W_i(\theta u, x) = \theta W_i(u,x)$. Next from theorem (3.3.6) we have

$$\begin{aligned} L(\theta u) &= \{x\colon 0 < W_i(\theta u, x) \leqq 1\} \\ &= \theta \cdot \{x/\theta\colon 0 < W_i(u, x/\theta) \leqq 1\} \\ &= \theta \cdot L(u). \ \blacksquare \end{aligned}$$

Theorems (8.2.6) and (8.2.7) yield the following definition of input scale efficiency

Definition: For $x \in L(u)$, $u \geq 0$, the Input Scale Efficiency Measure is $S_i(u, x) := K_i(u, x)/W_i(u, x)$. (8.2.8)

This definition clearly shows that the input scale efficiency measure $S_i(u,x)$ is a derived measure. In terms of Fig. 8–2, $S_i(u,x) = OR/OR'$. In Farrell's original framework (Farrell (1957)), constant returns to scale was assumed, and so $S_i(u,x) = 1$ by definition in his formulation.

Before stating the properties of the input scale efficiency measure we need to define what is meant by scale efficiency.

Definition: $x \in L(u)$, $u \geq 0$, is Input Scale Efficient if and only if $S_i(u,x) = 1$. (8.2.9)

The properties of the input scale efficiency measure are summarized in

Theorem: If $\overline{K(GR)}$ satisfies (GR.1–GR.5), then

$S_i.1$ $0 < S_i(u, x) \leqq 1$, $x \in L(u)$, $u \geq 0$,

$S_i.2$ $S_i(u, x) = 1$ if and only if (x, u) is input scale efficient, $x \in L(u)$, $u \geq 0$,

$S_i.3$ $S_i(u, \lambda x) = S_i(u, x)$, $\lambda > 0$. (8.2.10)

Proof: Property $S_i.1$ follows from the properties of $K_i(u,x)$ and $W_i(u,x)$, noting that $x \in L(u)$, $u \geq 0$. Property $S_i.2$ is true by definition. Property $S_i.3$ follows from properties $W_i.3$ and $K_i.3$. ■

Let $x \in L(u)$, $u \geq 0$, then we have the following decomposition of $K_i(u, x)$

$$K_i(u, x) = S_i(u, x) \cdot C_i(u, x) \cdot F_i(u, x), \tag{8.2.11}$$

where $S_i(u, x)$ measures scale efficiency, $C_i(u, x)$ measures congestion and $F_i(u, x)$ measures technical efficiency. In Farrell's 1957 work, he assumed the technology to satisfy (1) constant returns to scale and (2) strong disposability of inputs. These two assumptions imply that $S_i(u, x) = 1$ and $C_i(u, x) = 1$ by definition, therefore in his work, $K_i(u, x) = F_i(u, x)$.

8.3 The Output Scale Efficiency Measure

Prior to introducing a measure of output scale efficiency, we need to define a weak output measure of technical efficiency on the cone technology $P^K(x)$. Therefore, introduce the effective domain of $K_o(x, u)$, the weak output measure of technical efficiency for the cone technology

$$D(K_o) := \{(x, u) : \exists\ \theta \geqq 0 \text{ such that } \theta M(u) \cap P^K(x) \neq \emptyset\}, \tag{8.3.1}$$

where $M(u) := \{v : v \geqq u\}$. Now define

Definition: The function $K_o : R^n_+ \times R^m_+ \to R_+ \cup \{+\infty\}$ defined by (8.3.2)

$$K_o(x, u) := \begin{cases} \max\{\theta \geqq 0 : (\theta M(u) \cap P^K(x)) \neq \emptyset\}, & (x, u) \in D(K_o), \\ +\infty, & (x, u) \in \text{Complement } D(K_o), \end{cases}$$

is called the Weak Output Cone Measure of Technical Efficiency.

To illustrate the weak output cone measure of technical efficiency, consider Fig. 8–3, where $P(x) \subset P^K(x)$.

For $u \in P(x)$ at point P, the weak output cone efficiency measure $K_o(x, u) = \theta$, where $B = \theta M(u) \cap P^K(x)$. Verbally, $K_o(x, u)$ pushes the translated nonnegative orthant $M(u)$ as far out as possible along the ray OR through u under the condition that $\theta M(u)$ has a nonempty intersection with $P^K(x)$. Hence $\theta = OR/OP$.

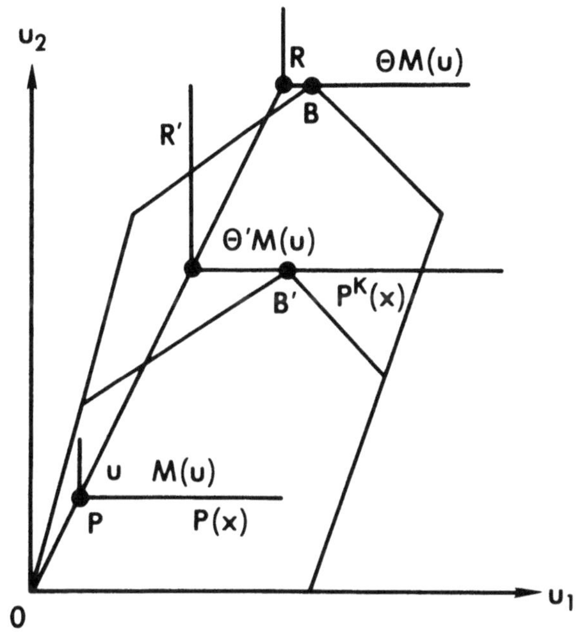

Figure 8-3

From the study of the weak output measure of technical efficiency in section 4.3, it is clear that $K_o(x, u)$ is well defined and has the following properties

Theorem: If $\overline{K(GR)}$ satisfies (GR.1–GR.5) then, (8.3.3)

$K_o.1$ $K_o(0, u) = +\infty$,

$K_o.2$ $0 < K_o(x, u) < +\infty$, $u \geq 0$, $(x, u) \in D(K_o)$,

$K_o.3$ $K_o(x, \theta u) = \theta^{-1} K_o(x, u)$, $\theta > 0$, $(x, u) \in D(K_o)$,

$K_o.4$ $K_o(\lambda x, u) \geqq K_o(x, u)$, $\lambda \geqq 1$,

$K_o.5$ $P^K(x) \subsetneqq \{u: K_o(x, u) \geqq 1\}$, $P^K(x) \neq \{0\}$,

$K_o.6$ WEff $P^K(x) = \{u: u \in P(x), K_o(x, u) = 1\}$.

An additional property of $K_o(x, u)$ is provided by the following

Theorem: If $\overline{\mathrm{K(GR)}}$ satisfies (GR.1–GR.5), then $K_o(\lambda x, u) = \lambda K_o(x, u)$, $\lambda > 0$, $(x, u) \in D(K_o)$. (8.3.4)

Proof: From theorem (8.1.5) we have that $\mathrm{P}^{\mathrm{K}}(\lambda x) = \lambda \cdot \mathrm{P}^{\mathrm{K}}(x)$. Thus, using definition (8.3.2) we obtain

$$\begin{aligned} K_o(\lambda x, u) &= \max\{\theta \geqq 0: \theta \mathrm{M}(u) \cap \mathrm{P}^{\mathrm{K}}(\lambda x) \neq \emptyset\} \\ &= \max\{\theta \geqq 0: \theta \mathrm{M}(u) \cap \lambda \cdot \mathrm{P}^{\mathrm{K}}(x) \neq \emptyset\} \\ &= \lambda \cdot \max\{\gamma \geqq 0: \gamma \mathrm{M}(u) \cap \mathrm{P}^{\mathrm{K}}(x) \neq \emptyset\} \\ &= \lambda K_o(x, u). \blacksquare \end{aligned}$$

In the case of strongly disposable outputs we also have

Theorem: If $\overline{\mathrm{K(GR)}}$ satisfies (GR.1–GR.5), then $\mathrm{P}^{\mathrm{K}}(x) = \{u: K_o(x, u) \geqq 1\}$, $\mathrm{P}^{\mathrm{K}}(x) \neq \{0\}$, if and only if outputs are strongly disposable (i.e., P.5.S holds). (8.3.5)

The proof of this theorem parallels the proof of theorem (4.3.7) and is thus omitted. The next two theorems show the relationship between $K_o(x, u)$ and $W_o(x, u)$

Theorem: If $\overline{\mathrm{K(GR)}}$ satisfies (GR.1–GR.5), then $K_o(x, u) = W_o(x, u)$ for all $(x, u) \in R^n_+ \times R^m_+$ if $\mathrm{P}(\lambda x) = \lambda \cdot \mathrm{P}(x)$. (8.3.6)

Proof: If the output correspondence is homogeneous of degree +1, then by corollary (8.1.7), $\mathrm{P}(x) = \mathrm{P}^{\mathrm{K}}(x)$. Thus from definitions (4.3.3) and (8.3.2), the result follows. $\blacksquare$

Regarding the converse of theorem (8.3.6) we have

Theorem: If $\overline{\mathrm{K(GR)}}$ satisfies (GR.1–GR.5) and if outputs are strongly disposable (i.e., P.5.S holds), then $K_o(x, u) = W_o(x, u)$ for all $(x, u) \in R^n_+ \times R^m_+$ implies that $\mathrm{P}(\lambda x) = \lambda \cdot \mathrm{P}(x)$. (8.3.7)

Proof: Since by assumption, $K_o(x, u) = W_o(x, u)$ for all $(x, u) \in R^n_+ \times R^m_+$, it follows from theorem (8.3.4) that $W_o(\lambda x, u) = \lambda W_o(x, u)$. Next from theorem (4.3.7) we have

$$\begin{aligned} \mathrm{P}(\lambda x) &= \{u: W_o(\lambda x, u) \geqq 1\} \\ &= \{\lambda u/\lambda: W_o(x, u/\lambda) \geqq 1\} \\ &= \lambda \cdot \mathrm{P}(x). \blacksquare \end{aligned}$$

Theorems (8.3.6) and (8.3.7) yield the following definition of output scale efficiency

Definition: For $u \in \mathrm{P}(x)$, $\mathrm{P}(x) \neq \{0\}$, the Output Scale Efficiency Measure is $S_o(x, u) := K_o(x, u)/W_o(x, u)$. (8.3.8)

In terms of Fig. 8–3, this derived efficiency measure measures $S_o(x, u) =$ OR/OR′, i.e., proportional output loss due to deviations from constant returns to scale.

Prior to stating the properties of the output scale efficiency measure we need the following definition.

Definition: $u \in \mathrm{P}(x)$, $\mathrm{P}(x) \neq \{0\}$, is Output Scale Efficient if and only if $S_o(x, u) = 1$. (8.3.9)

The properties of the output scale efficiency measure are summarized in

Theorem: If $\overline{\mathrm{K(GR)}}$ satisfies (GR.1–GR.5), then (8.3.10)

$S_o.1$ $S_o(x, u) \geqq 1$, $u \in \mathrm{P}(x)$, $u \geq 0$,

$S_o.2$ $S_o(x, u) = 1$ if and only if (x, u) is output scale efficient, $u \in \mathrm{P}(x)$, $u \geq 0$,

$S_o.3$ $S_o(x, \theta u) = S_o(x, u)$, $\theta > 0$.

Proof: Property $S_o.1$ follows from properties on $K_o(x, u)$ and $W_o(x, u)$, noting that $u \in \mathrm{P}(x)$, $u \geq 0$. Property $S_o.2$ is true by definition. Property $S_o.3$ follows from properties $W_o.3$ and $K_o.3$. ■

Let $u \in \mathrm{P}(x)$, $u \geq 0$, then the following decomposition of $K_o(x, u)$ is valid.

$$K_o(x, u) = S_o(x, u) \cdot C_o(x, u) \cdot F_o(x, u), \qquad (8.3.11)$$

where $S_o(x, u)$ measures scale efficiency, $C_o(x, u)$ measures output congestion, and $F_o(x, u)$ measures technical efficiency. If the technology exhibits constant returns to scale, then $S_o(x, u) = 1$ and if in addition outputs are freely disposable, $C_o(x, u) = 1$. Thus under these assumptions, $K_o(x, u) = F_o(x, u)$.

8.4 The Graph Scale Efficiency Measure

In order to introduce a measure of graph scale efficiency, we need to define a weak graph measure of technical efficiency for the cone technology $\overline{K(GR)}$. Introduce therefore, the effective domain of $K_g(x, u)$, the weak graph measure of technical efficiency for the cone technology

$$D(K_g) := \{(x, u): \exists\, \lambda \geqq 0 \text{ such that } (K(\lambda x) \times M(\lambda^{-1}u)) \cap \overline{K(GR)} \neq \emptyset\}. \tag{8.4.1}$$

Now define

Definition: The function $K_g: R^n_+ \times R^m_+ \rightarrow R_+ \cup \{+\infty\}$ defined by (8.4.2)

$$K_g(x, u) := \begin{cases} \min\{\lambda \geqq 0: (K(\lambda x) \times M(\lambda^{-1}u)) \cap \overline{K(GR)} \neq \emptyset\}, \\ \quad (x, u) \in D(K_g), \\ +\infty, \ (x, u) \in \text{Complement } D(K_g), \end{cases}$$

is called the Weak Graph Cone Measure of Technical Efficiency.

An illustration of this measure is given in Fig. 8–4. For $(x, u) \in GR$ at point P, the weak graph cone measure of technical efficiency pushes the set $(K(x) \times M(u))$ as far away from (x, u) as possible along the hyperbolic path PR under the condition that $(K(\lambda x) \times M(\lambda^{-1}u))$ has a nonempty intersection with the derived constant returns to scale graph $\overline{K(GR)}$.

From the discussion of the weak graph measure of technical efficiency (section 5.3) and the assumption that $\overline{K(GR)}$ satisfies (GR.1–GR.5), it is clear that $K_g(x, u)$ is well defined and has the following properties

Theorem: If $\overline{K(GR)}$ satisfies (GR.1–GR.5), then (8.4.3)

$K_g.1$ $K_g(0, 0) = 0$,

$K_g.2$ $0 < K_g(x, u) < +\infty$, $u \geq 0$, $(x, u) \in D(K_g)$,

$K_g.3$ $K_g(\theta x, \theta^{-1}u) = \theta^{-1}K_g(x, u)$, $\theta > 0$, $(x, u) \in D(K_g)$,

$K_g.4$ $K_g(\lambda x, u) \leqq K_g(x, u)$, $\lambda \geqq 1$,

$K_g.5$ $K_g(x, \theta u) \leqq K_g(x, u)$, $\theta \in [0, 1]$,

$K_g.6$ $\overline{K(GR)} \subseteqq \{(x, u): 0 < K_g(x, u) \leqq 1\}$, $u \geq 0$,

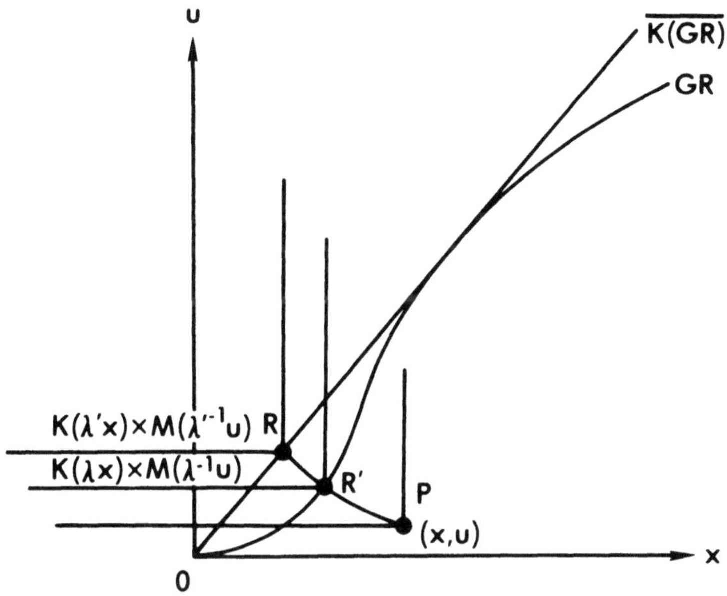

Figure 8-4

$K_g.7$ WEff $\overline{K(GR)} = \{(x, u): (x, u) \in \overline{K(GR)}, K_g(x, u) = 1\}$, $u \geq 0$.

In addition to properties ($K_g.1$–$K_g.7$) we have

Theorem: If $\overline{K(GR)}$ satisfies (GR.1–GR.5), then $K_g(\lambda x, u) = K_g(x, \lambda^{-1}u), \lambda > 0, (x, u) \in D(K_g)$. (8.4.4)

Proof: Note since $\overline{K(GR)}$ is a cone, $\lambda \cdot \overline{K(GR)} = \overline{K(GR)}, \lambda > 0$. Using this property of a cone and definition (8.4.2) we obtain

$$\begin{aligned} K_g(\lambda x, u) &= \min\{\delta \geqq 0: (K(\delta\lambda x) \times M(\delta^{-1}u)) \cap \overline{K(GR)} \neq \emptyset\} \\ &= \min\{\delta \geqq 0: ((\lambda \cdot K(\delta x)) \times M(\delta^{-1}u)) \cap \overline{K(GR)} \neq \emptyset\} \\ &= \min\{\delta \geqq 0: (K(\delta x) \times M((\delta\lambda)^{-1}u)) \cap \overline{K(GR)} \neq \emptyset\} \\ &= K_g(x, \lambda^{-1}u). \blacksquare \end{aligned}$$

In the case of strongly disposable inputs and outputs we also have

Theorem: If $\overline{K(GR)}$ satisfies (GR.1–GR.5), then $\overline{K(GR)} =$

$\{(x, u): 0 < K_g(x, u) \leqq 1\}$, $u \geq 0$, if and only if inputs and outputs are strongly disposable, i.e., GR.6 holds. (8.4.5)

The proof of this theorem follows the proof of theorem (5.3.6) and is thus omitted.

The next two theorems show the relationship between $K_g(x, u)$ and $W_g(x, u)$.

Theorem: If $\overline{\text{K(GR)}}$ satisfies (GR.1–GR.5), then $K_g(x, u) = W_g(x, u)$ for all $(x, u) \in R^n_+ \times R^m_+$ if $P(\lambda x) = \lambda \cdot P(x)$ or equivalently if $L(\theta u) = \theta \cdot L(u)$. (8.4.6)

The proof of this theorem follows from the fact that if the output or equivalently the input correspondence is homogeneous of degree +1, then $\overline{\text{K(GR)}} = \text{GR}$, being the smallest closed cone containing GR, in addition to the definitions (5.3.3) and (8.4.2).

Regarding the converse of theorem (8.4.6) we have

Theorem: If $\overline{\text{K(GR)}}$ satisfies (GR.1–GR.5, GR.6) then $K_g(x, u) = W_g(x, u)$ for all $(x, u) \in R^n_+ \times R^m_+$ implies that $P(\lambda x) = \lambda \cdot P(x)$ or equivalently that $L(\theta u) = \theta \cdot L(u)$. (8.4.7)

Proof: Since by assumption, $K_g(x, u) = W_g(x, u)$ for all $(x, u) \in R^n_+ \times R^m_+$, it follows from theorem (8.4.4) that $W_g(\lambda x, u) = W_g(x, \lambda^{-1} u)$. Next from theorem (4.3.7) we have

$$
\begin{aligned}
P(\lambda x) &= \{u: 0 < K_g(\lambda x, u) \leqq 1\} \\
&= \{\lambda u/\lambda: 0 < K_g(x, u/\lambda) \leqq 1\} \\
&= \lambda \cdot P(x). \blacksquare
\end{aligned}
$$

The last two theorems yield the following definition of graph scale efficiency.

Definition: For $(x, u) \in \text{GR}$, $u \geq 0$, the Graph Scale Efficiency Measure is $S_g(x, u) := K_g(x, u)/W_g(x, u)$. (8.4.8)

In terms of Fig. 8–4, this derived scale efficiency measure measures $S_g(x, u)$ along the hyperbolic path PR′R.

The next definition explains what is meant by graph scale efficiency.

Definition: $(x, u) \in \text{GR}$, $u \geq 0$, is Graph Scale Efficient if and only if $S_g(x, u) = 1$. (8.4.9)

The properties of the graph scale efficiency measure are summarized in

Theorem: If $\overline{K(GR)}$ satisfies (GR.1–GR.5), then (8.4.10)

$S_g.1$ $0 < S_g(x, u) \leqq 1$, $(x, u) \in GR$,

$S_g.2$ $S_g(x, u) = 1$ if and only if $(x, u) \in GR$ is scale efficient,

$S_g.3$ $S_g(\lambda x, \lambda^{-1}u) = S_g(x, u)$, $\lambda > 0$.

The proofs of properties $S_g.1$ and $S_g.3$ are omitted since they parallel those of $C_g.1$ and $C_g.3$. Property $S_g.2$ is true by definition.

Finally, let $(x, u) \in GR$, $u \geq 0$, then the following decomposition of $K_g(x, u)$ is valid.

$$K_g(x, u) = S_g(x, u) \cdot C_g(x, u) \cdot F_g(x, u), \qquad (8.4.11)$$

where $S_g(x, u)$ measures graph scale efficiency, $C_g(x, u)$ measures input and output losses due to lack of disposability and $F_g(x, u)$ measures technical efficiency.

8.5 Linear Programming Example

In this section we calculate scale efficiency for the data points used in chapter 5 on graph efficiency (see Table 8–1). Since the calculation of the input and output measures of scale efficiency are so similar, we will present

Table 8-1

	Outputs		*Input*
Firm	(u_1)	(u_2)	(x)
1	2	1.5	1
2	2	2	2
3	4	3	2
4	6	6	6
5	7	6	6
6	8	7	4
7	9	7	4

only the graph scale calculations here. We include all the components of the decomposition in equation (8.3.11), i.e.

$$K_g(x, u),\ S_g(x, u),\ C_g(x, u), \text{ and } F_g(x, u).$$

In order to calculate scale efficiency, we must first specify a technology that does not impose constant returns to scale. Assuming strong disposability of inputs and outputs, consider the following strongly disposable technology

$$\mathrm{P^S}(x) := \{u\colon z \in R^k_+,\ \sum_{i=1}^{k} z_i = 1,\ z \cdot \mathrm{M} \geqq u,\ x \geqq z \cdot \mathrm{N}\}, \tag{8.5.1}$$

or equivalently

$$\mathrm{L^S}(u) := \{x\colon z \in R^k_+,\ \sum_{i=1}^{k} z_i = 1,\ z \cdot \mathrm{M} \geqq u,\ x \geqq z \cdot \mathrm{N}\}, \tag{8.5.2}$$

where the z_i's are the intensity parameters and M and N represent output and input matrices, respectively. This technology differs from that used in previous chapters in that the z_i's now sum to one rather than being restricted to being nonnegative only.[1] This technology satisfies the basic assumptions P.1–P.5 (L.1–L.5). In addition, the graph of this technology is convex as before, but does not restrict the technology to satisfy constant returns to scale. In fact, in practice, this formulation of the technology as specified in (8.5.1) and (8.5.2), can even model increasing returns to scale if the zero input, zero output point is not included in the observations, as in Table 8–1, for example. With zero included as an observation, however, the technology specified above would construct convex combinations of all the observed points, which would then exhibit nonincreasing returns.

As in the strongly disposable technology, we can modify the weakly disposable technology to allow for nonconstant returns to scale by restricting the z's to satisfy $\sum_{i=1}^{k} z_i = 1$.

Based on this new technology (modified to allow for weak disposability of outputs and inputs) we can now specify the linear programming problem we will use to calculate $F_g(x, u)$, namely

minimize λ

subject to

$$\mu \cdot z \cdot \mathrm{M} = u^\circ/\lambda$$

$$z \cdot N = \lambda \cdot \delta \cdot x^\circ$$
$$\delta,\ \mu \in (0, 1]$$
$$\sum_{i=1}^{k} z_i = 1,\ z \in R^k_+, \qquad (8.5.3)$$

which can be transformed into the simpler problem

minimize Λ

subject to

$$z' \cdot M = \xi \cdot u^\circ$$
$$z' \cdot N = \Lambda \cdot x^\circ$$
$$\xi \geqq 1$$
$$\sum_{i=1}^{k} z_i' = \sigma,\ z' \in R^k_+,$$
$$\sigma \leqq 1 \qquad (8.5.4)$$

where $\Lambda = \lambda^2$, $z' = z(\lambda/\delta)$, and $\xi = 1/(\mu\delta)$, $\sigma = (\lambda/\delta)$.

We note that the restriction $\Sigma z_i' = \sigma$, is, in practice, $\Sigma z_i' = 1$. To see this, consider the reference technology being constructed by the problem. Clearly the technology is constructed from the observed inputs and outputs including (x°, u°). Ignoring the minimization of Λ for the moment, if $\Sigma z_i' < 1$, no observed x or u (including (x°, u°)) can have a weight (z_i') equal to unity. That implies that (x°, u°) will not be elements of the reference technology. Hence, we restrict $\sigma = 1$.

The specification of the linear programming problem to calculate $W_g(x, u)$ also employs the technology in (8.5.1):

minimize λ

subject to

$$z \cdot M \geqq u^\circ/\lambda$$
$$z \cdot N \leqq \lambda \cdot x^\circ$$
$$\sum_{i=1}^{k} z_i = 1,\ z \in R^k_+, \qquad (8.5.5)$$

which can be rewritten as

minimize Λ

subject to

$$z' \cdot \mathrm{M} \geqq u^\circ$$
$$z' \cdot \mathrm{N} \leqq \Lambda \cdot x^\circ$$
$$\sum_{i=1}^{k} z_i' = \lambda,\ z' \in R_+^k, \tag{8.5.6}$$

where $\Lambda = \lambda^2$ and $z' = \lambda \cdot z$. Again, in practice, the $\Sigma z_i'$ restriction becomes $\Sigma z_i' = 1$.

The cone measure $K_g(x, u)$, which uses as its reference the constant returns to scale technology, is calculated from the following linear programming problem[2]

minimize λ

subject to

$$z \cdot \mathrm{M} \geqq u^\circ/\lambda$$
$$z \cdot \mathrm{N} \leqq \lambda \cdot x^\circ$$
$$z \in R_+^k, \tag{8.5.7}$$

which can be transformed in a manner similar to (8.5.6).

In order to calculate the scale efficiency measure, we exploit theorem (8.4.8) and merely construct the ratio $K_g(x, u)/W_g(x, u)$. As before, the congestion measure is constructed as $W_g(x, u)/F_g(x, u)$. The various measures are summarized below in Table 8–2.

Table 8-2

Firm	$K_g(x, u)$	$S_g(x, u)$	$C_g(x, u)$	$F_g(x, u)$	$W_g(x, u)$
1	.87	.87	1.00	1.00	1.00
2	1.00	1.00	1.00	1.00	1.00
3	.87	1.00	.93	.94	.87
4	1.00	1.00	1.00	1.00	1.00
5	.93	1.00	1.00	.93	.93
6	.94	.94	1.00	1.00	1.00
7	.88	.94	1.00	.94	.94

8.6 Sources of Scale Efficiency

In the previous sections of this chapter, we introduced and discussed measures of scale efficiency. These measures determine when the scale of operations is nonoptimal (i.e., when returns to scale are not constant). However, those measures cannot identify the source of any scale inefficiency, in particular, they cannot distinguish between increasing and decreasing returns to scale. The purpose of this section is to introduce a means of determining whether scale inefficiency is due to increasing or decreasing returns to scale.

In order to make that distinction, we need to introduce a modified form of the technology used in the earlier sections of this chapter. In particular we introduce the star-closure of the graph

$$\overline{S(GR)} := \overline{\{(x, u): (x, u) = (\lambda y, \lambda v), (y, v) \in GR, \lambda \in [0, 1]\}}. \tag{8.6.1}$$

Technically, $\overline{S(GR)}$ is the smallest closed star-like set containing the graph GR. The distinction between $\overline{S(GR)}$ and $\overline{K(GR)}$ discussed earlier, is that in constructing $\overline{K(GR)}$, any point on the graph GR can be scaled up and down along a ray through the origin. $\overline{S(GR)}$, on the other hand, only allows for radial contraction back toward the origin. It should be noted that neither $\overline{S(GR)}$ nor $\overline{K(GR)}$ satisfy assumption GR.2 (see example (8.1.2) in section 1). However, since $\overline{S(GR)}$ satisfies (GR.1, GR.3–GR.5), we assume that $\overline{S(GR)}$ is a technology (as in chapter 2), which can be illustrated as in Fig. 8–5.

In this figure, the graph GR is bounded by the line OB and the x-axis. Its star-closure $\overline{S(GR)}$ is then bounded by OAB and the x-axis. The $\overline{K(GR)}$ would be bounded by the ray OA (and extended along the broken line).

The purpose of introducing the star-closure, is that it excludes increasing returns to scale, yet allows decreasing returns. To show this first define

Definition: The technology exhibits Non-Increasing Returns to Scale if $P(\lambda x) \subseteq \lambda \cdot P(x)$, $\lambda \geqq 1$. (8.6.2)

To show that the technology derived from $\overline{S(GR)}$ exhibits non-increasing returns to scale, define

$$P^*(x) := \{u: (x, u) \in \overline{S(GR)}\}, \tag{8.6.3}$$

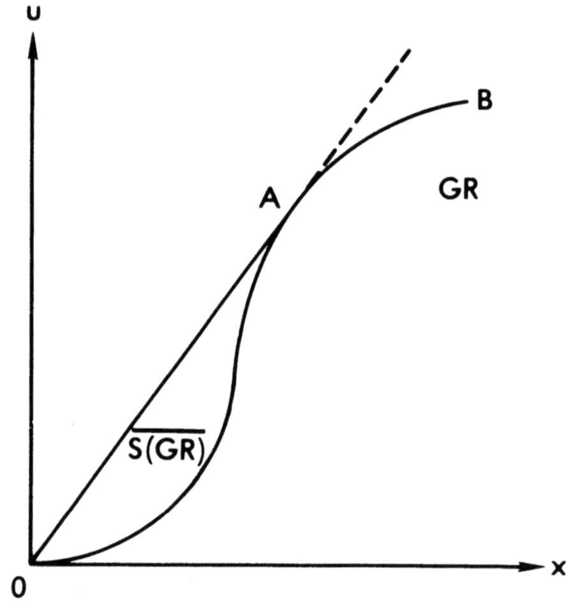

Figure 8-5

to be the star-closure output correspondence. Similarly, the star-closure input correspondence is given by

$$L^*(u) := \{x : (x, u) \in \overline{S(GR)}\}. \tag{8.6.4}$$

Theorem: Let $\overline{S(GR)}$ satisfy (GR.1–GR.5). The star-closure technology $P^*(x)$ exhibits non-increasing returns to scale. (8.6.5)

Proof: We note that for $\lambda \geqq 1$, $1/\lambda \cdot \overline{S(GR)} \subsetneqq \overline{S(GR)}$. Next, consider

$$\begin{aligned} P^*(\lambda x) &= \{u : (\lambda x, u) \in \overline{S(GR)}\}, \lambda \geqq 1, \\ &= \lambda \cdot \{v : (x, v) \in 1/\lambda \cdot \overline{S(GR)}\}, v := u/\lambda, \\ &= \lambda \cdot P^*(x). \blacksquare \end{aligned}$$

Regarding the converse of this theorem, we can prove

Theorem: Let P satisfy (P.1–P.5). If $P(\lambda x) \subsetneqq \lambda \cdot P(x)$, then $P(x) = P^*(x)$. (8.6.6)

Proof: Assume $u \in \mathrm{P}(x)$, then $(x, u) \in \mathrm{GR}$, and thus $(x, u) \in \overline{\mathrm{S(GR)}}$. Therefore, $u \in \mathrm{P}^*(x)$. To prove the converse, assume that $u \notin \mathrm{P}(x)$. Then $(x, u) \notin \mathrm{GR}$. If $(x, u) \notin \overline{\mathrm{S(GR)}}$, then $u \notin \mathrm{P}^*(x)$. Thus assume $(x, u) \in \overline{\mathrm{S(GR)}}$. We have two cases: (1) $(x, u) \in \mathrm{S(GR)}$ and (2) $(x, u) \in (\overline{\mathrm{S(GR)}} \setminus \mathrm{S(GR)})$. In the first case there exists a $\lambda \in [0, 1]$ and $(y, v) \in \mathrm{GR}$, such that $(x, u) = (\lambda y, \lambda v)$. But since $(\mathrm{P}(\lambda x) \subseteqq \lambda \cdot \mathrm{P}(x), \lambda \geqq 1) \Leftrightarrow (\mathrm{L}(\theta u) \supseteqq \theta \cdot \mathrm{L}(u), \theta \in [0, 1])$, $(x, u) \in \mathrm{GR}$, a contradiction. Thus only (2) is possible. If $(x, u) \in (\overline{\mathrm{S(GR)}} \setminus \mathrm{S(GR)})$, then there exists a sequence $(x^l, u^l) \subseteqq \mathrm{S(GR)}$ such that $(x^l, u^l) \to (x, u)$. Thus since $\mathrm{L}(\theta u) \supseteqq \theta \cdot \mathrm{L}(u)$, $\theta \in [0, 1]$, there is a sequence $(y^l, v^l) \subseteqq \mathrm{GR}$, such that $(x^l, u^l) = (\lambda^l y^l, \lambda^l v^l)$, $\lambda^l \in [0, 1]$, for all l and $(\lambda^l y^l, \lambda^l v^l) \to (x, u)$. Therefore, since the graph is closed, $(y^l, v^l) \to (y, v) \in \mathrm{GR}$, and since $\mathrm{L}(\theta u) \supseteqq \theta \cdot \mathrm{L}(u)$, $(x, u) \in \mathrm{GR}$. This contradiction completes the proof. ■

The next corollary follows immediately from the above theorem.

Corollary: Let L satisfy (L.1–L.5). If $\mathrm{L}(\theta u) \supseteqq \theta \cdot \mathrm{L}(u)$, $\theta \in [0, 1]$, then $\mathrm{L}(u) = \mathrm{L}^*(u)$. (8.6.7)

We are now ready to introduce a weak input efficiency measure on the star-input correspondence.

$$W_i^*(u, x) := \min\{\lambda \geqq 0 : (\lambda \mathrm{K}(x) \cap \mathrm{L}^*(u)) \neq \emptyset\}. \quad (8.6.8)$$

From theorems (8.6.5), (8.6.6), (3.3.6), and corollary (8.6.7) the next theorem follows.

Theorem: Let $\overline{\mathrm{S(GR)}}$ satisfy (GR.1–GR.5). $W_i^*(u, x) = W_i(u, x)$ for all $(u, x) \in R_+^m \times R_+^n$ if $\mathrm{L}(\theta u) \supseteqq \theta \cdot \mathrm{L}(u)$, $\theta \in [0, 1]$. If, in addition, inputs are strongly disposable (i.e., L.3.S holds), then $W_i^*(u, x) = W_i(u, x)$ for all $(u, x) \in R_+^m \times R_+^n$ implies that $\mathrm{L}(\theta u) \supseteqq \theta \cdot \mathrm{L}(u)$, $\theta \in [0, 1]$. (8.6.9)

From this theorem, we can conclude that if there is input scale inefficiency at (u, x), i.e., $S_i(u, x) \neq 1$, then it is caused by increasing returns to scale if and only if $W_i^*(u, x) < W_i(u, x)$, and it is caused by decreasing returns to scale if and only if $W_i^*(u, x) = W_i(u, x)$.

Regarding output scale inefficiency at (x, u), we can define

$$W_o^*(x, u) := \max\{\theta \geqq 0 : (\theta \mathrm{M}(u) \cap \mathrm{P}^*(x)) \neq \emptyset\} \quad (8.6.10)$$

and determine the source of scale inefficiency by comparing $W_o^*(x, u)$ and $W_o(x, u)$. If we have that $S_o(x, u) \neq 1$, then the inefficiency is caused by increasing returns to scale if and only if $W_o^*(x, u) > W_o(x, u)$, and by decreasing returns to scale if and only if $W_o^*(x, u) = W_o(x, u)$.

Finally, concerning the graph measure of scale efficiency, define the weak graph measure on the star-technology

$$W_g^*(x, u) := \min\{\lambda \geqq 0: (K(\lambda x) \times M(\lambda^{-1}u)) \cap \overline{S(GR)} \neq \emptyset\}. \tag{8.6.11}$$

We can now determine the source of scale inefficiency by comparing $W_g^*(x, u)$ and $W_g(x, u)$. Thus if $S_g(x, u) \neq 1$, i.e., the graph is scale inefficient at (x, u), then the source of inefficiency is increasing returns to scale if and only if $W_g^*(x, u) < W_g(x, u)$ and decreasing returns to scale if and only if $W_g^*(x, u) = W_g(x, u)$.

8.7 Computing Sources of Scale Inefficiency

In this section we present a simple numerical illustration of the technique described in section 8.6. For the illustration we employ the data used in section 8.5 to calculate scale efficiency. We restrict ourselves to the particular case of the graph measure of scale efficiency, in order to take advantage of the calculations in section 8.5.

In order to determine the sources of scale inefficiency, one must first determine whether scale inefficiency exists. For our example, we need to first calculate $W_g(x, u)$ and $F_g(x, u)$ in order to find $S_g(x, u)$, as in section 8.5. The next step is to calculate $W_g^*(x, u)$ based on the $\overline{S(GR)}$ technology. Similar to the technology of chapter 2, consider

$$\overline{S(GR)} := \{(x, u): z \cdot M \geqq u, x \geqq z \cdot N, \sum_{i=1}^{k} z_i \leqq 1, z \in R_+^k\}. \tag{8.7.1}$$

The specification of the technology differs from that in section 8.5 only in the restriction on the intensity parameters, z_i. Here, all of the z_i's could be equal to zero, whereas that possibility is excluded in the technology specified earlier (i.e., there the restriction was that $\Sigma z_i = 1$).

In order to calculate $W_g^*(x, u)$, consider the following linear programming problem minimize λ

subject to

$$z \cdot \mathrm{M} \geqq u^\circ/\lambda$$

$$z \cdot \mathrm{N} \leqq \lambda \cdot x^\circ$$

$$\sum_{i=1}^{k} z_i \leqq 1, \; z \in R^k_+, \qquad (8.7.2)$$

which can be transformed into the simpler problem

minimize Λ

subject to

$$z' \cdot \mathrm{M} \geqq u^\circ$$

$$z' \cdot \mathrm{N} \leqq \Lambda \cdot x^\circ$$

$$\sum_{i=1}^{k} z_i' \leqq 1, \; z' \in R^k_+, \qquad (8.7.3)$$

where $\Lambda = \lambda^2$ and $z' = \lambda \cdot z$.

As discussed in section 8.6, we need only compare $W_g(x, u)$ and $W_g^*(x, u)$ for scale inefficient points to determine whether increasing or decreasing returns are the source of scale inefficiency. The values for $W_g(x, u)$, $W_g^*(x, u)$, and $S_g(x, u)$ are summarized (for the data from Table 8–1) in Table 8–3. There are three firms which are scale inefficient: 1, 6, and 7. Note that for firm 1, $W_g^*(x, u) < W_g(x, u)$, therefore that firm exhibits increasing returns to

Table 8-3

Firm	$S_g(x, u)$	$W_g(x, u)$	$W_g^*(x, u)$	Returns to Scale
1	.87	1.00	.87	IRS
2	1.00	1.00	1.00	CRS
3	1.00	.87	.87	CRS
4	1.00	1.00	1.00	CRS
5	1.00	.93	.93	CRS
6	.94	1.00	1.00	DRS
7	.94	.94	.94	DRS

scale relative to the technology implied by the other firms. For firms 6 and 7, on the other hand, $W_g(x, u) = W_g^*(x, u)$, which implies that they have decreasing returns to scale, (see theorem 8.6.9).

Notes

1. We note that Afriat (1972) used this same restriction.
2. Note that this is identical to the calculation of $W_g(x, u)$ in chapter 5.

9 TOWARD EMPIRICAL IMPLEMENTATION

9.0 Introduction

In this brief concluding chapter we offer a summary of where we have been, where we are going, and how we might get there. In Section 9.1 we summarize the essential elements of efficiency measurement gleaned from the core of the book, chapters 3–8. In Section 9.2 we suggest two ways in which our work might be extended, to the development of dual efficiency measures, and to the measurement of dynamic efficiency. In Section 9.3 we provide a brief reader's guide to the various extant approaches to empirical implementation. This guide condenses and updates earlier surveys of Førsund, Lovell and Schmidt (1980) and Lovell and Schmidt (1983).

9.1 Summary of The Main Results

The basic purpose of this research has been to develop a coherent theory of production in the presence of inefficiency. The approach taken here to model productive behavior given inefficiency is axiomatic, and conforms in many aspects to modern production theory. In order to allow for inefficiency it has proved necessary, however, to start with a weaker set of axioms than those used, for example, in Debreu (1959). The relatively general framework used here follows that pioneered by Shephard (1970, 1974b).

In developing measures of various types of efficiency, we began with the radial measures of efficiency popularized by Farrell (1957). Input- and output-based radial efficiency measures were developed in chapters 3 and 4, respectively. In chapter 5 we introduced a natural complement of the input- and output-based measures, namely the graph measure of efficiency. This measure differs from the input- and output-based measures in that it is hyperbolic rather than radial. However these measures are related, which was the topic of chapter 6.

One potential disadvantage of the radial and graph measures of efficiency is that the point in the reference set (an element of the isoquant) relative to which efficiency is determined may not be a member of the efficient subset (see the definitions in chapter 2). This problem arises with these particular measures due to the radial (or hyperbolic) path used to determine efficiency. In chapter 7 we introduced a nonradial measure which is constructed to compare observations to the efficient subset. Input, output, and graph type nonradial measures were developed and compared to their radial (hyperbolic) counterparts.

Chapter 8 introduced input-, output-, and graph-based measures of scale efficiency. These measures capture departures from the scale of production consistent with long run competitive equilibrium. As such, this type of efficiency was shown to be one of the sources of technical efficiency.

This reference to sources of efficiency underscores one of the main contributions of our work, namely the development of a taxonomy of efficiency which allows us to decompose efficiency into a series of meaningful components (or sources) which are mutually exclusive and exhaustive.

As discussed in chapter 1, we suggest that efficiency can be usefully categorized as technical, structural, allocative, or social (i.e., scale efficiency). We can now illustrate that decomposition by synthesizing the decomposition derived in chapters 3–8. Specially, we now have

$$\mathrm{OE} = \mathrm{PTE} \cdot \mathrm{C} \cdot \mathrm{S} \cdot \mathrm{A}, \tag{9.1.1}$$

where OE is overall efficiency, PTE is purely technical efficiency, S is scale (i.e., social) efficiency, C is structural efficiency (i.e., congestion), and A is allocative efficiency.

This is perhaps best understood diagrammatically. Consider Fig. 9–1, which is an illustration using an input-based radial measure of efficiency. (The decomposition of the other measures is left to the reader.)

In Fig. 9–1, the observed input combination is at point V. Given input prices PP and the long run (scale) efficient reference technology denoted by $L^{SK}(u)$, the (overall) point of efficient production would be at point W. The input-based radial measure of overall efficiency would be

$$IOE = OT/OV. \tag{9.1.2}$$

Suppose that we would like to isolate the purely technical component of OT/OV, i.e., that part due to production in the interior of the input set, rather than on the isoquant. This is captured by

$$IPTE = OQ/OV. \tag{9.1.3}$$

The structural component, otherwise known as congestion, is due to production on a backward-bending segment of the isoquant (i.e., in the non-

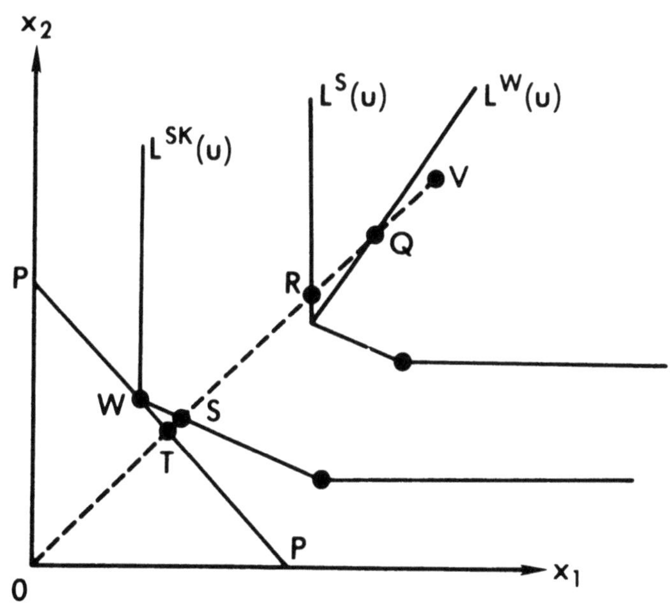

Figure 9-1

economic region where marginal product is negative). This is captured in Fig. 9–1 as

$$IC = OR/OQ. \tag{9.1.4}$$

Deviation from scale efficiency as defined here occurs because the firm is not operating at the scale of operations consistent with long-run competitive equilibrium, i.e., at a point consistent with constant returns to scale. At that point, the firm obtains maximum output for any given inputs. Stated differently, output u can be produced with the fewest possible inputs as in $L^{SK}(u)$ in Fig. 9–1. Thus scale efficiency is captured as

$$IS = OS/OR. \tag{9.1.5}$$

Allocative efficiency is price-dependent and is captured by an input-based radial measure of efficiency as

$$IA = OT/OS. \tag{9.1.6}$$

Thus the decomposition stated in (9.1.1) is confirmed for our example by

$$OT/OV = OQ/OV \cdot OR/OQ \cdot OS/OR \cdot OT/OS. \tag{9.1.7}$$

We note that in the calculations of the efficiency measures in chapters 3–8, scale efficiency was not included. Clearly, what we call scale efficiency was included in the technical component of efficiency in those cases. Another way of looking at the decomposition is to group the measures according to whether they are price-dependent or price-independent. We can construct an aggregate measure of price-independent efficiency (or overall technical efficiency) as

$$IOTE = IPTE \cdot IC \cdot IS, \tag{9.1.8}$$

which would be captured in Fig. 9–1 as

$$OS/OV = OQ/OV \cdot OR/OQ \cdot OS/OR. \tag{9.1.9}$$

Throughout this study, the various efficiency measures were defined, their properties as indicators of efficiency were derived, and their ability to characterize the underlying technology was investigated; all at a fairly high degree of rigor. In addition, the measures were illustrated at an intuitive level using simple diagrams and were given practical content in a series of linear programming examples used to calculate the measures.

9.2 Unfinished Business

In the previous chapters we have developed efficiency measures in the primal input-output space under the assumption of steady state. These measures can be extended into the dual price space and into a dynamic framework. Regarding dual efficiency measures and measuring, this research is partly underway, see e.g., Färe (1982), Färe and Grosskopf (1983c), Kopp and Diewert (1982), Muro (1982), and Zieschang (1983a). The aim in this research is twofold, namely (i) to use dual information to determine primal efficiency and (ii) to measure dual efficiency in the sense of shadow pricing. The first of these research goals is based on the knowledge of duality theory and that a technology, under certain assumptions, can be modeled both in the primal and the dual spaces. The second goal is to determine the efficiency of how prices are set. In public goods situations, when, e.g., the provision of goods is given, prices must be found such that costs are covered. In this situation, one can determine how efficient one price vector is in relation to a dual reference technology.

When the assumption of steady state is relaxed, and the production technology is given a dynamic interpretation, new problems of efficiency measuring occur. Following the dynamic production framework introduced by Shephard and Färe (1980), new notions of efficiency can be introduced. However, to obtain estimates of dynamic efficiency, one needs to formulate a dynamic reference technology and take into account "time substitution." The development of this type of reference technology is not yet completed.

9.3 Toward Empirical Implementation

The techniques of efficiency measurement developed in chapters 3–8 can be implemented empirically. In this section we provide a brief overview of the various approaches that have been developed for this purpose. In addition to an overview of the basic approaches, we also refer to a few empirical applications of each approach. Additional references to the empirical literature can be found in chapter 1.

Three tasks confront one who wishes to apply the techniques of efficiency measurement to empirical data. The first task is the specification of a behavioral objective for the production unit under observation. Obviously if no behavioral objective is specified one is restricted to an investigation of overall technical efficiency and its components. Just as clearly, if one is also interested in the measurement of the price-dependent notions of allocative and overall efficiency, then one must specify a behavioral objective. The choice of behavioral objective in turn determines the type of efficiency measure to be used. If cost minimization with exogenous outputs and input prices is the specified objective, then the input-based measures of chapter 3 and of chapter 7.1 are appropriate. If revenue maximization with exogenous inputs and output prices is the specified objective, then the output-based measures of chapter 4 and of chapter 7.2 are appropriate. If profit maximization with exogenous input prices and output prices is specified, then the graph measures of chapter 5 and of chapter 7.3 are appropriate.

The second task is the specification of technology. One option is to adopt a nonparametric representation of technology. This is the option we have chosen to illustrate the methods of efficiency measurement in this book. Our nonparametric piecewise linear technology was introduced in chapter 2.4, and used in chapters 3.7, 4.7, 5.8, 7.5, 8.5, and 8.7 for illustrative purposes. The other option is to select some parametric representation of technology. With this option, care must be taken to select a fairly flexible parametric representation, since the imposition of unwarranted parametric structure is likely to adversely affect the corresponding efficiency measures.

The third task is the selection of a computational method for measuring various types of efficiency relative to the specified (nonparametric or parametric) technology. Here again there are two options, with variations on each. Efficiency measures can be computed by mathematical programming techniques, or they can be estimated by statistical techniques. Since a nonparametric representation of technology leaves no parameters to be estimated in a statistical sense, efficiency measures must be computed by mathematical programming techniques when a nonparametric representation of technology is specified. However when a parametric representation of technology is specified, efficiency measures can be computed by mathematical programming techniques or estimated by statistical techniques.

This suggests three approaches to the specification of technology and the measurement of efficiency relative to that technology. For obvious reasons we call these three approaches the nonparametric programming approach, the parametric programming approach, and the parametric statistical approach. They are discussed briefly in section 9.3.1–9.3.3 below, and in more detail in Førsund, Lovell, and Schmidt (1980) and Lovell and Schmidt (1983).

9.3.1 The Nonparametric Programming Approach

This approach was apparently first utilized by Farrell (1957) and Farrell and Fieldhouse (1962). They constructed a nonparametric, piecewise-linear technology that was, however, very restrictive in its scale and disposability properties. Later Shephard (1970, 1974b), Afriat (1972) and others showed how to construct less restrictive nonparametric piecewise-linear technologies. These constructions have in turn been used for two related purposes: to test data sets for consistency with various regularity conditions on technology and behavior,[1] and to provide reference technologies against which to calculate the efficiency of observations in data sets.[2]

Our nonparametric piecewise-linear technologies were introduced in chapter 2.4. In subsequent chapters they were used as constraints in linear programming problems whose solutions provide measures of various types of efficiency. Varying the scale and disposability properties of the nonparametric piecewise-linear technologies generates different constraints in the linear programming problems, and this in turn yields measures of different types of efficiency (overall technical and its components, allocative, and scale).

Since the technologies, and the linear programming problems based on these technologies that are used to calculate efficiency measures, are laid out in some detail in chapters 2–8, they are not replicated here. Instead, we point out three noteworthy characteristics of this approach to efficiency measurement. First and foremost, the approach is extremely flexible. It can be used to calculate and decompose input-based efficiency measures, output-based efficiency measures, and measures of graph efficiency. Second, the nonparametric piecewise-linear technology constructed in this approach is the smallest set containing all the data and satisfying more or less stringent regularity conditions. Consequently the efficiencies calculated by this approach are upper bounds to the true efficiencies.[3] The third characteristic may provide a partial offset to the second. Since the data are enveloped by a deterministic technology, the entire deviation of an observation from the technology is attributed to inefficiency. All sorts of influences, favorable and unfavorable, beyond the control of the production unit, are lumped together with inefficiency and called inefficiency. Obviously this can cause an over- or under-statement of the true extent of inefficiency, unless one has a complete list of accurately measured variables, including exogenous conditioning or environmental variables.

9.3.2 The Parametric Programming Approach

This approach also was first proposed by Farrell (1957), and has been refined and extended by Aigner and Chu (1968) as well as by Førsund and his colleagues.[4] This approach also uses a sequence of linear (or quadratic) programs to compute efficiency measures relative to a deterministic technology. The only difference between the parametric and the nonparametric approaches is that the technology constructed by the parametric approach is parametric and smooth rather than nonparametric piecewise-linear.

To illustrate with a simple examle, suppose we observe a sample of k production units using inputs $x \in R^n_+$ available at prices $p \in R^n_{++}$ to produce scalar output $u \in R_+$. We posit the existence of a production function ϕ: $R^n_+ \rightarrow R_+$ satisfying (ϕ.1–ϕ.3) of chapter 2.3, relative to which the input correspondence $L(u) := \{x: u \leqq \phi(x)\}$ satisfies (L.1–L.5). The production function is given a specific functional form, say Cobb–Douglas for expository convenience, and so

$$L(u) = \{x: u \leqq \alpha_o \prod_{i=1}^{n} x_i^{\alpha_i}, \alpha_o > 0, \alpha_i > 0, i = 1, \ldots, n\}. \tag{9.3.2.1}$$

Next the parameters in ϕ are comuted by solving the program

$$\min\{\sum_{j=1}^{k} [ln\ \alpha_o + \sum_{i=1}^{n} \alpha_i\ ln\ x_i^j - ln\ u^j]\} \tag{9.3.2.2}$$

subject to

$$[ln\ \alpha_o + \sum_{i=1}^{n} \alpha_i\ ln\ x_i^j - ln\ u^j] \geqq 0, j = 1, \ldots, k, \alpha_o > 0,$$
$$\alpha_i > 0, i = 1, \ldots, n.$$

The Farrell measure of technical efficiency (note that overall technical efficiency equals purely technical efficiency, since there is no congestion in a Cobb–Douglas technology) is obtained from the functional constraints in (9.3.2.2) by defining

$$\varepsilon^j = \ln \alpha_o + \sum_{i=1}^{n} \alpha_i \ln x_i^j - \ln u^j, j = 1, \ldots, k, \tag{9.3.2.3}$$

so that

$$F_i(u^j, x^j) = \exp\{-\varepsilon^j\}, j = 1, \ldots, k, \tag{9.3.2.4}$$

which for small ε^j is approximately equal to $(1 - \varepsilon^j)$. The final step is to compute $Q(u^j, p^j)$ by solving the program

$$Q(u^j, p^j) = \min\{p^j x: [\ln \alpha_o + \sum_{i=1}^{n} \alpha_i \ln x_i - \ln u^j] \geqq 0,$$

$$\alpha_o > 0, \alpha_i > 0, i = 1, \ldots, n\}, \tag{9.3.2.5}$$

from which it follows that

$$O_i(u^j, x^j, p^j) = Q(u^j, p^j)/p^j x^j, j = 1, \ldots, k, \tag{9.3.2.6}$$

$$A_i(u^j, x^j, p^j) = O_i(u^j, x^j, p^j)/F_i(u^j, x^j), j = 1, \ldots, k. \tag{9.3.2.7}$$

Since the Cobb-Douglas production function used in this illustration is homogeneous and satisfies strong input disposability, the notion of scale efficiency is meaningless and congestion is absent. However both of these components of overall input efficiency can be restored simply by specifying a less restrictive functional form for the production function. The restriction to a single output can also be relaxed. One simply specifies a joint cost function for production units producing output vector $u \in R_+^m$, say Cobb-Douglas again for simplicity, the parameters of which are computed by solving the program

$$\min\{\sum_{j=1}^{k} [\ln(p^j x^j) - \beta_o - \sum_{l=1}^{m} \gamma_l \ln u_l^j - \sum_{i=1}^{n} \beta_i \ln p_i^j]\} \tag{9.3.2.8}$$

subject to

$$[\cdot] \geqq 0, j = 1, \ldots, k, \gamma_l > 0, l = 1, \ldots, m, \beta_i > 0, i = 1, \ldots, n,$$
$$\sum_{i=1}^{n} \beta_i = 1.$$

A measure of overall input efficiency is obtained for each observation as $O_i(u^j, x^j, p^j) = \exp\{-[\cdot]\}, j = 1, \ldots, k$. An alogorithm due to Kopp and

Diewert (1982) and Zieschang (1983a) decomposes $O_i(u^j, x^j, p^j)$ into its technical and allocative components.

It should be clear that output-based measures of efficiency and measures of graph efficiency can be obtained using this parametric programming approach, merely by replacing the parametric cost function of (9.3.2.8) with parametric revenue or profit functions and proceeding along similar lines.

The decomposition alogorithms of Kopp and Diewert, and of Zieschang, have improved the appeal of the parametric programming approach, but it still has two drawbacks. First, simple parametric specifications may impose unwarranted structure on technology and undesirable distortions in computed efficiencies. Second, like the nonparametric programming approach, the parametric programming approach is entirely deterministic. Since the parametric representation of technology is supported by a subset of the data, its shape and placement are highly sensitive to ostensibly efficient outliers. Consequently, so too are computed efficiencies.[5]

9.3.3 The Parametric Statistical Approach

In contrast to the nonparametric programming approach, this approach to efficiency measurement is parametric. In contrast to both programming approaches, this approach uses statistical techniques to estimate a parametric representation of technology, and to estimate efficiency relative to that technology. The seeds of this approach were sown by Aigner, Amemiya, and Poirier (1976), Aigner, Lovell, and Schmidt (1977), and Meeusen and van den Broeck (1977a,b).[6]

The approach can be illustrated by supposing that we observe a sample of k production units using inputs $x \in R^n_+$ available at prices $p \in R^n_{++}$ to produce scalar output $u \in R_+$. The actual output of a production unit can be expressed as

$$ln\ u^j = ln\ \alpha_o + \sum_{i=1}^{n} \alpha_i\ ln\ x_i^j + \varepsilon^j,\ j = 1, \ldots, k, \quad (9.3.3.1)$$

where the Cobb-Douglas parametric specification is arbitrary. The disturbance term ε^j consists of two parts

$$\varepsilon^j = \varepsilon_1^j + \varepsilon_2^j,\ j = 1, \ldots, k, \quad (9.3.3.2)$$

and so

$$ln\ u^j = ln\ \alpha_o + \sum_{i=1}^{n} \alpha_i\ ln\ x_i^j + \varepsilon_1^j + \varepsilon_2^j,\ j = 1, \ldots, k. \quad (9.3.3.3)$$

Here the symmetric disturbance term $\varepsilon_1 \gtreqless 0$ permits random variation of the production function across production units, and captures the effects of statistical noise, measurement error, and exogenous shocks beyond the control of the production unit. The production function is stochastic, varying randomly about a deterministic kernel. The one-sided disturbance term $\varepsilon_2 \leqq 0$ represents technical inefficiency relative to the stochastic production function. In constrast to the two programming approaches, in this approach the data are bounded, or enveloped, by a stochastic production function. Consequently the deviation of an observation from the deterministic kernel of the stochastic production function comes from two sources: random variation of the deterministic kernel across observations captured by the component ε_1, and technical inefficiency captured by the component ε_2.[7]

The next step is to estimate the parameters of $\phi(x)$, $f_1(\varepsilon_1)$ and $f_2(\varepsilon_2)$, the densities of ε_1 and ε_2. This requires the specification of parametric forms for ϕ (Cobb-Douglas in our illustration), f_1 (typically normal) and usually f_2 as well (truncated normal and exponential are popular choices). Estimation can then be conducted using either some type of corrected ordinary least squares technique or maximum likelihood.[8] Once the parameters have been estimated, the next step is to estimate technical efficiency. The sample mean value of technical efficiency is $E(\exp\{\varepsilon_2\}) \approx 1 + E(\varepsilon_2)$, which can be derived from the moments of the regression residuals. Jondrow, Lovell, Materov, and Schmidt (1982) have shown how to extract estimates of technical efficiency for each observation in the sample, by decomposing the composed error terms $(\varepsilon_1^j + \varepsilon_2^j)$ into ε_1^j and ε_2^j. This is accomplished by calculating the distribution of ε_2 conditional on $(\varepsilon_1 + \varepsilon_2)$; estimates of ε_2 are provided by the mean or the mode of the conditional distribution $(\varepsilon_2 \mid \varepsilon_1^j + \varepsilon_2^j)$.

The final step is to estimate allocative and overall efficiency. One way this can be done is to convert equation (9.3.3.3) into a system by appending a set of equations reflecting first-order conditions for cost minimization. Error terms on these equations represent allocative inefficiency. Assumptions on ϕ, f_1, f_2, and the distribution of the error terms on the first order conditions enable the system to the estimated by maximum likelihood, from which estimates of technical, allocative, and overall efficiency can be obtained. A second way this can be done is to estimate the dual stochastic cost function directly. In the Cobb-Douglas case this would be

$$ln(p^j x^j) = \beta_o + \beta_u ln\ u^j + \sum_{i=1}^{n} \beta_i\ ln\ p_i^j + \xi_i^j + \xi_2^j, j = 1, \ldots, k, \tag{9.3.3.4}$$

where ξ_1 is symmetric and $\xi_2 \geqq 0$ is one-sided and reflects the cost of technical and allocative inefficiency. This stochastic cost function can be estimated by corrected ordinary least squares or (in single equation or system form) by maximum likelihood. The Kopp-Diewert-Zieschang algorithm can then be adapted to the stochastic cost function context to provide estimates of technical, allocative, and overall inefficiency.[8]

The main disadvantage of the parametric statistical approach is that it is parametric. Possibly unwarranted structure is imposed on the production function, and on the distribution of inefficiency as well.[9] The main advantage of the parametric statistical approach is that it is statistical. It is the only approach that makes any accommodation for noise, measurement error, and exogenous shocks beyond the control of the production unit. Without such an accommodation these phenomena are counted as inefficiency.[10]

Notes

1. Among the more important contributions to the literature on nonparametric tests of regularity conditions and behavioral objectives in production theory are Afriat (1972), Hanoch and Rothschild (1972), Diewert and Parkan (1983), Varian (1984), and Banker and Maindiratta (1983).

2. The nonparametric approach to efficiency measurement is developed and applied by Banker (1984), Banker, Charnes, and Cooper (1983), Boyd and Färe (1984), Burley (1980), Byrnes, Färe, and Grosskopf (1984), Charnes, Cooper, and Rhodes (1978, 1979, 1981), Färe and Grosskopf (1983a,b), Färe, Grosskopf, Logan, and Lovell (1984), Lewin and Morey (1981), Lewin, Morey, and Cook (1982), and Zieschang (1983b) among others.

3. Piecewise log-linear technologies have also been developed; see Banker, Charnes, Cooper, and Schinnar (1981), Charnes, Cooper and Seiford (1982), and Charnes, Cooper, Seiford and Stutz (1982).

4. See Førsund and Hjalmarsson (1979a,b,c), and Førsund and Jansen (1977).

5. Timmer (1971) suggested dealing with efficient outliers by resorting to chance-constrained programming techniques. This approach involves discarding efficient observations until a certain percent of the observations lie outside the recomputed technology, or until the computed parameter values stabilize. Empirical experience with this technique has not been favorable.

6. Recent contributions to the parametric statistical approach include Jondrow, Lovell, Materov, and Schmidt (1982), Lee (1983), Lee and Tyler (1978), Pitt and Lee (1981), Schmidt and Lovell (1979, 1980), Stevenson (1980), and Tyler and Lee (1979).

7. A special case of this model is the so-called "full frontier" model in which $\varepsilon_1 = 0$. In this special case the parametric frontier is deterministic, and assuming a distribution for the density of ε_2 enables the model to be estimated by statistical techniques. See Richmond (1974) and Greene (1980a,b) for details, and see Schmidt (1976) on the relationship between parametric statistical models of the full frontier form and parametric programming models.

8. Details of these estimation techniques can be found in Førsund, Lovell, and Schmidt (1980) and Lovell and Schmidt (1983), as well as in references cited therein.

9. Some of the structure on the distribution of inefficiency can be relaxed in the presence of panel data; see Schmidt and Sickles (1984).

10. There are several comparisons of the alternative approaches to efficiency measurement in the literature, although no consensus has developed. See, for example, Banker, Charnes, Cooper, and Maindiratta (1982), Corbo and de Melo (1983), Cowing, Reifschneider, and Stevenson (1982), Kopp and Smith (1980), and van den Broeck, Førsund, Hjalmarsson, and Meeusen (1980).

APPENDIX

Standard Notations and Mathematical Appendix

A.1 Some Standard Notations

Let A and B be two sets, we mean by

$:=$	$A := B$	A is defined by B;
$\in$	$a \in A$	a is an element in A;
$\notin$	$a \notin A$	a is not an element in A;
$\subseteqq$	$A \subseteqq B$	A is a subset of B;
$\subset$	$A \subset B$	A is a true subset of B;
$\emptyset$	$A = \emptyset$	A is an empty set;
$\cap$	$A \cap B$	A intersection B;
$\setminus$	$A \setminus B$	$A \setminus B := \{x: x \in A, x \notin B\}$;

$+$	$A + B$ $A + B: = \{z: x \in A, y \in B, z = x + y\}$;
R^l	Euclidean space of dimension l;
$\geqq$	If x and $y \in R^l$, then $x \geqq y$ if and only if $x_i \geqq y_i$ for all $i = 1, 2, \ldots, l$;
$\geq$	$x \geq y$ if and only if $x \geqq y$ and $x \neq y$;
$>$	$x > y$ if and only if $x_i > y_i$ for all $i = 1, 2, \ldots, l$;
$\overset{*}{>}$	$x \overset{*}{>} y$ if and only if $x_i > y_i$ or $x_i = y_i = 0$, $i = 1, 2, \ldots, l$;
$\|\cdot\|$	$\|x\|: = (\sum_{i=1}^{l} (x_i)^2)^{½}$, Euclidean norm of $x \in R^l$;
R^l_+	$R^l_+: = \{x: x \in R^l, x \geqq 0\}$;
R^l_{++}	$R^l_{++}: = \{x: x \in R^l, x > 0\}$;
R^l_-	$R^l_-: = \{x: x \in R^l, x \leqq 0\}$;
$[\ ,\ ]$	$[a, b]: = \{x \in R: a \leqq x \leqq b\}$;
$[\ ,\ )$	$[a, b): = \{x \in R: a \leqq x < b\}$;
$\exists$	there exists;
$s^l \to s^\circ$	the sequence s^l converges to s°;
$\bar{A}$	closure of A;
px	$px = p_1x_1 + p_2x_2 + \ldots + p_nx_n$, p and $x \in R^n$;
ru	$ru = r_1u_1 + r_2u_2 + \ldots + r_mu_m$, r and $u \in R^m$;
$\odot$	$\lambda, x \in R^l, \lambda \odot x: = (\lambda_1x_1, \lambda_2x_2, \ldots, \lambda_lx_l)$;
$\Rightarrow$	$x \in A \Rightarrow x \in B$, x belongs to A only if x belongs to B;
$\Leftrightarrow$	$x \in A \Leftrightarrow x \in B$, x belongs to A if and only if x belongs to B;
$\to +\infty$	$x \to +\infty$, x tends to $+\infty$.

A.2 Mathematical Appendix

A.2.1 A set $A \subseteqq R^l$ is bounded if and only if $\sup\{\|x - y\|: x \in A, y \in A\} < +\infty$.

A.2.2 A set $F \subseteqq R^l$ is closed if and only if for every sequence $s^l \to s^\circ$ with $s^l \in F$ for all $l = 1, 2, \ldots, s^\circ \in F$.

A.2.3 A set $K \subseteqq R^l$ is compact if and only if it is closed and bounded.

A.2.4 A correspondence $S: R^l \to S(x) \subseteqq R^k$ is closed if and only if for every sequence $(x^l, y^l) \in R^l \times R^k$ such that $x^l \to x^\circ$ and $y^l \in S(x^l)$, $y^\circ \in S(x^\circ)$.

A.2.5 A function $\phi: R^n_+ \to R_+$ is upper semicontinuous if and only if for each $x^\circ \in R^n_+$ and each sequence $x^l \to x^\circ$, $\limsup_{l \to +\infty} \phi(x^l) \leqq \phi(x^\circ)$.

A.2.6 A function $f: R^l \to R$ is lower semicontinuous if and only if $-f$ is upper semicontinuous.

A.2.7 A class of sets A has the finite intersection property if and only if every finite subclass has a nonempty intersection.

A.2.8 A correspondence $S: R^l \to S(x) \subseteqq R^k$ is quasi-concave if and only if $S(\lambda x + (1-\lambda)x') \supseteqq S(x) \cap S(x')$, for all $x, x' \in R^l$ and $\lambda \in [0, 1]$.

Bibliography

Afriat, S. N. (1972) "Efficiency Estimation of Production Functions," *International Economic Review*, 13:3 (October), pp. 568–98.

Aigner, D. J., Amemiya, T., and Poirier, D. J. (1976) "On the Estimation of Production Frontiers: Maximum Likelihood Estimation of the Parameters of a Discontinuous Density Function," *International Economic Review*, 17:2 (June), pp. 377–96.

———, and Chu, S. F. (1968) "On Estimating the Industry Production Function," *American Economic Review*, 58:4 (September), pp. 826–39.

———, Lovell, C. A. K., and Schmidt, P. (1977) "Formulation and Estimation of Stochastic Frontier Production Function Models," *Journal of Econometrics*, 6:1 (July), pp. 21–37.

Al-Ayat, R., and Färe, R. (1979) "On the Existence of Joint Production Functions," *Naval Research Logistics Quarterly*, 26:4 (December), pp. 627–30.

Albach, H. (1980) "Average and Best-Practice Production Functions in German Industry," *Journal of Industrial Economics*, 29:1 (September), pp. 55–70.

Alchian, A. A. (1965) "Some Economics of Property Rights," *Il Politico*, 30:4 (December), pp. 816–29.

Atkinson, S. E., and Halvorsen, R. (1980) "A Test of Relative and Absolute Price Efficiency in Regulated Utilities," *Review of Economics and Statistics*, 62:1 (February), pp. 81–88.

Averch, H., and Johnson, L. L. (1962) "Behavior of the Firm Under Regulatory Constraint," *American Economic Review*, 52:5 (December), pp. 1052–69.

Banker, R. D. (1984) "Estimating Most Productive Scale Size Using Data Envelopment Analysis," *European Journal of Operational Research*, 17:1 (July), pp. 35–44.

———, Charnes, A., and Cooper, W. W. (1983) "Some Models for Estimating Technical and Returns to Scale Inefficiencies," *Management Science*, forthcoming.

———, Charnes, A., Cooper, W. W., and Maindiratta, A. (1982) "A Comparison of DEA and Translog Estimates of Production Frontier Using Simulated Observations From a Known Technology," unpublished manuscript.

———, Charnes, A., Cooper, W. W., and Schinnar, A. P. (1981) "A Bi-Extremal Principle for Frontier Estimation and Efficiency Evaluations," *Management Science*, 27:12 (December), pp. 1370–82.

———, and Maindiratta, A. (1983) "Nonparametric Estimation of Production Frontiers," unpublished manuscript.

Bardhan, P. K., and Srinivasan, T. N. (1971) "Cropsharing Tenancy in Agriculture: A Theoretical and Empirical Analysis," *American Economic Review*, 61:1 (March), pp. 48–64.

Baumol, W. J., and Klevorick, A. K. (1970) "Input Choices and Rate of Return Regulation: An Overview of the Discussions," *Bell Journal of Economics and Management Science*, 1:2 (Autumn), pp. 162–90.

———, Panzar, J. C., and Willig, R. D. (1982) *Contestable Markets and the Theory of Industry Structure*. New York: Harcourt Brace Jovanovich, Inc.

Becker, G. S. (1957) *The Economics of Discrimination*. Chicago: The University of Chicago Press.

Bergsman, J. (1974) "Commercial Policy, Allocative Efficiency, and 'X-efficiency'," *Quarterly Journal of Economics*, 88:3 (August), pp. 409–33.

Bharadwaj, K. (1974) *Production Conditions in Indian Agriculture*. London: Cambridge University Press.

Bol, G., and Moeschlin, O. (1975) "Isoquants of Continuous Production Correspondences," *Naval Research Logistics Quarterly*, 22:2 (June), pp. 391–98.

Borcherding, T. E., Pommerehne, W. W., and Schneider, F. (1982) "Comparing the Efficiency of Private and Public Production: The Evidence from Five Countries," *Zeitschrift für Nationalökonomie*, 42, Suppl. 2, pp. 127–56.

Boyd, G., and Färe, R. (1984) "Measuring the Efficiency of Decision Making Units: A Comment," *European Journal of Operational Research*, 15 (March), pp. 331–32.

van den Broeck, J. (1983) "Stochastic 'Frontier' Inefficiency and Firm Size for Selected Industries of the Belgian Manufacturing Sector: Some New Evidence," unpublished manuscript.

———, Førsund, F. R., Hjalmarsson, L. and Meeusen, W. (1980) "On the Estimation of Deterministic and Stochastic Frontier Production Functions: A Comparison," *Journal of Econometrics*, 13:1 (May), pp. 117–38.

Burley, H. T. (1980) "Production Efficiency in U.S. Manufacturing: A Linear Programming Approach," *Review of Economics and Statistics*, 62:4 (November), pp. 619–22.

Byrnes, P., Färe, R., and Grosskopf, S. (1984) "Measuring Productive Efficiency: An Application to Illinois Strip Mines," *Management Science*, forthcoming.

———, and Lovell, C. A. K. (1984) "The Effect of Unions on Productive Efficiency: U.S. Surface Mining of Coal," unpublished manuscript.

Carlson, S. (1939) *A Study on the Pure Theory of Production*. London: King.

Carlsson, B. (1972) "The Measurement of Efficiency in Production: An Application to Swedish Manufacturing Industries, 1968," *Swedish Journal of Economics*, 74:4 (December), pp. 468–85.

Caves, D. W., and Christensen, L. R. (1980) "The Relative Efficiency of Public and Private Firms in a Competitive Environment: The Case of Canadian Railroads," *Journal of Political Economy*, 88:5 (October), pp. 958–76.

Chamberlin, E. H. (1933) *The Theory of Monopolistic Competition*. Cambridge, Mass.: Harvard University Press.

Charnes, A., Cooper, W. W., Lewin, A. Y., Morey, R. C., and Rousseau, J. (1982) "An Approach to Positivity and Stability Analysis in DEA," Center for Cybernetic Studies, Report No. 434, Austin, Texas.

———, Cooper, W. W., and Rhodes, E. (1978). "Measuring the Efficiency of Decision Making Units," *European Journal of Operational Research*, 2:6 (November), pp. 429–44.

———, Cooper, W. W., and Rhodes, E. (1979) "Short Communication: Measuring Efficiency of Decision Making Units," *European Journal of Operational Research*, 3:4 (July), p. 339.

———, Cooper, W. W., and Rhodes, E. (1981) "Evaluating Program and Managerial Efficiency: An Application of Data Envelopment Analysis to Program Follow Through," *Management Science*, 27:6 (June), pp. 668–97.

———, Cooper, W. W., and Seiford, L. (1982) "A Multiplicative Model for Efficiency Analysis," *Socio-Economic Planning Sciences*, 16:5, pp. 223–24.

———, Cooper, W. W., Seiford, L., and Stutz, J. (1982) "Invariant Multiplicative Efficiency and Piecewise Cobb-Douglas Envelopments," unpublished manuscript.

———, Cooper, W. W., and Sherman, H. D. (1983) "A Comparative Study of Data Envelopment Analysis and Other Approaches to Efficiency Evaluation and Estimation," unpublished manuscript.

Cheung, S. N. S. (1969) *The Theory of Share Tenancy*, Chicago: The University of Chicago Press.

Corbo, V., and de Melo, J. (1983) "Measuring Technical Efficiency: A Comparison of Alternative Methodologies with Census Data," unpublished manuscript.

Cowing, T., Reifschneider, D., and Stevenson, R. E. (1982) "A Comparison of Alternative Frontier Cost Function Specifications," in A. Dogramaci (ed.), *Developments in Econometric Analyses of Productivity*. Boston: Kluwer-Nijhoff Publishing.

———, and Stevenson, R. E. (1982) "Automatic Adjustment Clauses and Allocative Efficiency in Public Utilities," *Journal of Economics and Business*, 34:4 (December), pp. 317–29.

Crain, W. M., and Zardkoohi, A. (1980) "X-Inefficiency and Nonpecuniary Rewards in a Rent-Seeking Society: A Neglected Issue in the Property Rights Theory of the Firm," *American Economic Review*, 70:4 (September), pp. 784–92.

Currie, J. M. (1981) *The Economic Theory of Agricultural Land Tenure*. New York: Cambridge University Press.

Danø, S. (1966) *Industrial Production Models.* New York: Springer-Verlag.

Davies, D. G. (1971) "The Efficiency of Public versus Private Firms: The Case of Australia's Two Airlines," *Journal of Law and Economics*, 19:1 (April), pp. 149–65.

Debreu, G. (1951) "The Coefficient of Resource Utilization," *Econometrica*, 19:3 (July), pp. 273–92.

———, (1959) *Theory of Value: An Axiomatic Analysis of Economic Equilibrium*. New York: John Wiley and Sons.

DeCanio, S. J. (1974) *Agriculture in the Post-Bellum South: The Economics of Production and Supply*. Cambridge, Mass.: The MIT Press.

Diewert, W. E. (1973) "Functional Forms for Profit and Transformation Functions," *Journal of Economic Theory*, 6:3 (June), pp. 284–316.

———, (1974) "Applications of Duality Theory," in Intriligator, M. D., and Kendrick, D. A., eds., *Frontiers of Quantitative Economics, Volume II*. Amsterdam: North-Holland Publishing Company.

——— (1982) "Duality Approaches to Microeconomic Theory," in Arrow, K. J., and Intriligator, M. D., eds., *Handbook of Mathematical Economics, Volume II*. Amsterdam: North-Holland Publishing Company.

———, and Parkan, C. (1983) "Linear Programming Tests of Regularity Conditions for Production Frontiers," in Eichhorn, W., Henn, R., Neumann, K., and Shephard, R. W., eds., *Quantitative Studies on Production and Prices.* Würzburg and Vienna: Physica-Verlag.

Eichhorn, W. (1972) "Effektivität von Produktionsverfahren," *Operations Research-Verfahren*, 12, pp. 98–115.

——— (1978a) "What is an Economic Index? An Attempt of an Answer," in Eichhorn, W., Henn, R., Opitz, O., and Shephard, R. W., eds., *Theory and Applications of Economic Indices.* Würzburg: Physica-Verlag.

——— (1978b) *Functional Equations in Economics*. Reading, Mass.: Addison-Wesley.

Färe, R. (1975) "Efficiency and the Production Function," *Zeitschrift für Nationalökonomie*, 35:3–4, pp. 317–24.

——— (1980) "On Three Joint Production Functions," Department of Economics, Southern Illinois University, Carbondale, Il.

——— (1981) "Simultaneous Input and Output Efficiency," *Operations Research Verfahren*, pp. 27–29.

——— "The Dual Measurement of Productive Efficiency," unpublished manuscript.

———, Grabowski, R., and Grosskopf, S. (1984) "Technical Efficiency of Philippine Agriculture," *Applied Economics*, forthcoming.

———, and Grosskopf, S., (1983a) "Measuring Output Efficiency," *European Journal of Operational Research*, 13, pp. 173–79.

______, and Grosskopf, S. (1983b) "Measuring Congestion in Production," *Zeitschrift für Nationalökonomie*, 43, pp. 257–71.
______, and Grosskopf, S. (1983c) "Measuring Dual Efficiency," unpublished manuscript.
______, Grosskopf, S., Logan, J., and Lovell, C. A. K. (1984) "Measuring Efficiency in Production: With an Application to Electric Utilities," in Dogramaci, A., and Adam, N., eds., *Current Issues in Productivity*. Boston: Kluwer-Nijhoff Publishing, forthcoming.
______, Grosskopf, S., and Lovell, C. A. K. (1983) "The Structure of Technical Efficiency," *Scandinavian Journal of Economics*, 85, pp. 181–90.
______, and Hunsaker, W. (1983) "Notions of Efficiency and their Reference Sets," unpublished manuscript.
______, and Lovell, C. A. K. (1978) "Measuring the Technical Efficiency of Production," *Journal of Economic Theory*, 19:1 (October), pp. 150–62.
______, and Lovell, C. A. K. (1981) "Measuring the Technical Efficiency of Production: Reply," *Journal of Economic Theory*, 25:3 (December), pp. 253–54.
______, Lovell, C. A. K., and Zieschang, K. (1983) "Measuring the Technical Efficiency of Multiple Output Production Technologies," in Eichhorn, W., Henn, R., Neumann, K., and Shephard, R. W. eds., *Quantitative Studies on Production and Prices*. Würzburg and Vienna: Physica-Verlag.
______, and Lyon, V. (1981) "The Determinateness Test and Economic Price Indices" *Econometrica* 49:1 (January), pp. 209–14.
______, and Shephard, R. W. (1977) "Ray-Homothetic Production Functions," *Econometrica*, 45:1 (January), pp. 133–46.
______, Svensson, L. (1980) "Congestion of Production Factors," *Econometrica*, 48:7 (November), pp. 1745–53.
Farrell, M. J. (1957) "The Measurement of Productive Efficiency," *Journal of the Royal Statistical Society*, Series A., General, 120, Part 3, pp. 253–81.
______, and Fieldhouse, M. (1962) "Estimating Efficient Production Under Increasing Returns to Scale," *Journal of the Royal Statistical Society*, Series A, General, 125, Part 2, pp. 252–67.
Førsund, F. R., and Hjalmarsson, L. (1974) "On the Measurement of Productive Efficiency," *Swedish Journal of Economics*, 76:2 (June), pp. 141–54.
______, and Hjalmarsson, L. (1979a) "Generalized Farrell Measures of Efficiency: An Application to Milk Processing in Swedish Dairy Plants," *Economic Journal*, 89:354 (June), pp. 274–315.
______, and Hjalmarsson, L. (1979b) "Frontier Production Functions and Technical Progress: A Study of General Milk Processing in Swedish Dairy Plants," *Econometrica*, 47:4 (July), pp. 883–900.
______, and Hjalmarsson, L. (1979c) "Analysis of Industrial Structure: A Production Function Approach." unpublished manuscript.
______, and Jansen, E. S. (1977) "On Estimating Average and Best Practice Homothetic Production Functions Via Cost Function," *International Economic Review*, 18:2 (June), pp. 463–76.
______, Lovell, C. A. K., and Schmidt, P. (1980) "A Survey of Frontier Production Functions and of their Relationship to Efficiency Measurement," *Journal of Econometrics*, 13:1 (May), pp. 5–25.
Frisch, R. (1965) *Theory of Production*. Chicago: Rand McNally and Company.
Fuss, M., and McFadden, D., eds. (1978) *Production Economics: A Dual Approach to Theory and Applications*. Amsterdam: North-Holland Publishing Company.
Gillis, M. (1982) "Allocative and X-Efficiency in State-Owned Mining Enterprises: Comparisons Between Bolivia and Indonesia," *Journal of Comparative Economics*, 6:1 (March), pp. 1–23.

Gollop, F. M., and Karlson, S. H. (1978) "The Impact of the Fuel Adjustment Mechanism on Economic Efficiency," *Review of Economics and Statistics*, 60:4 (November), pp. 574–84.

Greene, W. H. (1980a) "Maximum Likelihood Estimation of Econometric Frontier Functions," *Journal of Econometrics*, 13:1 (May), pp. 27–56.

——— (1980b) "On the Estimation of a Flexible Frontier Production Model," *Journal of Econometrics*, 13:1 (May), pp. 101–15.

——— (1982) "Maximum Likelihood Estimation of Stochastic Frontier Production Models," *Journal of Econometrics*, 18:2 (February), pp. 285–89.

Hall, M. L., and Winsten, C. B. (1959) "The Ambiguous Notion of Efficiency," *Economic Journal*, 69:1 (March), pp. 71–86.

Hanoch, G., and Rothschild, M. (1972) "Testing the Assumptions of Production Theory: A Nonparametric Approach," *Journal of Political Economy*, 80:2 (March/April), pp. 256–75.

Herdt, R. W., and Mandac, A. M. (1981) "Modern Technology and Economic Efficiency of Philippine Rice Farmers," *Economic Development and Cultural Change*, 29:2 (January), pp. 375–99.

Hicks, J. R. (1935) "Annual Survey of Economic Theory: Monopoly," *Econometrica*, 3:1 (January), pp. 1–20.

——— (1946) *Value and Capital*. Second Edition. Oxford: Clarendon Press.

Higgs, R. (1977) *Competition and Coercion: Blacks in the American Economy, 1865–1914*. New York: Cambridge University Press.

Hildenbrand, W. (1981) "Short-Run Production Functions Based on Microdata," *Econometrica*, 49:5 (September), pp. 1095–1125.

Holtman, A. G. (1983) "X-Inefficiency, Uncertainty, and Organization Form," *Journal of Economics and Business* 35:1 (February).

Jondrow, J., Lovell, C. A. K., Materov, I. S., and Schmidt, P. (1982) "On the Estimation of Technical Inefficiency in the Stochastic Frontier Production Function Model," *Journal of Econometrics*, 19:2/3 (August), pp. 233–38.

Jorgenson, D. W., and Lau, L. J. (1974a), "The Duality of Technology and Economic Behaviour," *Review of Economic Studies*, 41:2 (April), pp. 181–200.

———, and Lau, L. J. (1974b), "Duality and Differentiability in Production," *Journal of Economic Theory*, 9:1 (August), pp. 23–42.

Knight, F. H. (1965) *Risk, Uncertainty and Profit*. New York: Harper and Row.

Koopmans, T. C. (1951) "An Analysis of Production as an Efficient Combination of Activities," in T. C. Koopmans, ed., *Activity Analysis of Production and Allocation*, Cowles Commission for Research in Economics. Monograph No. 13, New York: John Wiley and Sons, Inc.

———(1957) *Three Essays on the State of Economic Science*. New York: McGraw Hill Book Company.

Kopp, R. J. (1981a) "The Measurement of Productive Efficiency: A Reconsideration," *Quarterly Journal of Economics*, 96:3 (August), pp. 477–503.

———(1981b) "Measuring the Technical Efficiency of Production: Comment," *Journal of Economic Theory*, 25:3 (December), pp. 251–52.

———, and Diewert, W. E. (1982) "The Decomposition of Frontier Cost Function Deviations into Measures of Technical and Allocative Efficiency," *Journal of Econometrics*, 19:2/3 (August), pp. 319–32.

———, and Smith, V. K. (1980) "Frontier Production Function Estimates for Steam Electric Generation: A Comparative Analysis," *Southern Economic Journal*, 46:4 (April), pp. 1049–1059.

Lau, L. J., and Yotopoulos, P. A. (1971) "A Test for Relative Efficiency and Applications to Indian Agriculture," *American Economic Review*, 61:1 (March), pp. 94–109.

Lecraw, D. J. (1979) "Choice of Technology in Low-Wage Countries: A Nonneoclassical Approach," *Quarterly Journal of Economics*, 93:4 (November), pp. 631–54.

Lee, L. -F. (1983) "A Test for Distributional Assumptions for the Stochastic Frontier Functions," *Journal of Econometrics*, 22:3 (August), pp. 245–67.

_____, and Tyler, W. G. (1978) "The Stochastic Frontier Production Function and Average Efficiency: An Empirical Analysis," *Journal of Econometrics*, 7:3 (June), pp. 385–89.

Leibenstein, H. (1966) "Allocative Efficiency vs. 'X-Efficiency'," *American Economic Review*, 56:3 (June), pp. 392–415.

_____ (1973) "Competition and X-Efficiency: Reply," *Journal of Political Economy*, 81:3 (May/June), pp. 765–77.

_____(1975) "Aspects of the X-Efficiency Theory of the Firm," *Bell Journal of Economics*, 6:2 (Autumn), pp. 580–606.

_____(1976) *Beyond Economic Man*, Cambridge: Harvard University Press.

_____(1978a) *General X-Efficiency Theory and Economic Development*, New York, London, and Toronto: Oxford University Press.

_____(1978b) "On the Basic Proposition of X-Efficiency Theory," *American Economic Review*, 68:2 (May), pp. 328–32.

Levy, V. (1981) "On Estimating Efficiency Differentials Between the Public and Private Sectors in a Developing Economy-Iraq," *Journal of Comparative Economics*, 5:3 (September), pp. 235–50.

Lewin, A. Y., and Morey, R. (1981) "Measuring the Relative Efficiency and Output Potential of Public Sector Organizations: An Application of Data Envelopment Analysis," *International Journal of Policy Analysis and Information Systems*, 5, pp. 267–85.

_____, Morey, R., and Cook, T. (1982) "Evaluating the Administrative Efficiency of Courts," *Omega*, 10, pp. 401–11.

Lovell, C. A. K., and Schmidt, P. (1983) "A Comparison of Alternative Approaches to the Measurement of Productive Efficiency," unpublished manuscript.

_____, and Sickles, R. (1983) "Testing Efficiency Hypotheses in Joint Production: A Parametric Approach," *Review of Economics and Statistics*, 65:1 (February), pp. 51–58.

Martin, J. P., and Page, J. M., Jr. (1983) "The Impact of Subsidies on X-Efficiency in LDC Industry: Theory and an Empirical Test," *Review of Economics and Statistics*, 65:4 (November), pp. 608–17.

Meeusen, W., and van den Broeck, J. (1977a) "Efficiency Estimation from Cobb-Douglas Production Functions with Composed Error," *International Economic Review*, 18:2 (June), pp. 435–44.

_____, and van den Broeck, J. (1977b), "Technical Efficiency and Dimension of the Firm: Some Results on the Use of Frontier Production Functions," *Empirical Economics*, 2, pp. 109–22.

Meller, P. (1976) "Efficiency Frontiers for Industrial Establishments of Different Sizes," *Explorations in Economic Research*, 3:3 (Summer), pp. 379–407.

Muro, J. D. (1982) "Dual Farrell Measures of Efficiency," unpublished manuscript.

Nishimizu, M., and Page, J. M., Jr. (1982) "Total Factor Productivity Growth, Technological Progress and Technical Efficiency Change: Dimensions of Productivity Change in Yugoslavia, 1965–78," *The Economic Journal*, 92:368 (December), pp. 920–36.

Pack, H. (1974) "The Employment-Output Trade-Off in LDC's: A Microeconomic Approach," *Oxford Economic Papers*, N.S., 26:3 (November), pp. 383–404.

_____ (1976) "The Substitution of Labour for Capital in Kenyan Manufacturing," *Economic*

Journal, 86:1 (March), pp. 45–58.
Page, J. M., Jr. (1979) "Firm Size, the Choice of Technique and Technical Efficiency: Evidence from India's Soap Manufacturing Industry," Studies in Employment and Rural Development, No. 59., The World Bank, Washington, D.C.
_____, and Martin, J. P. (1980) "Subsidized Industries, Managerial Effort and X-Efficiency," OECD, Paris.
Pelkmans, J. (1982) "Customs Union and Technical Efficiency," *De Economist*, 130:4, pp. 536–59.
Perrakis, S. (1980) "Factor-Price Uncertainty with Variable Proportions: Note," *American Economic Review*, 70:5 (December), pp. 1083–88.
Pitt, M. M., and Lee, L.-F. (1981) "The Measurement and Sources of Technical Inefficiency in the Indonesian Weaving Industry," *Journal of Development Economics*, 9:1 (August), pp. 43–64.
Primeaux, W. J. (1977) "An Assessment of X-Efficiency Gained Through Competition," *Review of Economics and Statistics*, 59:1 (February), pp. 105–08.
Ransom, R. L., and Sutch, R. (1977) *One Kind of Freedom: The Economic Consequences of Emancipation*. New York: Cambridge University Press.
Richmond, J. (1974) "Estimating the Efficiency of Production," *International Economic Review*, 15:2 (June), pp. 515–21.
Robinson, E. A. G. (1962) *The Structure of Competitive Industry*. Chicago: The University of Chicago Press.
Roumasset, J. A. (1976) *Rice and Risk*. Amsterdam: North-Holland.
Salter, W. E. G. (1966) *Productivity and Technical Change*. (Second Edition, with an addendum by W. B. Reddaway). Cambridge: The University Press.
Samuelson, P. A. (1947) *Foundations of Economic Analysis*. Cambridge: Harvard University Press.
_____ (1966) "The Fundamental Singularity Theorem for Non-Joint Production," *International Economic Review*, 7:1 (February), pp. 34–41.
Schmidt, P. (1976) "On the Statistical Estimation of Parametric Frontier Production Functions," *Review of Economics and Statistics*, 58:2 (May), pp. 238–39.
_____, and Lovell, C. A. K. (1979) "Estimating Technical and Allocative Inefficiency Relative to Stochastic Production and Cost Frontiers," *Journal of Econometrics*, 9:3 (February), pp. 343–66.
_____, and Lovell, C. A. K. (1980) "Estimating Stochastic Production and Cost Frontiers when Technical and Allocative Inefficiency are Correlated," *Journal of Econometrics*, 13:1 (May), pp. 83–100.
_____, and Sickles, R. (1984) "Production Frontiers and Panel Data," *Journal of Business and Economic Statistics*, forthcoming.
Schwartzman, D. (1973) "Competition and Efficiency: Comment," *Journal of Political Economy*, 81:3 (May/June), pp. 756–64.
Seitz, W. D. (1970) "The Measurement of Efficiency Relative to a Frontier Production Function," *American Journal of Agricultural Economics*, 52:4 (November), pp. 505–11.
_____ (1971) "Productive Efficiency in the Steam-Electric Generating Industry," *Journal of Political Economy*, 79:4 (July/August), pp. 876–86.
Sen, A. K. (1966) *Choice of Techniques*. 3rd. ed. Oxford: Blackwell.
_____ (1975) *Employment, Technology, and Development*. Oxford: Clarendon Press.
Shephard, R. W. (1953) *Cost and Production Functions*. Princeton: Princeton University Press.

_____ (1970) *Theory of Cost and Production Functions*. Princeton: Princeton University Press.
_____ (1974a) "Semi-Homogeneous Production Functions and Scaling of Production," in Eichhorn, W., Henn, R., Opitz, O., and Shephard, R. W. eds., *Production Theory*. Berlin, Heidelberg, New York: Springer-Verlag.
_____ (1974b) *Indirect Production Functions*. Mathematical Systems in Economics, No. 10, Meisenheim Am Glad: Verlag Anton Hain.
_____, and Färe, R. (1980) *Dynamic Theory of Production Correspondences*. Cambridge, Mass: Oelgeschlager, Gunn and Hain, Publishers, Inc.
Sidhu, S. S. (1974) "Relative Efficiency in Wheat Production in the Indian Punjab," *American Economic Review*, 64:4 (September), pp. 742–51.
Solow, R. M. (1957) "Technical Change and the Aggregate Production Function," *Review of Economics and Statistics*, 39:3 (August), pp. 312–20.
Stevenson, R. E. (1980) "Likelihood Functions for Generalized Stochastic Frontier Estimation," *Journal of Econometrics*, 13:1 (May), pp. 58–66.
Stewart, M. B. (1978) "Factor-price Uncertainty with Variable Proportions," *American Economic Review*, 68:3 (June), pp. 468–73.
Stigler, G. J. (1976) "The Xistence of X-Efficiency," *American Economic Review*, 66:1 (March), pp. 213–16.
Teusch, W. (1983) "Analysis and Construction of Uniformly Compact Production Correspondences," in Eichhorn, W., Henn, R., Neumann, K., and Shephard, R. W., eds., *Quantitative Studies on Production and Prices,* Würzburg, Vienna: Physica-Verlag.
Timmer, C. P. (1971) "Using a Probabilistic Frontier Production Function to Measure Technical Efficiency,"*Journal of Political Economy*, 79:4, (July/August), pp. 776–94.
Trosper, R. L. (1978) "American Indian Relative Ranching Efficiency," *American Economic Review*, 68:4 (September), pp. 503–16.
Tyler, W. G. (1979) "Technical Efficiency in Production in a Developing Country: An Empirical Examination of the Brazilian Plastics and Steel Industries," *Oxford Economic Papers*, N.S., 31:3 (November), pp. 477–95.
_____, and Lee, L. -F. (1979) "On Estimating Stochastic Frontier Production Functions and Average Efficiency: An Empirical Analysis with Colombian Micro Data," *Review of Economics and Statistics*, 61:3 (August), pp. 436–38.
Varian, H. R. (1984) "The Nonparametric Approach to Production Analysis," *Econometrica*, 52:3 (May), pp. 579–97.
Vincze, E. (1960) "Über das Problem der Berechnung der Wirtschaftlichkeit," *Acta Technica Academiae Scientiarum Hungaricae*, 28, pp. 33–41.
White, L. J. (1976) "Appropriate Technology, X-Efficiency, and a Competitive Environment: Some Evidence from Pakistan," *Quarterly Journal of Economics*, 90:4 (November), pp. 575–89.
Williamson, O. E. (1967) "Hierarchical Control and Optimum Firm Size," *Journal of Political Economy*, 75:2 (April), pp. 123–38.
Wu, C. C. (1979) "Price-Output Uncertainty and Allocative Efficiency: An Empirical Study of Small-Scale Farms," *Review of Economics and Statistics*, 61:2 (May), pp. 228–33.
Yotopoulos, P. A., and Lau, L. J. (1973) "A Test for Relative Economic Efficiency: Some Further Results," *American Economic Review*, 63:1 (March), pp. 214–29.
Zieschang, K. D. (1982) "Recovering Indices of Technical Efficiency from the Cost Function," BLS Working Paper, U.S. Bureau of Labor Statistics, Washington, D.C.

——— (1983a) "A Note on the Decomposition of Cost Efficiency into Technical and Allocative Components," *Journal of Econometrics*, 23:3, (December), pp. 401–05.

——— (1983b), "Measuring Technical Efficiency in DEA Models," unpublished manuscript.

——— (1984) "An Extended Farrell Technical Efficiency Measure," *Journal of Economic Theory*, forthcoming.

Author Index

Subject Index

MIX
Papier aus verantwortungsvollen Quellen
Paper from responsible sources
FSC® C105338
FSC
www.fsc.org

If you have any concerns about our products,
you can contact us on
ProductSafety@springernature.com

In case Publisher is established outside the EU,
the EU authorized representative is:
Springer Nature Customer Service Center GmbH
Europaplatz 3, 69115 Heidelberg, Germany

Printed by Libri Plureos GmbH
in Hamburg, Germany